BEYOND EGO

To Renew Books

PHONE 1

BEYOND EGO

Transpersonal
Dimensions
in Psychology

edited by
ROGER N. WALSH, M. D., Ph. D.
and
FRANCES VAUGHAN, Ph. D.

 JEREMY P. TARCHER, INC.
Los Angeles
Distributed by St. Martin's Press
New York

Dedicated to our teachers: the One and the many for the liberation of all beings

"Transpersonal Psychotherapy: Context, Content, and Process," by Frances Vaughan, and "The Possible Emergence of Cross-Disciplinary Parallels," by Roger Walsh, have appeared in the *Journal of Transpersonal Psychology 11* (1979). Portions of "What Is a Person?" and "A Comparison of Psychotherapies," by Roger N. Walsh and Frances Vaughan, have appeared in the *Journal of Humanistic Psychology*, Winter 1980.

Requests for such permissions should be addressed to:
J. P. Tarcher, Inc.
9110 Sunset Blvd.
Los Angeles, CA 90069

Library of Congress Catalog Card No.: 79–56299
ISBN: 0–87477–175–7

Design by Barbara Monahan

Manufactured in the United States of America

S 10 9 8 7 6

CONTENTS

PREFACE   9

ABOUT THE AUTHORS   10

ACKNOWLEDGMENTS   13

INTRODUCTION: THE EMERGENCE OF THE TRANSPERSONAL PERSPECTIVE   15

**1 WIDER VISION:
NEW PARADIGMS FOR OLD**   25

Perspectives on Psychology, Reality, and the Study of Consciousness   *Daniel Goleman*   29

Paradigms in Collision   *Roger N. Walsh, Duane Elgin, Frances Vaughan, Ken Wilber*   36

What Is a Person?   *Roger N. Walsh, Frances Vaughan*   53

Modern Physics and Eastern Mysticism   *Fritjof Capra*   62

2 THE NATURE OF CONSCIOUSNESS   71

Psychologia Perennis: The Spectrum of Consciousness   *Ken Wilber*   74

Realms of the Human Unconscious: Observations from LSD Research   *Stanislav Grof*   87

A Developmental Model of Consciousness   *Ken Wilber*   99

The Systems Approach to States of Consciousness   *Charles Tart*   115

**3   PSYCHOLOGICAL WELL-BEING:
      EAST AND WEST**   **119**

A Theory of Metamotivation: The Biological Rooting
  of the Value-Life   *Abraham Maslow*   122

Mental Health in Classical Buddhist Psychology
  Daniel Goleman   131

**4   MEDITATION: DOORWAY TO THE
      TRANSPERSONAL**   **135**

Relative Realities   *Ram Dass*   138

A Map for Inner Space   *Daniel Goleman*   141

Meditation: Aspects of Theory and Practice
  Jack Kornfield   150

Meditation Research: The Evolution and State of the
  Art   *Roger N. Walsh*   154

5   TRANSPERSONAL PSYCHOTHERAPY   **161**

A Comparison of Psychotherapies   *Roger N. Walsh,*
  Frances Vaughan   165

The Transpersonal Stance   *James Fadiman*   175

Transpersonal Psychotherapy: Context, Content,
  and Process   *Frances Vaughan*   182

Being Levels of Therapeutic Growth   *James Bugental*   190

**6   RIPPLES OF CHANGE:
      IMPLICATIONS FOR OTHER DISCIPLINES**   **196**

SCIENCE
States of Consciousness and State-Specific Sciences
  Charles Tart   200

Different Views from Different States   *Gordon Globus*   213

Eye to Eye: Science and Transpersonal Psychology
  Ken Wilber   216

The Possible Emergence of Cross-Disciplinary
  Parallels   *Roger N. Walsh*   221

EDUCATION
Education and Transpersonal Relations: A Research
    Agenda   *Thomas B. Roberts*   228

PHILOSOPHY
Two Modes of Knowing   *Ken Wilber*   234

PARAPSYCHOLOGY
The Societal Implications and Social Impact of Psi
    Phenomena   *Willis Harman*   240

SOCIAL SCIENCE
The Tao of Personal and Social Transformation
    Duane Elgin   248

EPILOGUE   **257**

GLOSSARY   **261**

SUGGESTED READING   **266**

INDEX   **270**

By their own theories of human nature psychologists have the power of elevating or degrading that same nature. Debasing assumptions debase human beings; generous assumptions exalt them.

GORDON ALLPORT

I have no doubt whatever that most people live, whether physically, intellectually or morally, in a very restricted circle of their potential being. They make use of a very small portion of their possible consciousness . . . much like a man who, out of his whole bodily organism, should get into a habit of using and moving only his little finger. . . . We all have reservoirs of life to draw upon, of which we do not dream.

WILLIAM JAMES

PREFACE

Despite its rapid growth, transpersonal psychology has lacked an introductory or comprehensive text. This volume is intended to fill this need by bringing together the outstanding papers and authors of the field. In doing this we had several goals in mind.

First, we wished to provide an introduction for those readers who were not previously familiar with the area. Therefore, we have provided introductions for each of the major sections, have sought out articles which avoid excessive technicalities, and have provided a glossary of technical terms.

Within the available space we wanted this volume to be as comprehensive as possible. Therefore we have tried to find outstanding papers in all the major areas of transpersonal psychology. Certain areas lacked appropriate reviews, and in some cases we filled this gap by writing new articles ourselves, for example, on meditation research. In order to include as many articles and areas as possible and to avoid redundancy, all articles have been edited and condensed. Readers may therefore sometimes wish to consult the original papers or books as well as the resources in the recommended reading list for more detailed discussions.

We also wanted to provide an overview and integration of the field. We have attempted to do this by choosing articles of broad integrative scope and by providing introductions and discussions that attempt to connect themes and uncover underlying common dimensions whenever possible. Such an attempt seems particularly important for a field that stands at the crossroads of an extraordinarily wide range of disciplines and points to the interconnectedness and interdependence of all things.

ABOUT THE AUTHORS

JAMES F. T. BUGENTAL, Ph.D. is a psychologist in private practice in San Rafael, California and a faculty member of the Humanistic Psychology Institute. He was the first president of the Humanistic Psychology Association and is best known for his writing on existential-humanistic psychotherapy. His books include *The Search for Authenticity*, *The Search for Existential Identity: Patient Therapist Dialogues in Humanistic Psychology*, and *Psychotherapy and Process*.

FRITJOF CAPRA, Ph.D. is a research physicist at the Lawrence Berkeley Laboratory of the University of California, Berkeley. He is the author of *The Tao of Physics*, and has lectured widely on this subject throughout the United States and in Europe.

DUANE ELGIN, M.A. is a social science researcher and futurist who has written extensively on alternative futures and contemporary trends toward voluntary simplicity. He is the author of *Voluntary Simplicity and co-author of Changing Images of Man*.

JAMES FADIMAN, Ph.D. is a lecturer at Stanford University and one of the founders of the Association for Transpersonal Psychology and the *Journal of Transpersonal Psychology*. He is the author of several books, including a textbook on *Personality and Personal Growth*.

GORDON GLOBUS, M.D. is professor of psychiatry at the University of California Medical School at Irvine. He has conducted extensive research on sleep, has written widely on phenomenology and philosophy, and is the editor of *Consciousness and the Brain*.

DANIEL GOLEMAN, Ph.D. is a writer and editor for *Psychology Today*. He conducted extensive research on meditation in India and Ceylon and taught meditation at Harvard University while working as a clinical psychologist. He is the author of *The Varieties of the Meditative Expeience* and a frequent contributor to the *Journal of Transpersonal Psychology*.

STANISLAV GROF, M.D., formerly chief of psychiatric research at the Maryland Psychiatric Center and assistant professor of Psychiatry at Johns Hopkins University School of Medicine, is now devoting full time to writing. Two recent books are *Realms of the Human Unconscious* and *The Human Encounter with Death*. He is a pioneer in the field of psychedelic research and transpersonal psychology and psychotherapy.

WILLIS HARMAN, Ph.D. is president of the Institute of Noetic Sciences, director of social research at Stanford Research Institute, and on the faculty of the School of Engineering at Stanford University. He is the author of *An Incomplete Guide to the Future* and *Changing Images of Man*.

JACK KORNFIELD, Ph.D. is a teacher of vipassana meditation whose training includes six years in Southeast Asia as a layman and monk in Theravada monasteries. He holds a doctorate in psychology and is author of *Living Buddhist Masters*.

ABRAHAM MASLOW, Ph.D. was professor of psychology at Brandeis University. He is considered the philosophical father of humanistic and transpersonal psychology and was the author of books relating humanistic psychology to education, religion, and industry.

RAM DASS was formerly a professor of psychology at Harvard University who has since deeply immersed himself in Eastern meditative and yogic practices. He is author of several books—including *Be Here Now*, *The Only Dance There Is*, and *Grist for the Mill* — and is a popular lecturer throughout the United States.

THOMAS B. ROBERTS, Ph.D. is professor of secondary education at Northern Illinois University. A pioneer in the field of transpersonal education, he published *Four Psychologies Applied to Education*, and has also written and lectured widely on teaching transpersonal techniques to secondary school teachers.

CHARLES TART, Ph.D. is professor of psychology at the University of California at Davis. Basically an experimental psychologist, he has conducted research on hypnosis, meditation, altered states of consciousness and paranormal phenomena. His books include *Altered States of Consciousness*, *Transpersonal Psychologies*, and *States of Consciousness*.

FRANCES VAUGHAN, Ph.D. is a clinical psychologist in independent practice in Mill Valley, California, and professor of psychology at the California Institute of Transpersonal Psychology. She is an editor for the *Journal of Transpersonal Psychology*, *Journal of Humanistic Psychology*, and *Re-Vision*, and was formerly president of the Association for Transpersonal Psychology. She is author of *Awakening Intuition* (Doubleday/Anchor, 1979).

ROGER N. WALSH, M.D., Ph.D. is on the faculty of the Department of Psychiatry, University of California, Irvine. He is author of *Toward an Ecology of Brain* and editor of *Environments as Therapy for Brain Dysfunction*, *The Science of Meditation: Research, Theory, and Experience* (in press), and *Beyond Health and Normality: Explorations of Extreme Psychological Well-being* (in press).

KEN WILBER, M.A. received his degree in biochemistry, and is a student of Zen meditation. His books, beginning with *The Spectrum of Consciousness*, constitute the major theoretical works in the field of transpersonal psychology. He is the editor of the journal *ReVision*.

ACKNOWLEDGMENTS

The editors wish to acknowledge with gratitude the support, encourage-ment, and assistance of many friends, colleagues, and co-workers, and the courage and work of those pioneers who have explored and opened to us the realms examined by transpersonal psychology. We are also grateful for the editorial assistance of Janice Gallagher and the long hours of typing by Sonja Hays as well as for the excellent feedback given to an earlier draft of this manuscript by Ken Wilber and Miles Vich.

The authors would like to thank the following publishers and authors for permission to reprint:

"Perspectives on Psychology, Reality, and the Study of Consciousness," by Daniel Goleman. Reprinted, by permission, from the *Journal of Trans-personal Psychology*, 1974, 6, 73–85. Copyright Transpersonal Institute; "Modern Physics and Eastern Mysticism," by Fritjof Capra. Reprinted, by permission, from the *Journal of Transpersonal Psychology*, 1976, 8, 20–40. Copyright Transpersonal Institute; "Psychologia Perennis: The Spectrum of Consciousness," by Ken Wilber. Reprinted, by permission, from the *Journal of Transpersonal Psychology*, 1975, 7, 105–132. Copyright Transper-sonal Institute; "Realms of the Human Unconscious: Observations from LSD Research," from *Realms of the Human Unconscious* by Stanislav Grof. Copyright © 1975 by Stanislav Grof and Joan Halifax-Grof. Reprinted by permission of Viking Penguin, Inc.; "A Developmental Model of Con-sciousness," by Ken Wilber. Reprinted by permission of the author. An expanded version of this paper is available in *The Atman Project* by Ken Wilber, Wheaton, Ill.: Theosophical Publishing House, 1980; "The Sys-tems Approach to States of Consciousness," from *States of Consciousness* by Charles T. Tart. Copyright © 1975 by Charles T. Tart. Reprinted by permission of the publisher, E. P. Dutton; "A Theory of Metamotivation: The Biological Rooting of the Value-Life," by A. H. Maslow. Excerpted by permission from the *Journal of Humanistic Psychology*, 1967, 7, 93–127; "Mental Health in Classical Buddhist Psychology," by Daniel Goleman.

THE EMERGENCE OF
THE TRANSPERSONAL
PERSPECTIVE

We are what we think.
All that we are arises with our thoughts.
With our thoughts we make the world.

                                         THE BUDDHA[1]

In recent years it has become apparent that our traditional assumptions and thinking about who and what we are and what we can become may not have been generous enough. Evidence from a wide range of disciplines — psychological and nonpsychological, traditional and non-traditional, Western and non-Western—suggests that we may have underestimated the human potential for psychological growth and well-being. Much of this new data is inconsistent with our traditional psychological models, and transpersonal psychology arose in response to these inconsistencies in an attempt to integrate suggestions of greater human capacity into the mainstream of the Western behavioral and mental health disciplines.

DEFINING TRANSPERSONAL PSYCHOLOGY

Transpersonal psychology thus aims at expanding the field of psychological inquiry to include areas of human experience and behavior associated with extreme health and well-being. As such it draws on both Western science and Eastern wisdom in an attempt to integrate knowledge from both traditions concerned with the fulfillment of human potentials. Its areas of interest extend widely, and the *Journal of Transpersonal Psychology*, first published in 1969, defines itself as being concerned with "the publication of theoretical and applied research, empirical papers, articles and studies in transpersonal process, values and states, unitive consciousness, metaneeds, peak experiences, ecstasy, mystical experience, being, essence, bliss, awe, wonder, transcendence of self, . . . the theories and practices of meditation, spiritual paths, compassion, transpersonal cooperation, transpersonal realization and actualization and related concepts, experiences, and activities."

The term *transpersonal* was adopted after considerable deliberation to reflect the reports of people practicing various consciousness disciplines who spoke of experiences of an extension of identity beyond both individuality and personality. Thus transpersonal psychology cannot strictly be called a model of personality because personality is considered only one aspect of our psychological nature; rather it is an inquiry into the essential nature of being.

Defining transpersonal psychology and therapy is difficult because transpersonal experiences are essentially altered states and this raises the problems of state dependency and cross-state communication. Since definitions, like models, can be constricting, it is useful to consider those for transpersonal psychology as still in evolution rather than complete. With these caveats in mind, the following definitions are offered.

> *Transpersonal psychology* is concerned with expanding the field of psychological inquiry to include the study of optimal psychological health and well-being. It recognizes the potential for experiencing a broad range of states of consciousness, in some of which identity may extend beyond the usual limits of the ego and personality.
>
> *Transpersonal psychotherapy* includes traditional areas and concerns, adding to these an interest in facilitating growth and awareness beyond traditionally recognized levels of health. The importance of modifying consciousness and the validity of transcendental experience and identity is affirmed.

With the introduction of a variety of consciousness altering technologies, an increasing number of people, including mental health professionals, are beginning to have a range of transpersonal experiences. Stanislav Grof has provided a useful definition of transpersonal experiences as those involving an expansion of consciousness beyond customary ego boundaries and beyond the ordinary limitations of time and space. In his research with LSD psychotherapy, Grof noted that all his subjects eventually transcended the psychodynamic level and entered transpersonal realms. This potential may also be achieved without chemicals, either spontaneously, by practicing various consciousness disciplines — e.g., meditation and yoga—or in advanced psychotherapy. It seems therefore that such experiences represent an essential aspect of human nature that must be taken into account in any psychological theory that attempts to delineate a model of the whole person. This book attempts to provide the major features of such a model. By way of introduction, the following paragraphs will examine the nature of models and psychologies, the evolution of Western psychology and the emergence of the transpersonal perspective, and the factors that have facilitated this emergence.

THE NATURE OF MODELS

Models are symbolic representations that describe the major features or dimensions of the phenomena they represent. As such they are extremely useful in breaking complex phenomena down into simpler and more readily comprehensible representations.

However, models come with certain prices attached to them. In recent years there has been an increasing awareness of the power of models and beliefs to shape perception. Especially when they are implicit, assumed, or unquestioned, models come to function as self-fulfilling, self-prophetic organizers of experience that modify perception, suggest areas of inquiry, shape investigation, and determine the interpretation of data and experience. The self-fulfilling, self-prophetic nature of this process indicates that models are self-validating. That is, their effects on perception and interpretation argue for their own validity, they shape perception in self-consistent ways. In other words, everything that we perceive tends to tell us that our models and beliefs are correct. But the greatest danger of this effect lies in the fact that most of it operates unconsciously. These factors are particularly important for our present discussion because all psychologies are models.

PSYCHOLOGIES AS MODELS

All psychologies are based on explicit or implicit models of human nature. Specific psychologies arise from the recognition and emphasis of specific areas or dimensions of this nature and tend to selectively perceive and interpret all behavior and experience from that perspective. For example, psychoanalysis and behavior modification hold very different views on the determination of behavior. For the psychoanalyst intrapsychic forces are the important determinants, whereas behaviorists emphasize the role of reinforcement from the environment.

As discussed above, any model tends to be self-validating, but this effect is magnified in psychological models due to the complex nature of the determination of behavior. Any behavior is overdetermined, that is, it is the result or end product of many different factors. Conversely any particular factor of motivation tends to enter into the determination of most or all behaviors. Thus anyone who searches for a particular motivation is likely to find it. For example, the Freudian analyst looking for sexual libido as the prime motivator, the Adlerian analyst searching for superiority strivings, and the behaviorist examining for environmental reinforcers, are all likely to be successful in their search.

Problems arise, however, when clinicians and researchers assume that finding the postulated motivator or factor provides exclusive support for their particular model. Such assumptions ignore the overdetermined complexity and richness of behavior and thus lose sight of alternate interpretations and models. Moreover, phenomena that lie outside the scope of the model will tend to be either excluded from consideration or misinterpreted. Thus for example, psychoanalysis does not entertain the possibility of transcendent states of consciousness and hence has tended to interpret these from its own perspective as being pathological ego regressions of near psychotic proportions. Thus, mystical experiences have been interpreted as "neurotic regressions to union with the breast,"[2] ecstatic states viewed as "narcissistic neurosis,"[2] and enlightenment dismissed as regression to intrauterine stages.[3]

Usually different psychological models have been seen as necessarily antagonistic and much heat has been generated by proponents of particular models arguing that theirs was the only true way. However, a broader perspective suggests that at least some models may be complementary, and we might hope that a sufficiently broad and unbiased view might encompass and integrate many of the major models.

The transpersonal model, therefore, is not necessarily expected to replace or challenge the validity of earlier ones but rather to set them within an expanded context of human nature. For example, since transpersonal psychology recognizes a broad hierarchical organization of motives, including commonly recognized ones such as sex and superiority strivings, the Freudian and Adlerian models may be seen as appropriate to specific levels of the hierarchy of motives. Similarly much of the psychodynamic wisdom about defenses is not necessarily abrogated by the recognition that defenses may exist only in conjunction with specific ego states. Rather, the psychodynamic formulations can now be seen as appropriate to specific states rather than as universal. With this in mind let us now examine the evolution of the major Western psychological models.

THE EVOLUTION OF WESTERN PSYCHOLOGY AND THE EMERGENCE OF THE TRANSPERSONAL PERSPECTIVE

Transpersonal psychology emerged in the sixties in response to a concern that the previous major models, the first three forces of Western psychology — behaviorism, psychoanalysis, and humanistic psychology — had been limited in their recognition of the upper reaches of psychological development. A growing number of mental health professionals felt that both behaviorism and psychoanalysis were limited in being derived largely from studies of psychopathology, in attempting to generalize from simple to more complex systems, in adopting a reductionistic approach to human nature, and in ignoring certain areas, concerns, and data relevant to a full study of human nature, such as values, will, consciousness, and seeking for self-actualization and self-transcendence. It was also felt that this neglect was sometimes accompanied by inappropriately reductionistic and pathologizing interpretations.

Indeed, the psychoanalytic perspective effectively made it impossible to consider or detect any health-oriented or health-motivated behavior except inasmuch as it represented a defense, or at the very best a compromise, with basic destructive forces. Thus, motivations and behaviors aimed toward self-actualization and self-transcendence, and even the possibility of attaining such goals, could not be accorded validity even though non-Western psychologies contained detailed descriptions of them. Similarly, such models allowed only for psychotherapy that essentially aimed at adjustment and did not include work at self-actualizing or self-transcending levels. As Gordon Allport noted, "We have on the psychology of liberation—nothing."[4] In fact, Freud's collected works contain over four hundred references to neurosis and none to health. Thus it was argued that while the behavioral and psychoanalytical models made major contributions, they also resulted in certain limitations for psychology and our concepts of human nature.

In the early sixties, humanistic psychology emerged in response to these concerns. It took as its major focus those areas that were uniquely human and particularly those aspects associated with health rather than pathology. For example, humanistic psychologists initiated studies of self-actualization and of those individuals who seemed to have matured furthest in these dimensions. Their concern with the whole person attempted to avoid compartmentalized views that reduced the human experience to mechanistic terms and lost the essence of both humanity and experience. Humanistic models recognized the drive toward self-actualization and explored ways in which this could be fostered in individuals, groups, and organizations. From this emerged the so-called human potential movement with its interest in actualizing the newly recognized potentials for development and well-being. Many humanistic ideas were incorporated in the evolving edge of a sizable counterculture and gained a considerable popular acceptance.

As more data became available on the farther reaches of well-being, the absence of relevant guidelines in traditional Western psychology became even more apparent. Indeed, the humanistic model itself began to show gaps and even the concept of self-actualization proved unable to encompass the newly recognized farther reaches of experience.

Toward the end of his life, Abraham Maslow, one of the major pioneers in humanistic psychology, called attention to possibilities beyond self-actualization in which the individual transcended the customary limits of identity and experience. In 1968 he concluded that, "I consider Humanistic, Third Force Psychology, to be transitional, a preparation for a still "higher" Fourth psychology, transpersonal, transhuman, centered in the cosmos rather than in human needs and interest, going beyond humanness, identity, self-actualization, and the like."[5]

Thus the humanistic model also revealed its limitations for encompassing the continuously broadening span of recognized human experience and potential. It should be noted that this recognition of limitations in models represents a necessary and desirable phase in their evolution that involves the continued recognition of the limits and biases of current models and their replacement by more comprehensive ones. Yesterday's model becomes a component of today's, what was context becomes content, and what was the whole set becomes an element or subset of the larger set. Furthermore, the new model is not all-encompassing, but hopefully a more accurate and comprehensive picture of the reality it attempts to describe. Unfortunately, with time we usually come to believe our own models rather than remembering that they are only approximate maps, and become attached to our models and resist their replacement, thereby slowing the evolutionary process.

Thus the transpersonal model presented in this book incorporates areas beyond the usual views of behaviorism, psychoanalysis, and humanistic psychology. However, this transpersonal model is not "the Truth," but only a larger though necessarily still limited, picture that in its turn will presumably be replaced by even more comprehensive models.

FACTORS FACILITATING THE EMERGENCE OF TRANSPERSONAL PSYCHOLOGY

In addition to the desire to complement and expand existing psychological models, several other factors facilitated the emergence of transpersonal psychology. Some of these occurred within the culture at large. The initial recognition of the inadequacy of the materialistic dream led some people to begin to look within for the source of satisfaction that external strivings had failed to provide. This shift resulted in the human potential movement, which nudged mental health practitioners to reassess their concepts of health and motivation.

The widespread use of psychedelics and consciousness altering techniques such as meditation also had a major impact. Suddenly, large numbers of people found themselves having extraordinarily powerful experiences of a range of states of consciousness quite outside the realm of daily living or of anything previously recognized by Western psychology. For some these included transcendental experiences, which historically had occurred only as rare, short-lived, spontaneous events, or even more rarely as gradual shifts in awareness among individuals who devoted major portions of their life to contemplative, meditative, or religous disciplines. Suddenly, what had for centuries appeared to Westerners as mystical, arcane, nonsensical, or even nonexistent became overwhelmingly real and sometimes central to the lives of a sizable minority.

Many such individuals developed compelling insights into the possible validity and importance of certain non-Western psychologies and religions. As theoretical understanding of altered states of consciousness evolved, it was gradually recognized that these traditions represented technologies designed for the induction of higher states of consciousness. It gradually became apparent that the capacity for transcendent states, which could be interpreted either religiously or psychologically as one chose, and the deep insights into self and one's relationship to the world that accompanied them, lay latent within us all.

For some individuals, the possibility of realizing an enduring state of being such as that glimpsed in moments of deep meditation or described by various non-Western disciplines proved a compelling attraction. Since just such an enduring state was the goal of the non-Western consciousness disciplines, increasing numbers of the most unlikely candidates began such practices. Many of them, who would have scoffed at the idea only a few years previously, found themselves sitting in meditation, practicing yoga, or studying texts that had previously been the preserve of Eastern mystics or an occasional Western intellectual philosopher or student of religion. The number of people involved in such practices continues to increase and has now extended into the millions in the United States alone.

Those not involved with such experiences sometimes reacted with bewilderment, concern, and judgment. Talk of altered states of consciousness, mystical unity, deep insight into the nature of being, expansion of identity beyond the ego and personality, may make little sense to one with no similar experience. One response has been to dismiss these experiences as nonsense at best or psychopathology at worst. This is a classical example of the difficulty of describing altered states to those with no experience of them. Communication across states of consciousness is a complex task limited by several factors. Unless these limitations are appreciated, the naive response is to dismiss such reports as nonsensical or pathological.[6]

Empirical research has gradually provided support and legitimization for certain claims about state-dependent and related phenomena. Both animal and human studies have validated the concept of altered states of consciousness and the unique properties of learning and communication that go with them.

Biofeedback has demonstrated the possibility of voluntary control of parts of the nervous system and body long thought to be automatic, e.g., heart rate, blood pressure, gastro-intestinal activity, and hormone secretion. Interestingly enough, Eastern yogis for centuries had claimed to be able to do just this, but their claims had been dismissed as impossible by

Western scientists whose theories and personal experience denied this possibility. This is an interesting example of a recurrent theme; namely that claims for capacities beyond our own currently recognized limits tend to be dismissed as deceptive.

Studies of meditation have also been supportive. Although still in an early stage, research lends preliminary support to ancient claims that meditation can enhance psychological development, modify physiological (including brain) processes, and induce a range of altered states.[7]

All of these factors have led to a renewed interest in the empirical investigation of consciousness. This is a relatively recent development in Western psychology, for although William James laid the groundwork for a psychology of consciousness at the turn of the century, there followed a period of some fifty years during which Western psychology shunned anything suggestive of introspection in an effort to secure its recognition as one of the objective hard sciences. Seen from one contemporary perspective: "Psychology is primarily the science of consciousness. Its researchers deal with consciousness directly when possible and indirectly, through the study of physiology and behavior, when necessary."[8] In recent years a gradual shift seems to be occurring toward a more balanced position that acknowledges both the importance of consciousness and the difficulties Western science faces in researching it directly.

Another supportive research area is, strangely enough, modern physics. In recent years the physicist's picture of the world has undergone a shift so radical and far-reaching in its implications as to shake the very foundations of science. For the reality revealed, especially at the subatomic level, is so paradoxical as to defy description in traditional terms and theories and to call into question some of the most fundamental assumptions of Western science and philosophy. Traditional descriptions were largely based on Greek philosophical concepts, and described the universe as atomistic, divisible, static, and nonrelativistic. These descriptions are being supplemented by models that acknowledge a holistic, indivisible, interconnected, dynamic, relativistic reality inseparable from, and a function of, the consciousness of the observer.[9]

Though these findings do not fit at all with our usual pictures or reality, they are strikingly reminiscent of descriptions given repeatedly across centuries and cultures by advanced practitioners of the consciousness disciplines. Indeed, physicists themselves have suggested that some discoveries can be viewed as a rediscovery of ancient wisdom.

> The general notions about human understanding... which are illustrated by discoveries in atomic physics are not in the nature of being wholly unfamiliar, wholly unheard of, or new. Even in our own culture they have a history, and in Buddhist and Hindu thought a more considerable and central place. What we shall find is an exemplification and encouragement, and a refinement of old wisdom.   —Oppenheimer[10]

For a parallel to the lesson of atomic theory [we must turn] to those kinds of epistemological problems with which already thinkers like the Buddha and Lao Tzu have been confronted, when trying to harmonize our position as spectators and actors in the great drama of existence.   —*Bohr*[11]

Sometimes it is difficult to decide whether descriptions of this reality are excerpted from textbooks of physics or the consciousness disciplines. Compare, for example, the description of space-time by the Buddhist master Suzuki, with that first introduced into physics by Hermann Minkowski in 1908:

We look around and perceive that...every object is related to every other object...not only spatially but temporally....As a fact of pure experience, there is no space without time, no time without space; they are interpenetrating.   —*Suzuki*[12]

The views of space and time which I wish to lay before you have sprung from the soil of experimental physics, and therein lies their strength. They are radical. Henceforth space by itself, and time by itself, are doomed to fade away into mere shadows, and only a kind of union of the two will preserve an independent reality.   —*Minkowski*[13]

At the most fundamental and sensitive levels of modern science, the emerging picture of reality resembles the most fundamental picture revealed by the consciousness disciplines.

This is not to say that the two disciplines are describing the same phenomena or that they have converged.[14] However, what is apparent is that a cutting edge of modern science is pointing to an underlying view of reality that parallels in certain ways the reality said by the consciousness disciplines to be revealed whenever our usual perceptual distortions are removed. Transpersonal psychology is interested in studying the nature of these distortions and the nature of self and reality revealed by their removal.

Notes

1. Byrom, T. *The dhammapada: The sayings of the buddha*. New York: Vintage, 1976.

2. Lewin, B. *The psychoanalysis of elation*. New York: *Psychoanalytic Quarterly*, 1961.

3. Alexander, F. In O. Strunk, *The psychology of religion*. New York: Abingdon, 1959, p. 59.

4. Allport, G. In H. Smith, *Forgotten truth: The primordial tradition*. New York: Harper & Row, 1976.

5. Maslow, A.H. *Toward a psychology of being*. 2nd ed. New York: Van Nostrand Reinhold, 1968.

6. Tart, C. States of consciousness and state-specific sciences. This volume.

7. Walsh, R. Meditation research: The evolution and state of the art. This volume.

8. Ornstein, R. *The psychology of consciousness*. San Francisco: Freeman, 1972.

9. Capra, F. Modern physics and eastern mysticism. This volume.

10. Oppenheimer, J.R. *Science and the common understanding*. New York: Oxford University Press, 1954, pp. 8–9.

11. Bohr, N. *Atomic physics and human knowledge*. New York: John Wiley, 1958, p. 20.

12. Suzuki, D.T. Preface to B.L. Suzuki, *Mahayana buddhism*. London: Allen and Unwin, 1959, p. 33.

13. Minkowski, H. Cited in A. Einstein, *The principle of relativity*. New York: Dover, 1923, p. 75.

14. Walsh, R. The possible emergence of cross-disciplinary parallels. This volume.

1

WIDER VISION: NEW
PARADIGMS FOR OLD

Projection makes perception. The world you see is what you gave it, nothing more than that. . . . It is the witness to your state of mind, the outside picture of an inward condition. As a man thinketh, so does he perceive. Therefore, seek not to change the world, but choose to change your mind about the world.

ANONYMOUS[1]

Every point of view rests on certain assumptions about the nature of reality. When this is recognized, assumptions function as hypotheses; when it is forgotten, they function as beliefs. Clusters of hypotheses create models or theories, and clusters of theories constitute paradigms.

A paradigm is a kind of general theory of such scope that it is capable of encompassing or providing a context for most of the known phenomena in its field.[2] For example, the theory that planets revolve around the sun is an example of a paradigm that guides astronomy. Any scientific theory or paradigm is supposedly continually accessible to modification or refutation. However, when theories are successful they tend eventually to be taken for granted. These "normative paradigms"[3] then become implicit unquestioned conceptual frameworks and filters that supply the "natural and sensible" way of looking at things. For example, before the Copernican revolution, the idea that the sun moved around the earth was unquestioned and was thought of as fact rather than theory or interpretation. Similarly, we tend to forget that the modern paradigm that the planets revolve around the sun is also only a theory or interpretation.

Once a paradigm becomes implicit, it acquires a tremendous yet unrecognized power over its adherents, who become believers.[4] In psychology this is known as a S-R (stimulus-response) bind, a condition in which the researcher is unable to admit any theory other than his or her own because it seems obvious that this is the only way it can be.[5] This condition is called "paradigm fixation."[6]

The introduction of a new paradigm can therefore be extraordinarily difficult, and may result in what Kuhn calls a paradigm clash.[2] In paradigm clashes, antagonism and poor communication between factions is common and accounts for the fact that even the greatest scientific innovators have frequently been discounted initially.

> If the communicating parties remain unaware that they are using different structures of reasoning, but are aware of their communication difficulties only, each party tends to perceive the communication difficulties as resulting from the other parties' illogicity, lack of intelligence, or even deceptiveness and insincerity. He may also fall into an illusion of understanding while being unaware of his misunderstandings.[7]

A paradigm may thus be viewed as a container or context for particular kinds of knowledge and investigation, thereby inevitably excluding other kinds of information. As with any theory or model, paradigms shape perception, inquiry, and interpretation in self-validating ways.[8, 9] That is, every paradigm argues for the truth of its own assumptions. Whatever lies outside its scope will still tend to be viewed from its perspective and thus be distorted or falsified. Thus paradigms, indeed any models, perform useful and necessary organizing functions, but when their hypothetical nature is forgotten, they act as distorting perceptual filters. (See also the discussion of models in the introduction.)

Members of a group tend to share common assumptions, both because they attract like-minded people and because they provide powerful selective reinforcement for their preferred assumptions. Any questioning of these assumptions is usually discouraged or, at best, not supported. Assumptions therefore function as beliefs that determine what will enter awareness and what will remain unconscious, hence determining cultural reality.[10] Seeing through one's cultural belief systems is extraordinarily difficult, but may be helped by exposure to other cultures and beliefs.

Transpersonal psychology represents a paradigm shift in Western psychology, resulting in part from exposure to cross-cultural beliefs about the nature of consciousness and reality. Guiding paradigms in Western psychology did not support the investigation of extreme psychological well-being and higher states of consciousness. In non-Western paradigms, investigators found sophisticated but radically different views of human nature and psychological potential. Once the cultural limitations of traditional Western paradigms were acknowledged, the way was open for an expanded view of psychological theory. Of course non-Western views of reality and human nature are not immune from analogous limitations, but there is now hope of creating new paradigms that can accommodate and ultimately go beyond both Eastern and Western world views.

At this stage we will merely mention some of the major dimensions in the hope of giving a flavor of some of the shifts currently being proposed. The readings in this section will provide more detailed accounts.

In the West the primary constituent of reality is held to be matter. Consciousness is seen as a product, even an epiphenomenon, of material processes, particularly brain processes. In the East, however, the opposite view is held. Consciousness is seen as primary and matter as its product and the material world is thus accorded less significance. One currently emerging viewpoint holds that neither is primary but rather that each is an expression of a higher order reality and that they are mutually interdependent.[11, 12, 13]

The traditional Western paradigm of the nature of the material universe has viewed it reductionistically and atomistically. That is, the fundamental nature of matter has been sought by breaking it down into its component parts and these parts have been assumed to exist as separate isolated entities. However, quantum physics is now revealing a picture that in many ways closely resembles the millennia-old descriptions of the East and of a holistic, interconnected, indivisible reality.[13, 14]

Indeed, in a "truth is stranger than fiction" development, recent evidence suggests that not only is each part connected to every other part of the universe, but that each part of the universe, in fact the whole universe, is enfolded in every other part.[15]

Western psychology has long regarded the ordinary waking state of consciousness as optimal. Various other psychologies, however, claim that more adaptive "higher" states exist and that the range of potentially available states is far broader than is usually appreciated. Traditional Western psychological models cannot encompass such claims since the "usual is best" assumption automatically excludes them from consideration. Hence a shift toward broader models is underway.

As new data becomes available from both non-Western traditions and modern science, such shifts are likely to continue. As Grof notes:

> The traditional paradigms have not been able to account for and accommodate a vast amount of challenging observations from many independent sources. In their totality these data ... indicate an urgent need for a drastic revision of our fundamental concepts about the human nature and the nature of reality.[16]

The specific dimensions of these paradigms and the social and intellectual forces that created them are the subject of the papers in this section. In his article, "Perspectives on Psychology, Reality, and the Study of Consciousness," Daniel Goleman points out that groups filter and structure beliefs and knowledge and hence create a shared reality. In the East the primary groups of explorers have recorded realms of psychological development that seem far beyond anything recognized as possible in the West, while Western scientists have mapped certain areas of psychopathology in great detail. Yet there are also areas of overlap recognizable to individuals with expertise in both systems.

In "Paradigms in Collision," Walsh, Elgin, Vaughan, and Wilber examine the attempts to compare and assess the consciousness disciplines and the Western behavioral sciences. Often previous assessments of the consciousness disciplines have concluded that their practitioners are suffering from various forms of psychopathology, even psychosis. "Paradigms in Collision," however, points out that these assessments have suffered from a number of methodological, conceptual, experiential, and paradigmatic errors. Failing to realize that the two systems may represent different paradigms, they have made the mistake of examining the Eastern model from within the Western one, a process certain to result in misunderstanding. Only by first becoming aware of, and taking into account, their own paradigmatic assumptions, can Western scientists avoid such pathologizing interpretations.

In "What Is a Person?" Walsh and Vaughan attempt to delineate the major dimensions of a transpersonal model of human nature. Examining the dimensions of consciousness, conditioning, personality, and identity, they point out common transpersonal assumptions about the psychological nature of humanity and contrast these with traditional Western and Eastern assumptions.

In "Modern Physics and Eastern Mysticism" Fritjof Capra points out in more detail the parallels between the picture of reality presented by modern physics and that of the Eastern mystics. He suggests that mystical insight and scientific experimentation may provide complementary views, both of which are essential for a full picture of reality.

Notes

1. Anonymous. *A course in miracles*. New York: Foundation for Inner Peace, 1975.

2. Kuhn, T. S. *The structure of scientific revolutions* (2nd ed.). Chicago: University of Chicago Press, 1970.

3. Wilson, T. Normative and interpretive paradigms in sociology. In J. Douglas (Ed.), *Understanding everyday life*. Chicago: Aldine, 1970, pp. 57–79.

4. Tart, C. (Ed.). *Transpersonal psychologies*. New York: Harper & Row, 1975.

5. Rychlak, J. F. *A philosophy of science for personality theory*. Boston: Houghton Mifflin, 1968.

6. Scriven, M. Psychology without a paradigm. In L. Berger (Ed.), *Clinical cognitive psychology*. Englewood Cliffs, N.J.: Prentice-Hall, 1969.

7. Maruyana, M. Paradigms and communication. *Technol. Forecasting Soc. Change*, 1974, *6*, 3.

8. Allport, G. W. *Personality: A psychological interpretation*. New York: Holt, 1937.

9. Bandura, A. The self system in reciprocal determination. *Amer. Psychol.*, 1978, *33*, 344–357.

10. Fromm, E., Suzuki, D. T., and DeMartino, R. *Zen Buddhism and psychoanalysis*. New York: Harper & Row, 1970.

11. Bohm, D. An interview with David Bohm. *ReVision*, 1979, *1*, 10.

12. Elgin, D. *Voluntary simplicity*. New York: William Morrow, in press.

13. d'Espagnat, B. *Conceptual Foundations of Quantum Mechanics*. W. A. Benjamin, 1976.

14. d'Espagnat, B. The quantum theory and reality. *Scientific American*, 1979, *241*, 158–181.

15. Beynam, L. The emergent paradigm in science. *ReVision*, 1978, *1*, 56–72.

16. Grof, S. Modern consciousness research and the quest for the new paradigm. *ReVision*, 1979, *2*, 41–52.

Perspectives on Psychology, Reality, and the Study of Consciousness

DANIEL GOLEMAN

In his sociology of knowledge, Mannheim (1936) describes how reality is...shaped by the structured tone and ethos of society. Human groups construct a reality according to innumerable implicit assumptions; Whorf (1964) demonstrates how these reality-shaping assumptions operate in language. Each language offers an arbitrary set of categories and syntactic rules for the interrelationships of those categories, and in so doing artificially slices the continuous spread and flow of existence in a unique way. Within the broader context of culture, science further codifies and organizes experiences.... Like the central nervous system and like a given culture, science too is tuned to some aspects of reality but out of focus for others. Within science in general each branch and specialty represents an even finer focus, and is to some degree a self-contained subculture with its own language and special view of the world.

Kuhn (1970) describes the element of arbitrariness implicit in the natural history of scientific schools and the manner in which they come to see the world and practice science in it. Assumptions such as the nature of the fundamental entities which compose the universe, the interaction of those entities with the senses, and the legitimate questions to be asked and techniques employed in seeking answers come to constitute the basis of educational initiation into a field of activities of research, as do the conceptual categories supplied during professional education into which the scientist subsequently attempts to divide nature. The assumption underlying what Kuhn calls "normal science" is that the scientific community knows what the world is like. A corollary of this assumption is that normal science often suppresses novelties which are subversive of its basic commitments. An example of such suppression within psychology is the early reaction of Viennese medical circles to the work of Freud; a more recent example is the struggle within the AAAS [American Association for the Advancement of Science] in recognizing parapsychology as a legitimate area for scientific inquiry. While normal science legitimizes some areas of inquiry, it can also discredit others.

Kuhn uses the term "paradigm" in one sense to denote "the entire constellation, values, techniques, and so on shared by the members of a given community." In this sense — as a set of shared constructs — a paradigm in science is on the same order as other community-shared world views — e.g., Buddhism. The means by which paradigms are perpetuated and transmitted are akin to the process of socialization into any other group-specific reality. Professional training is a secondary socialization whereby the fledgling scientist acquires a role-specific paradigm.

This socialization into a paradigm is by no means limited to science, but applies equally well, for example, to the novitiate lama as to the budding scientists: both acquire the implicit rules of their respective roles, games and cosmologies along with their formal training. Both the scientist and the lama enter a role-specific, socially differentiated, subuniverse of meaning which is esoteric relative to the common stock of knowledge, and which is carried by a particular collectivity. And in both cultural contexts the function of the lore entered is to comprehend and organize reality for the layman.

To a degree, psychological theory is shaped by autobiography, the personal history of theoreticians directly influencing their articulation of and emphasis in theory. Freud, for example, in his introduction to *Civilization and Its Discontents* tells of receiving a letter from the poet Romain Rolland, who had become a student of the great Indian saint Sri Ramakrishna. Rolland described a feeling of something "limitless and unbounded," which he saw as "the physiological basis of much of the wisdom of mysticism." Freud labeled the feeling "oceanic," and, admitting his puzzlement and failure to discover this oceanic feeling in himself, went on to reinterpret this fact of experience in a manner consonant with his own world view, positing as its origins a feeling of infantile helplessness which he saw as a source of religious feeling. In doing so, Freud explicitly applied a template which he had derived for understanding experience of a different order than Rolland was describing, but which seems to have rendered the data more comfortable for Freud.

Attempts to forge a systematic and inclusive understanding of human behavior by no means originated with contemporary Western psychology. Our formal psychology as such is less than a hundred years old, and so represents a recent version of an endeavor probably as old as human history. It is also the product of European and American culture, society, and intellectual history, and as such is only one of innumerable "psychologies" (though for us by far the most familiar and comfortable) which have been articulated as an implicit or explicit part of the fabric of reality in every culture, present and past. If we are to arrive at the fullest possible understanding of human psychology, it behooves us to turn to these other systems of psychology, not as curiosities to be studied from our own vantage point, but as alternative lenses on man through which we may be allowed visions and insights which our own psychological viewpoints might obscure. While we may subsequently find some alternative viewpoints irrelevant to our own situation, we may also find much of value.

Individuals in each culture, observes Dorothy Lee (1950), codify experience in terms of the categories of their own linguistic system, grasping reality only as it is presented in code. Each culture punctuates and categorizes experience differently. The anthropologist recognizes that the study of a code different from our own can lead us to concepts and aspects of reality from which our own way of looking at the world excludes us.

One significance of Carlos Castaneda's (1969, 1971, 1972) works is in his sharing with the reader the personal struggle undergone in shedding his standard Western view of reality and his professional anthropologist's assumptions in order to finally accept the teachings of his Yaqui shaman "informant" on their own terms. A similar openness on the part of contemporary psychology may be a requisite to gaining what wisdom and insights regarding consciousness are contained in traditional psychologies. Each culture has a specialized vocabulary in those areas of existence which are most salient to its own mode of experiencing the world. In this light it is intriguing that our own culture has as its major technical vocabulary for describing inner experience a highly specialized nosology of psychopathology, while Asian cultures such as India have equally intricate vocabularies for altered states of consciousness and stages in spiritual development.

LaBarre (1947) points out that the outward expression of emotion is susceptible to great cross-cultural variation, even those expressions such as laughing and crying which are generally considered biologically determined. So with the experience and communication of states of awareness: culture molds awareness to conform to certain norms, limits the types of experience or categories for experience available to the individual, and determines the appropriateness or acceptability of a given state of awareness or its communication in the social situation.

Our normative cultural reality is state-specific. Insofar as "reality" is a consensually validated, but arbitrary, convention, an altered state of consciousness can represent an anti-social, unruly mode of being. . . . This fear of the unpredictable may have been a major motivating force behind the repression in our own culture of means for inducing altered states — e.g., psychedelics — or for a more general suspicion of techniques such as meditation.

While the cultural value system which has led to the preeminence of the waking state and the preclusion of altered states (except for alcohol intoxication) from the cultural norm has proved functional in terms of say, . . . economic growth, they have also rendered us as a culture relatively unsophisticated in terms of altered states of consciousness (ASC). Other "primitive" and traditional cultures, while less materially productive than our own, are far more knowledgeable than we in the intracacies of consciousness. Some cultures explicitly educate some or all members in altering consciousness, and many have developed "technologies" for this purpose — e.g., the Bushmen are trained to enter a trance via dancing, and to use the trance state for healing (Katz, 1973); a Yaqui Indian "warrior" retrains his perceptual habits so as to apprehend messages and natural forces ordinarily unsensed (Castaneda, 1973); the Malaysian Senoi systematically utilize dream contents to maintain harmonious interpersonal relations in community life (Stewart, 1969).

The religious teachings of the East contain psychological theories, just as our own psychologies reflect cosmologies. Within the context of their own respective cosmologies these traditional psychologies of the East are equal to our own in terms of an "empirical" adequacy determined not by the procedural canons of empirical science, but rather as interpretive schemes applicable to the experiential phenomena of everyday life. Berger and Luckmann (1967, p. 178) observe:

> Insofar as psychological theories are elements of the social definition of reality, their reality-generating capacity is a characteristic they share with other legitimate theories. . . . If a psychology becomes socially established (that is, becomes generally recognized as an adequate interpretation of objective reality), it tends to realize itself forcefully in the phenomena it purports to interpret. . . . Psychologies produce a reality, which in turn serves as the basis for their verification.

. . . The domain of many traditional psychologies encompasses the familiar territory of normal waking awareness, but extends also into states of consciousness of which the West has only recently become cognizant (and the existence of which may yet remain a mystery for most Western psychologists and laymen who have not themselves heard of or experienced them). The models of contemporary psychology, for example, foreclose the acknowledgement or investigation of a mode of being which is the central premise and *summum bonum* of virtually every Eastern psycho-spiritual system. Called variously "enlightenment," "Buddha-hood," "liberation," the "awakened state," and so on, there is simply no fully equivalent category in contemporary psychology.[1] The paradigms of traditional Asian psychologies, however, are capable of encompassing the major categories of contemporary psychology as well as this other mode of consciousness.

The Tibetan Wheel of Life, for example, depicts pictorially six realms of existence, each a metaphor for a different psychological state.[2] One realm, that of the "stupid beast," stands for the level of behavior which is totally conditioned, and corresponds to the world studied by behaviorism, where habit and simple stimulus-response is the principle determinant of action and thought. The hell realms represent aggression and anxiety states, and are emblematic of all anxiety-based behavior; this is the realm of psychopathology as mapped by contemporary psychologists like Freud, Sullivan, and Laing. The realm of the *pretas*, or hungry ghosts, corresponds to insatiable appetite or needfulness — what Maslow has characterized as "deficiency motivation." The realm of heaven depicts god-like beings who represent sensual bliss and gratification of the highest order; the "peak experience" would be subsumed by this category as would many of the experiences which have emerged from humanistic psychology.... Shown at war with the gods of the heaven realm are the "jealous gods" who represent an attitude shaped not by needfulness, but by envy; these reflect a motivational state of overweening competitiveness and self-aggrandizement—a state of mind studied widely within Western social science, e.g., Veblen and Lorenz. The sixth realm is that of human beings, and denotes the potential for insight into the human condition; this insight is very similar to the understanding formulated in Freud's tragic vision: that suffering is inescapable.

Freud, in articulating this insight, saw no way out of suffering but to beat it; the Buddhist psychologist, in stating the same insight as the "First Noble Truth," offers an alternative: alter the processes of ordinary consciousness and thereby end suffering. The state of consciousness which transcends all the ordinary realms of being is the "Buddha realm...." Buddhahood is attained by transforming ordinary consciousness, principally through meditation, and once attained is characterized by the extinction of all those states—e.g., anxiety, needfulness, pride—which mark the ordinary realms of existence.... Buddhahood is a higher-order integration than any suggested by the developmental schema of contemporary psychology.

What is particularly intriguing about the Buddhist developmental schema is that it not only expands the constructs of contemporary psychology's view of what is possible for man, but also gives details of the means whereby such a change can occur . . . namely, that via meditation—an attentional manipulation — one can enter an altered state, and that through systematic retraining of attentional habits one can alter consciousness as a trait of being. Such an enduring alteration of the structure and process of consciousness is no longer an ASC, but represents an altered *trait* of consciousness, or ATC, where attributes of an ASC are assimilated in ordinary states of consciousness.

. . . Though traditional and contemporary psychologies may partially overlap — e.g., in a common interest in attentional processes, or in an understanding of the inescapable nature of human suffering — each also thoroughly explores territory and techniques the other ignores or barely touches on. Psychoanalytic thought, for example, has charted aspects of what would be called "karma" in the East in far greater detail and complexity than any Eastern school of psychology, just as Eastern schools have developed an array of techniques for voluntarily altering consciousness and stabilizing in an ATC, and so establish a technology for dealing with realities beyond the mind as it is conceptualized in contemporary psychology or experienced in our usual state of consciousness.

To the extent that biography is the progenitor of psychology, these paradigmatic differences between traditional Eastern and contemporary Western psychology reflect differing experiences of being-in-the-world. Psychoanalytic thought, for example, gives a prominent place to the concept of reality-testing, which from the viewpoint of the relativity of states of consciousness is a state-bound test of "reality," but does not deal with a conception of levels of reality or ASC, as is depicted in the Tibetan Wheel of Life. "Reality-testing" entails an "either-or" dichotomatization; the Tibetan view allows for a "both-and" outlook on states of awareness. The Western pathology of view is to equate "reality" with the world as perceived in waking state awareness, so denying access or credibility to reality as perceived in other states of consciousness. The complementary Eastern pathology is to see reality as wholly other than that of waking awareness, and so dismisses the physical world as illusory.

As in the evolution of science generally, in resolving any seeming conflicts in vision, paradigm, or world view between Eastern and Western psychologies, an integratory effort may generate resolutions which would be higher order formulations offering an understanding of states of consciousness and state-dependent realities at once more complex and more solidly grounded than any at present. . . . The key for a progressive transfer to wider modes of apprehension for psychology as a whole as for the individual:

> . . . is the recognition, as William James said, that there is "always more," outgrowing the bonds of present self-limitation for the apprehension of present reality, and the developing of *openness* upon which the germinal — or not yet germinal — potentialities for new reals may come into existence . . . not

only with the real which can be independently shown to be real by . . . more sober methods, but with the real which newly comes into existence as evolution goes on.

Notes

1. Maslow's (1970) "plateau experience" is one near approximation in contemporary psychology; Sutich's (1973) concept of "ultimate states" may also subsume this category.
2. This interpretation is based on explanations by Chögyam Trungpa Rimpoche, Herbert Guenther, and Bhagvan Das (all personal communications). The final extrapolations to contemporary psychology are my own. A more complete and authoritative account of the Wheel of Life is given by Chögyam Trungpa (1973).

References

Berger, P. L., & Luckmann, T. *The social construction of reality.* New York: Anchor, 1967.

Casteneda, C. *The teachings of Don Juan.* New York: Simon and Schuster, 1969.

Casteneda, C. *A separate reality.* New York: Simon and Schuster, 1971.

Casteneda, C. *Journey to Ixtlan.* New York: Simon and Schuster, 1972.

Goleman, D. The Buddha on meditation and consciousness. Part I: The teachings, *J. Transpersonal Psychol.* 1972, *4*, 1, 1–44.

James, W. *Psychology: Briefer course.* New York: Holt and Co., 1910.

Katz, R. Education for transcendence: Lessons from the !Kung Zhū/twāsi, *J. Transpersonal Psychol.*, 1973, *5*, 2, 136–155.

Kuhn, T. S. *The structure of scientific revolutions.* Chicago: University of Chicago Press, 1970.

LaBarre, W. The cultural basis of emotions and gestures, *J. Pers.*, 1947, *16*, 49–68.

Lee, D. Codification of reality: Lineal and nonlineal, *Psychosom. Med.*, 1950, 12, 2, 89–97.

Mannheim, K. *Ideology and utopia.* London: Routledge and Kegan Paul, 1936.

Maslow, A. Theory Z, *J. Transpersonal Psychol.*, 1970, 2, 1, 31–47.

Stewart, K. Dream theory in Malaya, in C. Tart (Ed.), *Altered states of consciousness.* New York: Wiley and Sons, 1969.

Sutich, A. J. Transpersonal therapy, *J. Transpersonal Psychol.*, 1973, *5*, 1, 1–6.

Trungpa, C. *Cutting through spiritual materialism.* Berkeley: Shambhala, 1973.

Whorf, B.L. *Language, thought, and reality.* Cambridge: M.I.T. Press, 1964.

Paradigms in Collision

ROGER N. WALSH, DUANE ELGIN,
FRANCES VAUGHAN, KEN WILBER

Western behavioral scientists have made a number of attempts in recent years to evaluate the consciousness disciplines. However, almost all evaluations have suffered from serious conceptual and methodological deficiencies that render their conclusions questionable. The aim of this paper is to point to the inadequacies that have marred previous attempts and to delineate the conceptual, informational, and experiential criteria that must be met in order to allow adequate examination.

To do this we will first examine and compare the models of human nature posited by the consciousness disciplines and Western science, and show that what Thomas Kuhn (1970) has called a "paradigm clash" must inevitably result when the former model is examined from the Western perspective. Many of the conclusions some reports have drawn will be seen to be derived from paradigmatic assumptions. Moreover, due to insufficient depth of study and personal experience most investigators have mistakenly focused on epiphenomena of these practices and have fallen into traps that advanced practitioners explicitly warn against. Finally, we will point to recent advances in the Western sciences, both psychological and physical, that are essential to an adequate assessment.

The major focus of this paper will be on the process of assessment and comparison. Although their basic assumptions will be examined, no attempt will be made to perform a detailed critique of the consciousness disciplines. As will become apparent, such an undertaking is necessarily a very major task. The failure to undertake a critique here should not be seen as advocating a blanket acceptance of these disciplines. There is no shortage of inconsistencies associated with them, but the first step in adequately examining these is to first examine the process of examination.

It seems appropriate to begin with some definitions, because words associated with various disciplines are frequently misunderstood and confused with a variety of occult popularisms. The term "consciousness disciplines" and other terms such as "spiritual disciplines," "Eastern traditions" and "mysticism" are often used interchangeably. They can be defined as doctrines and practices that assert the possibility of obtaining, through mental training, the most profound insight into consciousness, mental processes, and reality. This training is usually an extraordinarily intense and arduous one, often demanding decades if not a major portion of life to reach complete fruition. The training constitutes the basis for a wide range of meditative and yogic practices. Meditation can be defined as the training and practice of control of attention and awareness, while yoga is a more generic term applied to several types of practice that may include meditation and sometimes the physical postures (asanas) with which it is usually identified in the West. Some of these practices have traditionally been associated with Eastern religions, e.g., Buddhism and Hinduism, but they must be carefully differentiated from the items of faith and dogma to which believers adhere. Rather, they represent *practices* that individuals may employ to obtain insights into self and reality that may in turn enhance religious understanding (Goleman, 1979; Smith, 1958).

TENETS OF THE CONSCIOUSNESS DISCIPLINES

Most traditions posit models of human nature that show a degree of consistency across cultures and ages and that have been variously named "the perennial philosophy" (Huxley, 1944), "the perennial religion" (Smith, 1976), or the "perennial psychology" (Wilber, 1977). Obviously we cannot hope to do full justice to them here, but we will attempt to delineate some of the dimensions underlying such models and refer the interested reader elsewhere for more complete descriptions (e.g., Walsh and Vaughan, this volume; Wilber, 1977).

Many traditions view consciousness as their central concern and make several claims that run counter to Western assumptions. These include statements that (1) our usual state of consciousness is severely suboptimal, (2) that multiple states including true "higher" states exist, (3) that these states are attainable through training but, (4) that verbal communication about them is necessarily limited. We will now examine these tenets in more detail.

Fully developed mystics state unequivocally that our usual state of consciousness is not only suboptimal, it is dreamlike and illusory. They assert that whether we know it or not, we, as untrained individuals, are prisoners of our own minds, totally and unwittingly trapped by a continuous inner fantasy-dialogue that creates an all-consuming illusory distortion of perception or reality (*maya* or *samsara*). However, this condition goes unrecognized until we begin to subject our perceptual-cognitive processes to rigorous scrutiny such as in meditation.

Thus, the "normal" person is seen as "asleep" or "dreaming." When the "dream" is especially painful or disruptive it becomes a nightmare and is recognized as psychopathology, but since the vast majority of the population "dreams," the true state of affairs goes unrecognized. When the individual permanently disidentifies from or eradicates this dream he or she is said to have awakened and can now recognize the true nature of both his or her former state and that of the population. This awakening or enlightenment is the aim of the consciousness disciplines (e.g., Goldstein, 1976; Goleman, 1977; Ram Dass, 1975b, 1976, 1977, 1978; Wilber, 1977).

To some extent this is an extension rather than a denial of the perspective of Western psychology and psychiatry, which have long recognized that careful experimental observation reveals a broad range of perceptual distortions unrecognized by naive subjects. The consciousness disciplines merely go further in asserting that we are all subject to distortions, that they affect all aspects of our perception, that without specific remedial mental training all remain unaware of them, and that the consensual reality we share is thus illusory. This has also been suggested by a number of Western investigators (e.g., Fromm, 1970).

The implications of this are awesome. Within the Western model, we recognize and define psychosis as a suboptimal state of consciousness that views reality in a distorted way and does not recognize that distortion. It is therefore significant to note that from the mystical perspective, our usual state fits all the criteria of psychosis in that it is suboptimal, has a distorted view of reality, and does not recognize that distortion. Indeed, from the ultimate mystical perspective, psychosis can be defined as being trapped in, or attached to, any *one* state of consciousness, each of which by itself is necessarily limited and only relatively real (Ram Dass, 1977, 1978).

To hold this as an interesting objective concept is one thing. To consider it as something directly applicable to our own experience is of course considerably more difficult. As Tart (1975a) notes:

> We have studied some aspects of samsara (illusion, maya) in far more detail than the Eastern traditions that originated the concept of samsara. Yet almost no psychologists apply this idea to themselves. They assume ... that their own states of consciousness are basically logical and clear. Western psychology now has a challenge to recognize this detailed evidence that our "normal" state is a state of samsara. (p. 286)

Of course, it is very difficult, if not impossible, to recognize the limitations of the usual state of consciousness if that is all one has ever known. However, mystics repeatedly claim that anyone who is willing to undertake the strenuous but necessary training to extricate their awareness from the conditioned tyranny of the mind will be able to look back and see the formerly unrecognized limitations within which they lived. A common present-day analogy is that of the people who live in a chronically smog-ridden urban environment but only see the full extent of the pollution once they get out of it.

Most traditions acknowledge a wide spectrum of states of consciousness. In some disciplines, especially those emphasizing the importance of meditation, e.g., Buddhist psychology, this spectrum is described in considerable detail. Descriptions of the phenomenology of individual component states, and the techniques for attaining them, provide an articulate cartography of altered states (Brown, 1977; Kornfield, 1977; Wilber, 1977).

While knowledge of this multiplicity of states is best obtained by direct experience, their existence has been recognized and acknowledged by some nonpractitioners. Perhaps the earliest and most eminent psychologist was William James (1958), who around the turn of the century remarked:

> ... our normal waking consciousness ... is but one special type of consciousness, whilst all about it parted from it by the filmiest of screens, there lie potential forms of consciousness entirely different. We may go through life without suspecting their existence; but apply the requisite stimulus and at a touch they are there in all their completeness....
>
> No account of the universe in its totality can be final which leaves these other forms of consciousness quite disregarded. How to regard them is the question.... At any rate, they forbid a premature closing of our accounts with reality.

It is not just the existence of multiple states that is held to be important, but the fact that they may be associated with state-specific properties, functions, and abilities. Perceptual sensitivity and clarity, attention, responsivity, sense of identity, affective, cognitive, and perceptual processes may all vary with the state of consciousness in apparently precise and predictable ways (Brown, 1977; Goleman, 1977).

Some of these states are held to be functionally specific and a few to be true higher states. Functionally specific states are those in which specific functions can be performed better than in the usual state, though other functions may be less effective. True higher states are those that possess all the effective functions of the usual condition plus additional ones (Tart, 1972, 1975a). Such states may be accompanied by perceptions, insights, and affects outside the realm of day-to-day untrained experience, some of which are held to be central to the growth of true higher wisdom.

Different traditions emphasize different techniques and combinations of techniques to obtain control over consciousness and perception, and the interested reader is referred elsewhere for a detailed classification of these practices (e.g., Goleman, 1977, Wilber, 1977, in press b). In summary it can be said that all involve training in controlling one or more aspects of perceptual sensitivity, concentration, affect, or cognition. The intensity and duration of training usually needed to attain mastery in these disciplines may be quite extraordinary by Western standards, and is usually reckoned in decades. In the words of Ramana Maharshi, perhaps the most respected Hindu teacher of the last few centuries: "No one succeeds without effort. Mind control is not your birthright. Those who succeed owe their liberation to perseverance." (Kornfield, 1977).

The Swiss existential psychiatrist Medard Boss (1963), one of the first Westerners to examine both the Eastern and Western literature *and practice* noted that compared with the extent of the yogic self-exploration "even the best Western training analysis is not much more than an introductory course" (p. 188).

The different levels and aims of psychotherapeutic intervention may be broadly categorized as traditionally therapeutic (reducing pathology and enhancing adjustment), existential (confronting the questions and problems of existence and one's response to them), and soteriological (enlightenment, liberation, freedom, transcendence of the problems first confronted at the existential level). Western psychologies and therapies focus on the first two levels and "on the psychology of liberation — nothing" (Allport, cited by Smith, 1976, p. 160–161; Thetford, Schuman, and Walsh, in press). Yet the human condition appears to include further possibilities: "what has been called 'salvation' by the Christians, 'liberation' and 'enlightenment' by the Buddhists, and love and union by the non-theistic humanist" (Fromm & Xirau, 1968). It is this latter level that is the primary goal of the consciousness disciplines (Brown, 1977).

Interestingly enough, although these disciplines may start from different places and employ different approaches, they all aim for an enduring final common soteriological state of consciousness, known by a variety of names, such as "enlightenment," "samadhi," "nirvana," "liberation"(Goleman, 1977; Johansson, 1969; Ram Dass, 1975a, 1976, 1977; Smith, 1976; Wilber, 1975). This might be seen in general systems terms as "equifinality," in which a common end stage is reached independent of the original state (Bertalanffy, 1968).

Although the instructions for attaining them may be quite explicit, the verbal descriptions of the states themselves are often considerably less so. This brings us to the last tenet of the consciousness disciplines that we will list in this section, namely the claim that language and even thought are inappropriate and inadequate modes with which to fully comprehend some of these phenomena. For example the Buddha, although clearly capable of the most sophisticated logical analysis (Owens, 1976) and "a thinker of unexcelled philosophic power" (Burtt, 1955), repeatedly stated that "the deepest secrets of the world and of man are inaccessible to abstract philosophical thinking" (Govinda, 1969, p. 36). Rather, students are told that they must experience these things directly for themselves if they are to have any true understanding.

We may now be confronting a paradigm clash between traditional Western psychological models and the models of the consciousness disciplines. If this is so, then our first task before judging the validity of the consciousness disciplines' paradigm is to examine the assumptions and logic of our own paradigm.

TENETS OF THE BEHAVIORAL SCIENCES

> There is nothing more difficult than to become critically aware of the presuppositions of one's own thoughts. . . . Every thought can be scrutinized directly except the thought by which we scrutinize.
>
> —*Schumacher, 1977, p. 44*

What, then, are some of these relevant implicit assumptions of Western science? Concerning consciousness, the behavioral sciences recognize only a limited number of normal states, such as waking, dreaming, and nondreaming sleep. Very few others are recognized and are inevitably held to be pathological, e.g., delirium, psychosis. In addition the usual waking state is held to be optimal, predominantly rational, and under good intellectual control (Frank, 1977; Tart, 1975b). Thus, no serious consideration is given to the possibility of the existence of either functionally specific or true higher states. As King (1963) wryly puts it, "we all convince one another that the waking condition is a healthy and proper one, for no other reason than that we are all its common victims."

A similar situation exists for perception, for it is commonly assumed that ordinary perception is as close to optimum as is humanly possible. For example, concentration, the ability to consciously focus and fix perception, has been tacitly assumed to be only slightly trainable ever since William James at the turn of the century suggested an upper limit of three seconds for concentration on any one object (James, 1950). This is very different from the statements of advanced yogis from a variety of cultures and disciplines who have frequently been observed to remain motionless for hours or days, and who claim that during this time they remained unshakably concentrated on their object of meditation (Brown, 1977; Goleman, 1977; Shapiro and Walsh, in press).

In the Western sciences the intellect and objectivity reign supreme. All phenomena are held to be ultimately capable of examination by intellectual analysis and such analysis is viewed as the optimal path to knowledge. A corollary of this is that all experiences are usually thought to be essentially verbally encodable and communicable. A final premise, which Western critics of mysticism almost invariably practice, is that an intellectual, nonexperiential, nonpractical examination and appraisal of other traditions and practices represents an adequate approach for determining their worth.

PARADIGMS IN COLLISION

Now let's examine what must necessarily happen when the claims and models of the consciousness disciplines are examined from within this Western framework. First, as regards consciousness, all claims for the existence of true higher states will automatically be disallowed because we know the usual state to be optimal and there is thus no place in the Western model for anything better. Not only are they disallowed, but because some of these experiences are unknown to the usual state, they are necessarily viewed as pathological. For example, the experience of satori or enlightenment or shorter lived transcendental experiences include a sense or unity or at-oneness with the universe (Kapleau, 1967; Walsh and Shapiro, in press; Wilber, 1977), which Western psychiatrists and psychologists have tended to interpret as a regressive retreat to a primitive infantile state, e.g.:

> The obvious similarities between schizophrenic regressions and the practices of yoga and Zen merely indicate that the general trend in oriental cultures is to withdraw into the self from an overbearingly difficult physical and social reality.   —*Alexander & Selesnich, 1966, p. 457*

On the other hand, the yogi's claim that our usual state of consciousness is limited, fantasy filled, unclear, and illusory, necessarily makes little sense to the Western scientist or mental health practitioner who has neither experienced clearer states nor examined his or her own consciousness with any rigor. Fortunately, this is one claim where personal testing is relatively easy by any individual willing to undertake intensive practice of any of those meditative disciplines that aim at examining the workings of the mind. Even within a few days of intensive investigation, the irrational, unclear, and uncontrollable nature of the untrained mind will rapidly become apparent, and the investigators will find themselves amazed that they had previously remained so unaware of these phenomena (Goldstein, 1976; Kornfield, 1977; Walsh, 1977, 1978).

The claim that the intellect is an inadequate and inappropriate epistemological tool for the comprehension of the reality revealed by the consciousness disciplines will meet with little understanding among traditional behavioral sciences. However, those who have examined the implications of recent advances in physics and neuroscience will be less surprised (Capra, this volume).

Western philosophy, traditionally, has recognized three distinct modes of acquiring knowledge: perception, cognition, and contemplation/meditation (Wilber, 1979; this volume b). Each of these modes has its own unique properties and areas that are not fully overlapping and cannot be fully reduced one to another without producing what is called category error. Thus, in Western epistemological language, the consciousness disciplines' claim for the inappropriateness of the intellect as the sole judge of yogic insights may be seen as a plea against category error.

When the yogi claims that physical empirical approaches are always erroneous, or the scientist denies the validity of contemplation, then both are guilty of category error, meditation becomes pseudophilosophy, and science becomes scientism. It may be that these modes and types of knowledge are complementary, just as the wave and particle descriptions of subatomic particles are complementary. Thus, neither mode of knowing may encompass the totality, but rather may see only that portion for which it is adequate, so that what is required for a fuller picture is a "dynamic epistemology" (Globus & Franklin, 1978).

The claim that mystical experiences cannot be verbally communicated has traditionally met with little sympathy. However, this statement may be reasonable if we remember that language is conceptual and hence may result in category error when applied to nonconceptual material. Also, language may be excellent for communicating about experiences people have in common, but otherwise surprisingly inefficient (Maslow, 1966). No overlapping experience means very little or no communication, e.g., the description of the color green for a blind person. This limitation is particularly evident in communication about altered states of consciousness, and will be discussed in more detail subsequently.

However, mystics are not the only ones who claim that it is impossible to fully conceptualize and communicate symbolically the fundamental nature of reality. A number of scientists, working at the frontiers of their fields, have reached the same conclusion. Consider, for example, the words of the renowned physicists Eddington and Heisenberg:

> We have two kinds of knowledge which I call symbolic knowledge and intimate knowledge. . . . [The] more customary forms of reasoning have been developed for symbolic knowledge only. The intimate knowledge will not submit to codification and analysis; or, rather, when we attempt to analyze the intimacies are lost and it is replaced by symbolism.
> —*Eddington, 1969, cited by Wilber, 1977*

> In quantum theory . . . we have at first no simple guide for correlating the mathematical symbols with concepts of ordinary language; and the only thing we know from the start is the fact that our common concepts cannot be applied to the structure of atoms. —*Heisenberg, 1958, cited by Wilber, 1977*

In addition, it seems that English is poorly equipped to deal with precise descriptions and analyses of consciousness, having a very limited descriptive vocabulary in this area compared to some other languages, e.g., Pali (Tart, 1975a). Thus, we may be victims of "linguistic relativism," in which we create our language and are limited by it in turn. "We dissect nature along lines laid down by our native languages" (Whorf, 1956, p. 213).

It should be noted that the consciousness disciplines model is inherently a broader one than that of the Western behavioral sciences, since it involves a significantly wider range of states of consciousness and perceptual modes. Indeed the Western model might be seen as a limiting case of the mystical model. The Western model, then, may have a position vis-à-vis the mystical model comparable to the Newtonian model vis-à-vis an Einsteinian model in physics. The Newtonian case applies to macroscopic objects moving at relatively low velocities compared to the speed of light. When applied to high velocity objects the Newtonian model no longer fits. The Einsteinian model, on the other hand, encompasses both low and high speeds and from this broader perspective, the Newtonian model, and its limitations, are all perfectly logical and understandable (employing Einsteinian and not Newtonian logic, of course). However, the reverse is definitely untrue, for the Einsteinian logic is not comprehensible within a

Newtonian framework. Furthermore, from a Newtonian perspective, reports of incongruous findings such as the constancy of the speed of light and objects increasing in mass at high speed are incomprehensible and suspect.

In terms of abstract set theory the Newtonian model can be seen as a subset nested within the larger Einsteinian set. The properties of the subset are readily comprehensible from the perspective of the set but the reverse is necessarily untrue. The general principle is that to try to examine the larger model or set from the perspective of the smaller is inappropriate and necessarily productive of false conclusions.

The implications of this for the comparison and assessment of the consciousness disciplines and Western behavioral sciences should now be clear. From a multiple-states-of-consciousness model the traditional Western approach is recognized as a relativistically useful model provided that, because of the limitations imposed by state dependency, it is not applied inappropriately to altered states outside its scope. From the Western perspective, however, the consciousness disciplines' model must necessarily appear incomprehensible and nonsensical.

METHODOLOGICAL PROBLEMS IN THE APPRAISAL OF THE CONSCIOUSNESS DISCIPLINES

In addition to the paradigmatic clash described above, a significant number of deficiencies of logic, knowledge, and experience mar most appraisals. Western investigators of the mystical literature almost invariably focus on the powerful, dramatic, and unusual experiences that yogis encounter. These span the whole range of human experience from unpatterned sensations to muscular spasms, complex images, and intense effects. Such experiences are quite common for individuals commencing intensive practices. What investigators have not realized is that such experiences are not the goal of mystical traditions. Advanced practitioners view them merely as epiphenomena to be treated with detachment and benign neglect (Deikman, 1977).

Thus, a well-known Zen story tells of a student being taught to meditate on his breath who one day rushed to his master saying that he had seen images of a golden Buddha surrounded by light. "Ah yes," said the master. "But did you also keep your mind on the breath?"

Western investigators have tended to base their assessment of mysticism on the very phenomena the mystics themselves warn against taking seriously!

This assessment has also been founded on an intellectual analysis of the mystical *literature* without examination or personal experience of mystical *practice*. However, mystics have explicitly warned against this, stating that deep conceptual understanding is dependent on adequate personal practice.

Without practice, without contemplation, a merely intellectual, theoretical, and philosophical approach to Buddhism is quite inadequate. ... Mystical insights ... cannot be judged by unenlightened people from the worm's-eye view of book learning, and a little book knowledge does not really entitle anyone to pass judgement on mystical experiences.

—*Vimalo 1974, pp. 70 and 73*

Several lines of evidence lend support to this claim. Several initially skeptical Western behavioral scientists with personal experience of these disciplines have remarked that only after they began practice did some of the statements and claims that initially made little or no sense gradually become comprehensible (e.g., Deikman, 1977). The earlier discussion that noted the different modes and types of knowledge (Eddington, 1969; Heisenberg, 1958; Wilber, 1979, this volume b) is also supportive since it recognizes that to equate conceptual and contemplative knowledge may result in category error. Similarly, the recent recognition of state-dependent phenomena, such as state-dependent learning and communication (to be discussed in more detail shortly), is consistent with the claim that this is learning in which a basic requirement is a change in consciousness (Rajneesh, 1975, p. 9).

Two philosophical principles are also relevant. The first is *adequatio* (adequateness), which states that the understanding of the knower must be adequate to the thing to be known (Schumacher, 1977). Closely related is the concept of "grades of significance." The same phenomenon may hold entirely different grades of meaning and significance to different observers with different degrees of adequatio. Thus, for an animal, a particular phenomenon may be merely a colored object (which it is), to a savage it may represent only marked paper (which it is). For the average educated adult it may be a book (which again it is) that makes patently ridiculous claims about the nature of the world, while for the physicist it is a brilliant treatise on relativity revealing new insights and depths to reality. In each case the phenomenon remained the same, but its level of meaning and significance was a function of the capacity and training (adequatio) of the observer. The facts themselves do not carry labels indicating the appropriate level at which they ought to be considered. Nor does the choice of an inadequate level lead to factual error or logical contradiction. All levels of significance up to the highest are equally factual, equally logical, equally objective. The observer who is not adequate to the higher levels of significance will not know that they are being missed (Schumacher, 1977). "If I don't know I don't know I think I know" (Laing, 1970). This is precisely the claim of the consciousness disciplines: namely, that only through personal mental training does the average person become adequate to the knowledge that is the concern of these disciplines. This claim, then, is no different in principle than the claim that scientific research is best judged by those with appropriate scientific training, only the type of training is different.

Does this mean that *only* advanced practitioners can make assessments of the consciousness disciplines, or that Western scientists must all first become yogis? Obviously not! But it does mean that Western-trained scientists must recognize that without specific preparation there may be epistemological and paradigmatic limits to their ability to comprehend and assess these disciplines, that scientific objectivity may need to be balanced (in at least some researchers) by personal experience and training, and that cautious openmindedness to yogic claims may be a more skilfull stance than automatic rejection of anything not immediately logical and comprehensible.

RELEVANT ADVANCES IN WESTERN SCIENCE

Any examination of the consciousness traditions should take into consideration certain recent advances in Western science. These areas include transpersonal psychology, state-dependent learning, meditation research, clinical and sociological studies of peak and transcendental experiences, advanced psychedelic therapy, as well as the frontiers of quantum and particle physics.

Transpersonal psychology has been especially concerned with topics such as states of consciousness, meditation, models of psychological health, peak experiences, mystical experiences, implications of modern physics, etc. It has already examined many of the issues raised anew by investigators of the consciousness disciplines, who should thus be familiar with this literature.

A second area concerns research and theorizing in the field of altered states of consciousness. Both animal and human studies have shown that learning, understanding, and recall may be dependent on, and limited by, the state of consciousness (Overton, 1971). Thus, information acquired in one state by an individual may be neither recallable nor comprehensible by that same individual when in another state. Similarly, another individual may be quite unable to understand the communication from someone else in an altered state ("state-dependent communication"), but may be able to do so if he or she enters that same state also (Tart, 1972, 1975a). In some cases information initially available in only one state may subsequently be retained or more easily be learned in others (cross-state communication, cross-state retention).

Because the mystical traditions employ a range of altered states, the relevance of these recent findings is readily apparent. Mystics may enter altered states and acquire formerly inaccessible knowledge. However, due to the limits set by cross-state communication, this information may make little sense to another individual with no experience of that state. The easiest but also most superficial judgment would then be that the mystic was speaking incomprehensible nonsense resulting from either psychopathology or an impaired state of consciousness. However, such a conclusion is premature because only by experiencing that same state will the observer be able to rule out the possibility that the mystic is expounding valid though state-dependent knowledge.

It has not infrequently been suggested that mystical phenomena, even the supposedly highest and most illumined transcendental experiences, are essentially pathological, representing psychotic or near psychotic ego regressions toward an undifferentiated infantile state of consciousness (Ostow, 1969). Thus, for example, Freud (1962) interpreted oceanic experiences as indicative of infantile helplessness, Alexander (1931) saw meditation training as self-induced catatonia, and The Group for the Advancement of Psychiatry (1976) saw "forms of behavior intermediate between normality and psychosis." Such interpretations do not seem to consider the problem of paradigm clash or the now sizable body of experimental data on the psychology and sociology of transcendental experiences.

For the purposes of this discussion the term transcendental experience will be confined to an experience of an altered state of consciousness characterized by

1. Ineffability: the experience is of such power and so different from ordinary experience as to give the sense of defying description.
2. Noetic: a heightened sense of clarity and understanding.
3. Altered perception of space and time.
4. Appreciation of the wholistic, unitive integrated nature of the universe and one's unity with it.
5. Intense positive affect including a sense of the perfection of the universe.

Such experiences have been called by many names, including cosmic consciousness (Bucke, 1972) and peak experience (Maslow, 1964, 1971).

Several lines of evidence suggest that these experiences tend to occur most often among those who are psychologically most healthy. Clients working at advanced stages of psychotherapy may experience them (Bugental, 1978; Walsh & Shapiro, in press) as may self-actualizers, those individuals identified by Maslow (1971) as most healthy. Incipient experiences may occur in most people but may be repressed or misinterpreted due to fears of loss of control and intolerance of ambiguity. Indeed, those who report such experiences tend to score lower on intolerance of ambiguity scales (Maslow, 1964; Thomas & Cooper, 1977). Sociological surveys suggest that transcenders tend to be widespread in the population (greater than 1 percent), and are likely to be better educated, more economically successful, less racist, and substantially higher on scores of psychological well-being (Allison, 1967; Greeley, 1975; Hood, 1974, 1976, Thomas & Cooper, 1977).

Such experiences may apparently produce long-lasting beneficial changes in the individual (Chaudhuri, 1975; Roberts, 1977). Livingston (1975) lists 129 positive residual effects that may occur and concludes that positive residue may be a defining characteristic of transcendental phenomena. This echoes the ideas of Jung, who was the first Western therapist to affirm the importance of transcendental experience for mental health and wrote, "the fact is that the approach to the numinous is the real therapy and inasmuch as you attain to the numinous experiences you are released from the curse of pathology" (1973, p. 377).

Maslow (1972, p. 357, 361–363) states that the transcendental, or as he called it "peak" experience, is "so profound and shaking . . . that it can change the person's character . . . forever after." Upon his return, the person "feels himself more than at other times to be the responsible, active, the creative center of his own activities and of his own perceptions, more self-determined, more of a free agent, with more 'free will' than at other times." In his final formulation of the concept of "the hierarchy of needs" Maslow came to see the seeking of transcendence as the highest of all goals, even above self-actualization (Roberts, 1978).

It therefore seems inappropriate to equate transcendental experiences with psychopathology and psychosis. This is not to say that similar experiences cannot occur in the mentally ill, or even that they might not be harmful for some individuals. Only further research will tell. What is clear is that it is no longer tenable to view them as necessarily, or even usually, pathological.

Empirical research on meditation is still in a very early stage (for reviews see Shapiro & Giber, 1978; Shapiro & Walsh, in press). Preliminary evidence supports its potential for inducing altered states and greater mental health. However, as yet there is little information on who is most likely to benefit or whether it is sometimes harmful. Likewise we have little data on its effects on more advanced practitioners.

A further relevant area is the recently emerging, and as yet little known, evidence from in-depth research with psychedelics. It is necessary to stress the words *in depth* because it is now clear that while the usual experiments employing either low doses, relatively few sessions, or subjects suffering from some form of psychopathology may provide extremely interesting information on perception and psychodynamics, this is far from being the whole story. In fact, this area of research appears to provide an independent line of evidence supporting the existence and availability of states of consciousness similar to those described by the consciousness disciplines, as well as the phenomenon of state-dependent learning. For discussions of the relevance of in-depth research on psychedelics see Grof, chapter 2, and for physics see Capra, later in this chapter.

ADEQUATE ASSESSMENTS OF THE CONSCIOUSNESS DISCIPLINES

What then must Western behavioral scientists do if they are to conduct truly adequate investigations of the consciousness disciplines? First and foremost they will have to recognize that the task they are undertaking is considerably more demanding than previously thought. Recognizing the possibility of paradigm clash, the first essential step will require a thoroughgoing examination of the beliefs, models, and paradigms they themselves bring to the investigation. Along with this goes the need for a willingness to be open to the possibility that these disciplines may represent systems and paradigms in many ways, although in different ways, as sophisticated as our own. Thus, initially unfamiliar or incomprehensible phenomena are not to be immediately assumed to be evidence of either inferior intelligence or psychopathology. Rather, the first response must be to inquire whether both the investigator and the investigation process are adequate to the task.

Thus for example, it will be especially important to remember such factors as state-dependent learning, the different modes of acquiring knowledge, and the difference between intimate and symbolic knowledge. Investigators will therefore wish to directly examine both the literature *and practices* of these disciplines and will recognize the need for at least some investigators to have personal experience of these practices.

It may be necessary to adopt new research paradigms as suggested by Tart (1972, 1975a). In this design the subject would be a participant/experimenter or "yogi-scientist" trained in both the behavioral sciences and the consciousness disciplines. This is obviously an extremely exacting requirement, but one that may be necessary for the fullest possible understanding of these practices.

It seems prudent to heed the warnings of the advanced practitioners of these traditions, and, at least initially, to focus on those phenomena that they consider central. It will also be necessary to distinguish between the central consciousness disciplines and the degenerate popularisms with which they are so often confused.

One of the most subtle yet important tasks facing investigators may be the recognition that they may experience active resistances to some of the ideas and experiences presented by these disciplines, because their most fundamental beliefs and world views may be called into question (Deikman, 1977; Goleman, 1974; Rajneesh, 1975; Wilber, 1977, in press b; this volume a).

> This is why it is so difficult to explain the path to one who has not tried: he will see only his point of view of today or rather the loss of his point of view. And yet if we only knew how each loss of one's viewpoint is a progress and how life changes when one passes from the stage of the closed truth to the

stage of the open truth — a truth like life itself, too great to be trapped by points of view, because it embraces every point of view ... a truth great enough to deny itself and pass endlessly into a higher truth.

—*Satprem, 1968, p. 84*

This advice from the mystics is curiously similar to the solution suggested by William James (1910). He proposed that the key to the progression to broader perspectives for both the individual and for psychology as a whole lay in the recognition that

> ... there is "always more," outgrowing the bonds of present self-limitation for the apprehension of present reality, and the developing of openness upon which the germinal — or not yet germinal — potentialities for new reals may come into existence ... not only with the real which can be independently shown to be real by ... now sober models, but with the real which newly comes into existence as evolution goes on.

It is this openness to the "always more," this willingness to at least temporarily go beyond one's current viewpoint, that, when combined with the best of the behavioral scientists' conceptual and empirical rigor, will enable us to optimally examine the paradigm of the consciousness disciplines, and perhaps our own.

References

Alexander, F. Buddhistic training as an artificial catatonia (the biological meaning of psychic occurences). *Psychoanal. Rev.*, 1931, *18*, 129–145.

Alexander, F. G., & Selesnich, S. T. *The history of psychiatry*. New York: New American Library, 1966.

Allison, J. Adaptive regression and intense religious experience. *J. Nerv. Ment. Dis.*, 1967, *145*, 452–463.

Allport, G. W. *Personality: A psychological interpretation*. New York: Holt, 1937.

Bandura, A. The self system in reciprocal determinism. *Amer. Psychol.*, 1978, *33*, 344–357.

Bertalanffy, V. *General systems theory*. New York: Braziller, 1968.

Boss, M. *A psychiatrist discovers India*. New York: Basic Books, 1963.

Brown, D. A model for the levels of concentrative meditation. *Int. J. Clin. Exp. Hypnosis*, 1977, *25*, 236–273.

Bucke, W. From self to cosmic consciousness. In J. White (Ed.), *The highest state of consciousness*. Garden City, N.Y.: Doubleday, 1972.

Buddhagosa, P. M. Tin (Trans.) *The path of purity*. Sri Lanka: Pali Text Society, 1923.

Bugental, J. *Psychotherapy and process*. Reading, Mass.: Addison-Wesley, 1978.

Burtt, E. *The teachings of the compassionate Buddha*. New York: Mentor, 1955.

Capra, F. *Modern physics and eastern mysticism*. This volume.

Chaudhuri, H. Psychology: Humanistic and transpersonal. *J. Humanistic Psychol.*, 1975, *15*, 7–15.

Deikman, A. Comments on the GAP report on mysticism. *J. Nerv. Men. Dis.*, 1977, *165*, 213–217.

Frank, J. D. Nature and function of belief systems: Humanism and transcendental religion. *Amer. Psychol.*, 1977, *32*, 555–559.

Freud, S. *Civilization and its discontents*. New York: Norton, 1962.

Fromm, E., DeMartino, R., Suzuki, D. T. *Zen Buddhism and psychoanalysis*. New York: Harper & Row, 1970, 98–99, 104.

Fromm E., & Xirau, R. *The nature of man*. New York: Macmillan, 1968.

Goldstein, J. *The experience of insight*. Santa Cruz, Calif.: Unity Press, 1976.

Goleman, D. Perspectives on psychology, reality, and the study of consciousness. *J. Transpersonal Psychol.*, 1974, *6*, 73–85. Reprinted in this volume.

Goleman, D. *The varieties of the meditative experience*. New York: E. P. Dutton, 1977. Reprinted in this volume as A map for inner space.

Goleman, D. Buddhism and personality theory. In C. Hall & G. Lindsey (Eds.), *Theories of personality* (3rd ed.). New York: John Wiley, 1979.

Goleman, D. Meditation and well-being: An eastern model of psychological health. In R. Walsh & D. Shapiro (Eds.), *Beyond health and normality: An exploration of extreme psychological well-being*. New York: Van Nostrand Reinhold, in press.

Globus, G., & Franklin, S. *Thought, meditation, and knowledge*. Unpublished manuscript, 1978.

Govinda, L. A. *Psychological attitude of early Buddhist philosophy*. New York: Weiser, 1969.

Greeley, A. M. *The sociology of the paranormal*. Beverly Hills, Calif.: Sage, 1975.

Group for the Advancement of Psychiatry. *Mysticism: Spiritual quest or psychic disorder?* New York: Group for the Advancement of Psychiatry, 1976.

Hood, R. W. Psychological strength and the report of intense religious experience. *J. Sci. Study Religion*, 1974, *13*, 65–71.

Hood, R. Conceptual criticisms of regressive explanations of mysticism. *Rev. Religious Res.*, 1976, *17*, 179–188.

Huxley, A. *The perennial philosophy*. New York: Harper & Row, 1944.

James. W. *Psychology: Briefer course*. New York: Holt & Co., 1910.

James, W. *The varieties of religious experience*. New York: New American Library, 1958, 298.

Johannson, R. *The psychology of nirvana*. London: George Allen and Unwin, 1969.

Jung, C.G., *Letters* (G. Adler, Ed.) Princeton, N.J.: Princeton University Press, 1973.

Kapleau, P. *The three pillars of zen*. Boston: Beacon Press, 1967.

King. C D. *The states of human consciousness*. New York: Unity Books, 1963.

Kornfield, J. *Living Buddhist masters*. Santa Cruz, Calif.: Unity Press, 1977.

Kuhn, T. S. *The structure of scientific revolutions*. (2nd ed.) Chicago: University of Chicago Press, 1970.

Laing, R. D. *Knots*. New York: Pantheon, 1970.

Livingston, D. Transcendental states of consciousness and the healthy personality: An overview. Unpublished doctoral dissertation, University of Arizona, 1975.

Maruyana, M. Paradigms and communications. *Technol. Forecasting Soc. Change*, 1974, *6* 3–32.

Maslow, A. H. *Religions, values, and peak experience*. New York: Viking, 1964.

Maslow, A. H. *The psychology of science*. Chicago: Gateway, 1966.

Maslow, A. H. *The farther reaches of human nature*. New York: Viking, 1971.

Oppenheimer, J. R. *Science and the common understanding*. New York: Oxford University Press, 1954.

Ostow, M. Antinomianism, mysticism, and psychosis. *Psychedelic Drugs*, 1969, 177–185.

Overton, D. A. Discriminative control of behavior by drug states. In T. Thompson & R. Pickens (Eds.), *Stimulus properties of drugs*. New York: Appleton-Century-Crofts, 1971.

Owens, C. M. Zen Buddhism. In C. Tart (Ed.), *Transpersonal psychologies*. New York: Harper & Row, 1976, pp. 156–202.

Pahnke, W., & Richards, W. Implications of LSD and experimental mysticism. *J. Religion Health*, 1966, *5*, 175–208.

Rajneesh, B. S. *Just like that*. Poona, India: Rajneesh Foundation, 1975.

Ram Dass. Assoc. Transpersonal Psychol. Newsletter (Winter), 1975, 9. (a)

Ram Dass. *The only dance there is*. New York: Doubleday, 1975. (b)

Ram Dass. Talk given at Rowe, Ma., tapes from Hanuman Foundation, Tape Library, P.O. Box 835, Santa Cruz, CA 95061, 1975. (c)

Ram Dass. Freeing the mind. *J. Transpersonal Psychol.*, 1976, *8*, 133–140.

Ram Dass. *Grist for the mill*. Santa Cruz, Calif.: Unity Press, 1977.

Ram Dass. *Journey of awakening: A meditator's guidebook*. New York: Doubleday, 1978.

Roberts, T. Education and transpersonal relations: A research agenda. *Simulations and Games*, 1977, *8*, 7–28.

Roberts, T. Beyond self-actualization. *ReVision*, 1978, *1*, 42–46.

Satprem. *Sri Aurobindo or the adventure of consciousness*. New York: Harper & Row, 1968.

Schumacher, E. F. *A guide for the perplexed*. New York, Harper & Row, 1977.

Shapiro, D., & Giber, D. Meditation: Self control strategy and altered states of consciousness. *Arch. Gen. Psychiat.*, 1978, *35*, 294–302.

Shapiro, D., & Walsh, R., (Eds.). *The Science of Meditation: Research, Theory, and Practice*. Chicago: Aldine Press, in press.

Smith, H. *The religions of man*. New York: Harper & Row, 1958.

Smith, H. *Forgotten truth*. New York: Harper & Row, 1976.

Stace, W. T. *Mysticism and philosophy*. Philadelphia: Lippincott, 1960.

Tart, C. States of consciousness and state-specific sciences. *Science*, 1972, *176*, 1203-1210. Reprinted in this volume.

Tart, C. *States of consciousness*. New York: E. P. Dutton, 1975. (a) Reprinted in this volume as The systems approach to states of consciousness.

Tart, C. (Ed.). *Transpersonal psychologies*. New York: Harper & Row, 1975. (b)

Thetford, W., Schucman, H., & Walsh, R. Other psychological theories. In A. Freedman, H. Kaplan, & B. Sadock (Eds.), *Comprehensive textbook of psychiatry* (3rd ed.), Baltimore: Williams and Wilkins, in press.

Thomas, L., & Cooper, P. Incidence and psychological correlates of intense spiritual experiences. Paper presented East. Psychol. Assoc. Meet., Boston, 1977.

Vimalo, B. Awakening to the truth. Visaka Puja, Thailand: Annual Publication Buddhist Assoc., Thailand, 1974, 53–79.

Walsh, R. Initial meditative experiences: I. *J. Transpersonal Psychol.*, 1977, *9*, 151–192.

Walsh, R. Initial meditative experiences: II. *J. Transpersonal Psychol.*, 1978, *10*, 1–28.

Walsh, R. *Towards an ecology of brain*. New York: Spectrum Press, 1980.

Walsh, R., & Shapiro, D., (Eds.). *Beyond health and normality: Explorations of extreme psychological well-being*. New York: Van Nostrand Reinhold, in press.

Walsh, R., & Vaughan, F. What is a person? This volume.

Whorf, B. L. *Language, thought, and reality*. Cambridge: M.I.T. Press, 1956.

Wilber, K. The ultimate state of consciousness. *J. Altered States Consciousness*, 1975, *2*, 231–242.

Wilber, K. *The spectrum of consciousness*. Wheaton, Ill.: Theosophical Publishing House, 1977.

Wilber, K. Eye to Eye: Transpersonal psychology and science. *ReVision*, 1979, *2*, 3–25.

Wilber, K. Where it was, there I shall be. In R. Walsh and D. Shapiro (Eds.), *Beyond health and normality: An exploration of extreme psychological well-being*, New York: Van Nostrand Reinhold, in press. (a)

Wilber, K. *The atman project*. Wheaton, Ill., Theosophical Publishing House, in press. (b)

Wilber, K. A developmental model of consciousness. This volume. (a)

Wilber, K. Eye to eye. This volume. (b)

What Is a Person?

Roger N. Walsh, Frances Vaughan

What is a person? This is the most fundamental question confronting all psychologies. Different psychologies assume different perspectives and emphasize different dimensions. From these they construct what often seem to be radically different images of human nature. Usually these views are seen as oppositional, more likely they represent parts of a complex multidimensional whole. The transpersonal model presented here is not intended to negate other models, but rather to set them in a larger context that includes states of consciousness and levels of well-being not encompassed by previous psychological models.

The four major dimensions of this model are consciousness, conditioning, personality, and identity. Using these headings, we will summarize what seem to us to represent the basic tenets of a transpersonal model and compare them with traditional Western assumptions.

CONSCIOUSNESS

This transpersonal model holds consciousness as being a central dimension that provides the basis and context for all experience. Traditional Western psychologies have held differing positions with regard to consciousness. These range from behaviorism, which prefers to ignore it because of the difficulty of researching it objectively, to psychodynamic and humanistic approaches, which acknowledge it but generally pay more attention to the contents than to consciousness per se, as the context of experience.

A transpersonal model views our usual consciousness as a defensively contracted state. This usual state is filled to a remarkable and unrecognized extent with a continuous flow of largely uncontrollable thoughts and fantasies in accordance with our needs and defenses. In the words of Ram Dass, "We are all prisoners of our minds. This realization is the first step on the journey of freedom."[1]

Optimum consciousness is viewed as being considerably greater, and potentially available at any time, should the defensive contraction be relaxed. The fundamental perspective on growth is therefore one of letting go this defensive contraction and removing obstacles to the recognition of the expanded ever-present potential through quieting the mind and reducing perceptual distortion. [2, 3, 4, 5, 6]

> The fundamental task which gives the key to many realizations is the silence of the mind. . . . All kinds of discoveries are made, in truth, when the mental machinery stops, and the first is that if the power to think is a remarkable gift, the power not to think is even more so.[7]

The transpersonal perspective holds that a large spectrum of altered states of consciousness exist, that some are potentially useful and functionally specific (i.e., possessing some functions not available in the usual state but lacking others), and that some of these are true "higher" states. Higher is here used in Tart's [8, 9] sense of possessing all the properties and potentials of lower states, plus some additional ones. Furthermore, a wide range of literature from a variety of cultures and growth disciplines attest to the attainability of these higher states.[10, 11, 12, 13, 14] On the other hand, the traditional Western view holds that only a limited range of states exists, e.g., waking, dreaming, intoxication, delerium. Furthermore, nearly all altered states are seen as detrimental and "normality" is considered optimal.

Viewing our usual state from an expanded context results in some unexpected implications. The traditional model defines psychosis as a distorted perception of reality that does not recognize the distortion. From the perspective of this multiple-states model, our usual state fits this definition, being suboptimal, providing a distorted perception of reality, and failing to recognize that distortion. Indeed, any one state of consciousness is necessarily limited and only relatively real. Hence, from the broader perspective psychosis might be defined as attachment to, or being trapped in, any single state of consciousness.[5, 15]

Since each state of consciousness reveals its own picture of reality,[16] it follows that reality as we know it (and that is the only way we know it) is also only relatively real. Put another way, then, psychosis is attachment to any one reality. In the words of Ram Dass:

> We grow up with one plane of existence we call real. We identify totally with that reality as absolute, and we discount experiences that are inconsistent with it. . . . What Einstein demonstrated in physics is equally true of all other aspects of the cosmos: all reality is relative. Each reality is true only within given limits. It is only one possible version of the way things are. There are always multiple versions of reality. To awaken from any single reality is to recognize its relative reality.[15]

Thus the reality we perceive reflects our own state of consciousness and we can never explore reality without at the same time exploring ourselves, both because we are, and because we create, the reality we explore.

CONDITIONING

With regard to conditioning, the transpersonal perspective holds that people are vastly more ensnared and trapped in their conditioning than they appreciate, but that freedom from this conditioning is possible.[14] The aim of transpersonal psychotherapy is essentially the extraction of awareness from this conditioned tyranny of the mind. This is described in more detail in the section on identity.

One form of conditioning Eastern disciplines have examined in detail is attachment. Attachment is closely associated with desire and signifies that nonfulfillment of the desire will result in pain. Attachment therefore plays a central role in the causation of suffering, and letting go of attachment is central to its cessation.[17, 18]

> Whenever there is attachment
> Association with it
> Brings endless misery.[15]

> Whenever we are still attached, we are still possessed;
> and when one is possessed, it means the existence of some-
> thing stronger than oneself.[19]

Attachment is not limited to external objects or persons. In addition to the familiar forms of attachment to material possessions, special relationships and the prevailing status quo, there may be equally strong attachments to a particular self-image, a pattern of behavior, or a psychological process. Among the strongest attachments noted in the consciousness disciplines are those to suffering and to unworthiness. Insofar as we believe that our identity is derived from our roles, our problems, our relationships, or the contents of consciousness, attachment is reinforced by fear for personal survival. "If I give up my attachments, who and what will I be?"

PERSONALITY

Personality has been accorded a central place in most previous psychologies and indeed many psychological theories hold that people are their personality. Interestingly enough, the most common title given to books on psychological health and well-being has been *The Healthy Personality*. [20] Health has usually been viewed as primarily involving a modification of personality. From a transpersonal perspective, however, personality is accorded relatively less importance. Rather, it is seen as only one aspect of being with which the individual may, but does not have to, identify. Health is seen as primarily involving a shift from exclusive identification with personality rather than a modification of it.

Likewise, the personal drama or story each person has to tell about him/herself is also seen in a different perspective. According to Fadiman,[21] personal dramas are an unnecessary luxury and interfere with full functioning. They are part of our emotional baggage, and it is usually beneficial for a person to gain some detachment or disidentification from his/her dramas, as well as from the personal dramas of others.

IDENTITY

Identity is seen as a crucial concept and is conceptually extended beyond traditional Western limits. Traditional psychologies have recognized identification with external objects and have defined it as an unconscious process in which the individual becomes like or feels the same as something or someone else.[22] Transpersonal and Eastern psychologies also recognize external identification but maintain that identification with internal (intrapsychic) phenomena and processes is even more significant. Here identification is defined as the process by which something is experienced as self. Furthermore, this type of identification goes unrecognized by most of us, including psychologists, therapists, and behavioral scientists, because we are all so involved in it. That is, we are so identified that it never even occurs to us to question that which it seems so clear that we are.

Consensually validated identifications go unrecognized because they are not called into question. Indeed, any attempt to question them may meet with considerable resistance from others. "Attempts to awake before our time are often punished, especially by those who love us most. Because they, bless them, are asleep. They think anyone who wakes up, or ... realizes that what is taken to be real, is a dream, is going crazy."[23]

The process of disidentification has far-reaching implications. The identification of awareness with mental content renders the individual unconscious of the broader context of consciousness that holds this content. When awareness identifies with mental content this content becomes the context from which all other mental content and experience are viewed. Thus the content become context now interprets other content, and determines meaning, perception, belief, motivation, and behavior, all in a manner that is consistent with and reinforces this context. Furthermore, the context sets in motion psychological processes that also reinforce it.[24, 25, 26]

For example, if a thought "I'm scared" arises and this thought is observed and seen to be what it is, i.e., just another thought, then it exerts little influence. However, if it is identified with, then the reality at that moment is that the individual is scared and is likely to generate and identify with a whole series of fearful thoughts and emotions, to interpret nondescript feelings as fear, to perceive the world as frightening, and to act in a fearful manner. Thus, identification sets in motion a self-fulfilling, self-prophetic process in which experience and psychological processes validate the reality of that which was identified with. For the person identified with the thought "I'm scared," everything seems to prove the reality and validity of his/her fear. Remember that with identification the person is unaware of the fact that his/her perception stems from a thought "I'm scared." This thought is now not something that can be seen, rather it is that from which everything else is seen and interpreted. Awareness, which could be transcendent and positionless, has now been constricted to viewing the world from a single self-validating perspective. This is similar to the process that occurs with unrecognized models as described earlier "We are dominated by everything with which our self becomes identified. We can dominate and control everything from which we disidentify."[27] "As long as we are identified with an object, that is bondage."[28]

It may be that thoughts and beliefs constitute the operators or algorithms that construct, mediate, guide, and maintain the identificatory constriction of consciousness and act as limiting models of who we believe ourselves to be. As such, they must be opened to identification in order to allow growth. It may be that beliefs are adopted as strategic, defensive decisions about who and what we must be in order to survive and function optimally.

When it is remembered that the mind is usually filled with thoughts with which we are unwittingly identified, it becomes apparent that our usual state of consciousness is one in which we are, quite literally, hypnotized. As in any hypnotic state, there need not be any recognition of the trance and its attendant constriction of awareness, or memory of the sense of identity prior to hypnosis. While in the trance, who we think we are are the thoughts with which we are identified! Put another way, those thoughts from which we have not yet disidentified create our state of consciousness, identity and reality!

> We are what we think.
> All that we are arises with our thoughts.
> With our thoughts we make the world.   —*The Buddha*[29]

> We uphold the world with our internal dialogue.[30]

The general mechanisms underlying the hypnotic nature of our usual state are probably similar for all of us, although the contents vary between individuals and between cultures. Within cultures common beliefs and realities tend to be powerfully inculcated and shared.[31, 16]

> What is unconscious and what is conscious depends ... on the structure of society and on the patterns of feelings and thoughts it produces. ... The effect of society is not only to funnel fictions into our consciousness, but also to prevent awareness of reality.... Every society ... determines the forms of awareness. This system works, as it were, like a *socially conditioned* filter; experience cannot enter awareness unless it can penetrate the filter.[32]

From this perspective, ego appears to come into existence as soon as awareness identifies with thought, to represent the constellation of thoughts with which we tend to identify, and to be fundamentally an illusion produced by limited awareness. This is a sobering thought both in its personal implications and inasmuch as our traditional Western psychologies are ego psychologies and hence are studies of illusion.

BEYOND IDENTIFICATION

The task of awakening can thus be viewed from one perspective as a progressive disidentification from mental content in general and thoughts in particular. This is evident in practices such as insight meditation, where the student is trained to observe and identify all mental content rapidly and precisely.[33, 14] For most, this is a slow, arduous process in which a gradual refinement of perception results in a peeling away of awareness from successively more subtle layers of identification.[34, 35, 36, 26]

Finally, awareness no longer identifies exclusively with anything. This represents a radical and enduring shift in consciousness known by various names, such as enlightenment or liberation. Since there is no longer any exclusive identification with anything, the me/not me dichotomy is transcended and such persons experience themselves as being both nothing and everything. They are both pure awareness (no thing) and the entire universe (every thing). Being identified with both no location and all locations, nowhere and everywhere, they experience having transcended space and positionality.

A similar transcendence occurs for time. The mind is in constant flux. At the most sensitive levels of perception attainable by perceptual training such as meditation, all mind, and hence the whole phenomenal universe, is seen to be in continuous motion and change, with each object of awareness arising out of void into awareness and disappearing again within minute fractions of a second. [33, 13, 17] This is the fundamental recognition of the Buddhist teaching of impermanence, i.e., that everything changes, nothing remains the same. [34, 35, 36] This realization can become one of the major motivating forces for advanced meditators to transcend all mental processes and attain the changeless, unconditioned state of nirvana.

In this final state of pure awareness, since there is no longer identification with mind, there is no sense of being identified with change. Since time is a function of change, this results in an experience of being outside, or transcendent to, time. This is experienced as eternity, the eternity of the unchanging now, and from this perspective time is perceived as an illusory product of identification.

> Time is of your own making
> Its clock ticks in your head.
> The moment you stop thought
> Time too stops dead. [37]

Mental contents and processes occur largely as a result of conditioning, a fact recognized by both Western and non-Western psychologies. Identification with these contents results in the experience of a self that is controlled by conditioning. Once their identification is transcended then so are the effects of conditioning. Conditioned thoughts and emotions still pass through the mind, but without identification with them awareness may now be experienced as unconditioned.

The experience of unconditioned pure awareness is apparently a blissful one, described in the Hindu tradition as comprised of sat-chit-ananda: awareness, being, and bliss. Without identification with painful thoughts and emotions there is no experience of suffering. Thus, from this perspective the cause of suffering is identification.

Freed of unconscious distorting and limiting identifications and contexts, awareness is now capable of clear, accurate perception. Hence, in Tibetan Buddhism it is called a "crystal mirror" because of its clear, faithful reflection of reality. Furthermore, with no exclusive identification, mirror and that which it perceives, subject and object, are perceived as one and the same thing. Awareness now perceives itself as being that which it formerly looked at, for the observer or ego, which was an illusory product of identification, is no longer experienced as a separate entity.

Furthermore, since a person in this state experiences him/herself as being pure awareness at one with everything yet being no thing, each person also experiences him/herself as being exactly the same as, or identical with, every other person. From this state of consciousness the words of the mystics proclaiming "we are one" make perfect sense as literal experience. With nothing except one's self in existence the thought of harming "others" makes no sense whatsoever, and it is said that such thoughts may not even occur.[14] Rather, the natural expressions of this state toward others are love and compassion.

Descriptions of the experience of this state make it clear that these experiences are known to most of us only in those moments of transcendent insight afforded by peak experiences.[38] Thus, our capacity for understanding is limited by the constraints of cross-state communication and lack of direct experience. Hence, it is apparent that descriptions of these states may be partially incomprehensible to the rest of us and may be uninterpretable from the frameworks of traditional psychology. It then becomes very easy to superficially dismiss such phenomena as nonsensical or even pathological, a mistake made even by some of the most outstanding Western mental health professionals. However, the transpersonal model attempts to provide for the first time a psychological framework capable of comprehending religious experiences and disciplines.

Inasmuch as people in the state of consciousness known as enlightenment experience themselves as being pure awareness, everything and nothing, the entire universe, unconditioned, unchanging, eternal, and one with all others, they also experience themselves as being one with God. Here, God does not imply some person or thing "out there," but rather represents the direct experience of being all that exists. In the utmost depths of the human psyche, when all limiting identifications have been droppped, awareness experiences no limits to identity and directly experiences itself as that which is beyond limits of time or space, that which humanity has traditionally called God. "To me, God is a word used to point to our ineffable subjectivity, to the unimaginable potential which lies within each of us.[39]

Thus, at the highest levels of psychological well-being, the transpersonal model can only point to that which is beyond both models and the personal.

Notes

1. Ram Dass. Assoc. Transpersonal Psychol. Newsletter (Winter), 1975, 9.

2. Ouspensky, P. D. *In search of the miraculous*. New York: Harcourt, Brace and World, 1949.

3. Rajneesh, B. S. *The way of the white cloud*. Poona, India: Rajneesh Center, 1975.

4. Ram Dass. A talk at the San Francisco Gestalt Institute. In J. Downing (Ed.), *Gestalt awareness*. New York: Harper & Row, 1976.

5. Ram Dass. *Grist for the mill*. Santa Cruz, Calif.: Unity Press, 1977.

6. Vaughan, F. *Awakening intuition*. New York: Doubleday, 1979.

7. Satprem. *Sri Aurobindo or the adventure of consciousness*. New York: Harper & Row, 1968.

8. Tart, C. (Ed.). *Transpersonal psychologies*. New York: Harper & Row, 1975.

9. Tart, C. *States of consciousness*. New York: E. P. Dutton, 1975.

10. Kapleau, P. *The three pillars of zen*. Boston: Beacon Press, 1967.

11. DeRopp, R. S. *The master game*. New York: Delta, 1968.

12. Riordan, K. Gurdjieff. In C. Tart (Ed.), *Transpersonal psychologies*, New York: Harper & Row, 1975, pp. 281–328.

13. Goleman, D. Meditation and consciousness: An Asian approach to mental health. *Amer. J. Psychother.*, 1976, 41–54.

14. Goleman, D. *The varieties of the meditative experience*. New York: E. P. Dutton, 1977. Reprinted in this volume as A map for inner space.

15. Ram Dass. *A meditator's guidebook*. New York: Doubleday, 1978.

16. Wilber, K. *The spectrum of consciousness*. Wheaton, Ill.: Theosophical Publishing House, 1977.

17. Buddhagosa. P. M. Tin (Trans.) *The path of purity*. Sri Lanka: Pali Text Society, 1923.

18. Guenther, H. V. *Philosophy and psychology in the Abhidharma*. Berkeley, Calif.: Shambhala, 1976.

19. Jung, C. G. *The secret of the golden flower*. (Rev. ed.). New York: Harcourt, Brace and World, 1962, p. 114.

20. Chiang, H., & Maslow, A. H. (Eds.). *The healthy personality*. New York: Van Nostrand Reinhold, 1969.

21. Fadiman, J. The transpersonal stance. This volume.

22. Brenner, C. *An elementary textbook of psychoanalysis*. New York: Anchor, 1974.

23. Laing, R. D. *The politics of the family*. New York: Pantheon, 1971. p. 82.

24. Erhard, W. Workshop for Psychotherapists, San Francisco, 1977.

25. Erhard, W. Who is it who is healthy? In R. Walsh & D. Shapiro (Eds.), *Beyond health and normality: Explorations of extreme psychological well-being*, New York: Van Nostrand Reinhold, in press.

26. Walsh, R. Initial meditative experiences: I. *J. Transpersonal Psychol.*, 1977, *9*, 151–192.

27. Assagioli, R. *Psychosynthesis: A manual of principles and techniques*. New York: Hobbs Dorman, 1965.

28. Wei Wu Wei. *All else is bondage*. Hong Kong: Hong Kong University Press, 1970.

29. Byrom, T. *The Dhammapada: The sayings of the Buddha*. New York: Vintage, 1976.

30. Castaneda, C. *Tales of Power*. New York, Simon and Schuster, 1974.

31. Elgin, D. *Voluntary simplicity*. New York, William Morrow, in press.

32. Fromm, E., Suzuki, D. T., & DeMartino, R. *Zen Buddhism and psychoanalysis*. New York, Harper & Row, 1970, 98–99, 104.

33. Goldstein, J. *The experience of insight*. Santa Cruz, Calif.: Unity Press, 1976.

34. Sayadaw, M. *Practical insight meditation*. Kandy, Sri Lanka: Buddhist Publication Society, 1976.

35. Sayadaw, M. *The progress of insight*. Kandy, Sri Lanka: Buddhist Publication Society, 1978.

36. Kornfield, J. *Living Buddhist masters*. Santa Cruz, Calif.: Unity Press, 1977.

37. Frank, F. *The book of Angelus Silesius*. New York: Vintage, 1976, p. 40.

38. Maslow, A. H. *The farther reaches of human nature*. New York: Viking, 1971.

39. Bugental, J. F. T. *Psychotherapy and process*. Reading, Mass.: Addison-Wesley, 1978.

Modern Physics and Eastern Mysticism

FRITJOF CAPRA

Twentieth-century physics has had a profound influence on general philosophical thought, because it has revealed an unsuspected limitation of classical ideas and has necessitated a radical revision of many of our basic concepts. The concept of matter in subatomic physics, for example, is totally different from the traditional material substance of classical physics, and the same is true for concepts like space, time, or causality. These concepts, however, are fundamental to our outlook on the world around us, and with their radical transformation our whole world view has begun to change.

These changes brought about by modern physics all seem to lead towards a view of the world which is very similar to that of Eastern mysticism.

A detailed analysis of the parallels between the principal theories of modern physics and the mystical traditions of the Far East can be found in *The Tao of Physics* (Capra, 1975). In this paper, I want to concentrate on two ideas which are emphasized throughout Eastern mysticism and which are recurring themes in the world view of modern physics: the unity and mutual interrelation of all things and events, and the intrinsically dynamic nature of the universe.

After presenting a brief juxtaposition of the mechanistic world view of classical physics and the 'organic' view of Eastern mysticism, I shall show how the notion of a fundamental interconnectedness of nature arises in quantum theory and how it acquires an essential dynamic character in relativity theory, implying a new conception of particles which is closely related to the Eastern conception of the material world.

MECHANISTIC AND ORGANIC WORLD VIEWS

The traditional world view of classical physics is a mechanistic view of the world. It has its roots in the philosophy of the Greek atomists, ... who saw matter as being made of several 'basic building blocks,' the atoms, which are purely passive and intrinsically dead. The atoms were thought to be moved by some external force which was often assumed to be of spiritual origin, and thus fundamentally different from matter. This image became an essential part of the Western way of thinking. It gave rise to the dualism between spirit and matter, between the mind and the body, which is characteristic of Western thought. This dualism was formulated in its sharpest form in the philosophy of Descartes who based his view of nature on a fundamental divison into two separate and independent realms, that of mind (*res cogitans*), and that of matter (*res extensa*). The Cartesian division allowed scientists to treat matter as dead and completely separate from themselves, and to see the material world as a multitude of different objects assembled into a huge machine. Such a mechanistic world view was held by Newton who constructed his mechanics on its basis and made it the foundation of classical physics.

Opposed to the mechanistic conception of the world is the view of the Eastern mystics which may be characterized by the word 'organic,' as it regards all phenomena in the universe as integral parts of an inseparable harmonious whole. For the Eastern mystic, all things and events perceived by the senses are interrelated, connected, and are but different aspects or manifestations of the same ultimate reality. Our tendency to divide the world we perceive into individual and separate 'things' and to experience ourselves in this world as isolated egos is seen as an 'illusion' which comes from our measuring and categorizing mentality. The division of nature into separate objects is, of course, useful and necessary to cope with our everyday environment, but it is not a fundamental feature of reality. For the Eastern mystic, any such objects have therefore a fluid and ever-changing character. The Eastern world view is thus intrinsically dynamic, and contains time and change as essential features. The cosmos is seen as one inseparable reality—forever in motion, alive, organic—spiritual and material at the same time. Motion and change being essential properties of things, the forces causing motion are not outside the objects, as in the classical Greek view, but are an intrinsic property of matter. I shall now show how the main features of this picture appear in modern physics.

QUANTUM THEORY

One of the main insights of quantum theory has been the recognition that probability is a fundamental feature of the atomic reality which governs all processes, and even the existence of matter. Subatomic particles do not exist with certainty at definite places, but rather show — as Heisenberg (1963) has put it— "tendencies to exist." Atomic events do not occur with certainty at definite times and in definite ways, but rather show "tendencies to occur." Henry Stapp (1971) has emphasized that these tendencies, or probabilities, are not probabilities of 'things,' but rather probabilities of interconnections. Any observed atomic 'object' constitutes an intermediate system connecting the preparation of the experiment and the subsequent measurement. It exists and has meaning only in this context—not as an isolated entity, but as an interconnection between the processes of preparation and measurement. The properties of the object cannot be defined independently of these processes. If the preparation or the measurement is modified, the properties of the object will also change.

On the other hand, the fact that we speak about an 'object'—an atom, an electron, or any other observed system — shows that we have some independent physical entity in mind which is first prepared and then measured. The basic problem, then, with observation in atomic physics is—in the words of Stapp (1971)—that "the observed system is required to be isolated in order to be defined, yet interacting in order to be observed." This problem is resolved in quantum theory in a pragmatic way by requiring that the preparing and measuring devices be separated by a large distance so that the observed object be free from their influence while travelling from the area of preparation to the area of measurement.

In principle, this distance must be infinite. In the framework of quantum theory, the concept of a distinct physical entity can be defined precisely only if this entity is infinitely far away from the agencies of observation. In practice, this is of course not possible, nor is it necessary. We have to remember, here, the basic attitude of modern science that all its concepts and theories are approximate. In the present case, this means that the concept of a distinct physical entity need not have a precise definition, but can be defined approximately. For large distances between the preparing and measuring devices, their disturbing effects on the observed object are small and can be neglected, and one can speak of a distinct physical entity being observed. Such a concept, therefore, is merely an idealization. When the measuring devices are not placed far enough apart, their influence can no longer be neglected, and the whole macroscopic system forms a unified whole and the notion of an observed object breaks down.

Quantum theory thus reveals an essential interconnectedness of the universe. It shows that we cannot decompose the world into independently existing smallest units. As we penetrate into matter, we find it is made of particles, but these are not 'basic building blocks' in the sense of Democritus and Newton. They are merely idealizations which are useful from a practical point of view, but have no fundamental sigificance. In the words of Niels Bohr (1934, p. 57):

> Isolated material particles are abstractions, their properties being definable and observable only through their interaction with other systems.

THE COSMIC WEB

At the atomic level, then, the solid material objects of classical physics dissolve into patterns of probabilities, and these patterns do not represent probabilities of things, but probabilities of interconnections. Quantum theory forces us to see the universe not as a collection of physical objects, but rather as a complicated web of relations between the various parts of a unified whole. In the words of Werner Heisenberg (1963, p. 96):

> The world thus appears as a complicated tissue of events, in which connections of different kinds alternate or overlap or combine and thereby determine the texture of the whole.

This, however, is the way in which the Eastern mystics experience the world, and they often express their experience in words which are almost identical to those used by atomic physicists. Take, for example, the following quotation from a Tibetan Buddhist, Lama Govinda (1973, p. 93):

> The external world and his inner world are for (the Buddhist) only two sides of the same fabric, in which the threads of all forces and of all events, of all forms of consciousness and of their objects, are woven into an inseparable net of endless, mutually conditioned relations.

These words by Govinda bring out another feature which is of fundamental importance both in modern physics and in Eastern mysticism. The universal interconnectedness of nature always includes the human observer and his or her consciousness in an essential way. In quantum theory, the observed 'objects' can only be understood in terms of the interaction between the processes of preparation and measurement, and the end of this chain of processes lies always in the consciousness of the human observer. The crucial feature of quantum theory is that the human observer is not only necessary to observe the properties of an object, but is necessary even to define these properties. In atomic physics, we can never speak about nature without, at the same time, speaking about ourselves. As Heisenberg has put it (1963, p. 75):

> Natural science does not simply describe and explain nature; it is a part of the interplay between nature and ourselves.

In modern physics, then, the scientist cannot play the role of a detached observer, but becomes involved in the world he or she observes. John Wheeler (1974) sees the involvement of the observer as the most important feature of quantum theory, and he has therefore suggested replacing the word 'observer' by the word 'participator.' But this, again, is an idea which is well known to any student of a mystical tradition. Mystical knowledge can never be obtained just by observation, but only by full participation with one's whole being. The notion of the participator is thus basic to the mystical traditions of the East.

RELATIVITY THEORY

The second basic theory of modern physics, relativity theory, has forced us to change our concepts of space and time in a drastic way. It has shown that space is not three-dimensional and that time is not a separate entity. Both are intimately connected and form a four-dimensional continuum called 'space-time.' In relativity theory, therefore, we can never talk about space without talking about time and vice versa. We have now been living with the theory of relativity for a long time and have become thoroughly familiar with its mathematical formalism. But this has not helped our intuition very much. We have no direct sensory experience of the four-dimensional space-time continuum, and whenever this 'relativistic' reality manifests itself we find it very hard to deal with it at the level of intuition and ordinary language.

A similar situation seems to exist in Eastern mysticism. The mystics seem to be able to attain non-ordinary states of consciousness in which they transcend the three-dimensional world of everyday life to experience a higher, multidimensional reality, a reality which, like that of relativistic physics, is impossible to describe in ordinary language. Govinda (1973, p. 136) talks about this experience when he writes:

> An experience of higher dimensionality is achieved by integration of experiences of different centres and levels of consciousness. Hence the indescribability of certain experiences of meditation on the plane of three-dimensional consciousness.

The dimensions of these states of consciousness may not be the same as the ones we are dealing with in relativistic physics, but it is striking that they have led the mystics towards notions of space and time which are very similar to those implied by relativity theory. Throughout Eastern mysticism, there seems to be a strong intuition for the 'space-time' character of reality. The fact that space and time are inseparably linked, which is so characteristic of relativistic physics, is stressed again and again. Thus the Buddhist scholar D. T. Suzuki writes (1959, p. 33):

> As a fact of pure experience, there is no space without time, no time without space.

In physics, the concepts of space and time are so basic for the description of natural phenomena that their modification entails a modification of the whole framework we use to describe nature. The most important consequence of this modification is the realization that mass is nothing but a form of energy, that every object has energy stored in its mass.

These developments — the unification of space and time and the equivalence of mass and energy — have had a profound influence on our picture of matter and have forced us to modify our concept of a particle in an essential way. In modern physics, mass is no longer associated with a material substance, and hence particles are not seen as consisting of any basic 'stuff,' but as bundles of energy. Energy, however, is associated with activity, with processes, and this implies that the nature of subatomic particles is intrinsically dynamic. In a relativistic theory, where space and time are fused into a four-dimensional continuum, these particles can no longer be pictured as static three-dimensional objects, like billiard balls or grains of sand, but must be conceived as four-dimensional entities in space-time. Their forms have to be understood dynamically, as forms in space and time. Subatomic particles are dynamic patterns which have a space aspect and a time aspect. Their space aspect makes them appear as objects with a certain mass, their time aspect as processes involving the equivalent energy. Relativity theory thus gives the constituents of matter an intrinsically dynamic aspect. It shows that the existence of matter and its activity cannot be separated. They are but different aspects of the four-dimensional space-time reality.

The Eastern mystics seem to be aware of the intimate connection of space and time, and consequently their view of the world, like that of modern physicists, is intrinsically dynamic. ... In their non-ordinary states of consciousness, [they] seem to be aware of the unity of space and time at a macroscopic level, and thus they see the macroscopic objects in a way which is very similar to the physicists' conception of subatomic particles. Suzuki (1968a, p. 33), for example, writes in one of his books on Buddhism:

> Buddhists have conceived an object as an event and not as a thing or substance.

The two basic theories of modern physics thus exhibit all the main features of the Eastern world view. Quantum theory has abolished the notion of fundamentally separated objects, has introduced the concept of the participator to replace that of the observer, and has come to see the universe as an interconnected web of relations whose parts are only defined through their connections to the whole. Relativity theory, so to speak, has made the cosmic web come alive by revealing its intrinsically dynamic character, and by showing that its activity is the very essence of its being.

Current research in physics aims at unifying quantum theory and relativity theory into a complete theory of the subatomic world. We have not yet been able to formulate such a complete theory, but we do have several partial theories which describe certain aspects of subatomic phenomena very well. All of these theories express, in different ways, the fundamental interrelatedness and the intrinsically dynamic character of the universe, and they all involve philosophical conceptions which are strikingly similar to those used in Eastern mysticism.

THE BOOTSTRAP

The basis of the bootstrap philosophy is the idea that nature cannot be reduced to fundamental entities, like fundamental building blocks of matter, but has to be understood entirely through self-consistency. All of physics has to follow uniquely from the requirement that its components be consistent with one another and with themselves.

This idea constitutes a radical departure from the traditional spirit of basic research in physics which had always been bent on finding the fundamental constituents of nature. The bootstrap philosophy abandons not only the idea of fundamental building blocks of matter, but accepts no fundamental entities whatsoever — no fundamental laws, equations, or principles. The universe is seen as a dynamic web of interrelated events. None of the properties of any part of this web is fundamental; they all follow from the properties of the other parts, and the overall consistency of their mutual interrelations determines the structure of the entire web.

It is evident that this idea is very much in the spirit of Eastern thought. An indivisible universe, in which things and events are interrelated, would hardly make sense unless it were self-consistent. In a way, the requirement of self-consistency, which forms the basis of the bootstrap hypothesis, and the unity and interrelation of all phenomena, which are so strongly emphasized in Eastern mysticism, are just different aspects of the same idea. This becomes particularly clear in Chinese philosophy. Joseph Needham, in his thorough study of Chinese science and civilization, discusses at great length how the Western concept of fundamental laws of nature has no counterpart in Chinese thought (Needham, 1956, pp. 528ff). According to Needham, the Chinese did not even have a word corresponding to the classical Western idea of a 'law of nature.' The term which comes closest to it is *li*, which Needham translates as 'dynamic pattern ' He says that, in the Chinese view

> The cosmic organisation ... is in fact, a Great Pattern in which all lesser patterns are included, and the 'laws' which are involved in it are intrinsic to these patterns. [Needham, 1956, p. 567]

This is exactly the idea of the bootstrap philosophy: everything in the universe is connected to everything else and no part of it is fundamental. The properties of any part are determined, not by some fundamental law, but by the properties of all the other parts.

CONCLUSION

In conclusion, I want to make a few remarks concerning the question: what can we learn from these parallels? Is modern science, with all its sophisticated machinery, merely rediscovering ancient wisdom, known to the Eastern sages for thousands of years? Should physicists, therefore, abandon the scientific method and begin to meditate? Or can there be a mutual influence between science and mysticism — perhaps even a synthesis?

I think that all these questions have to be answered in the negative. I see science and mysticism as two complementary manifestations of the human mind, of its rational and intuitive faculties. The modern physicist experiences the world through an extreme specialization of the rational mind; the mystic through an extreme specialization of the intuitive mind. The two approaches are entirely different and involve far more than a certain view of the physical world. However, they are 'complementary,' as we have learned to say in physics. Neither is comprehended in the other, nor can either of them be reduced to the other, but both of them are necessary, supplementing one another for a fuller understanding of the world. To paraphrase an old Chinese saying, mystics understand the roots of the *Tao* but not its branches; scientists understand its branches but not its roots. Science does not need mysticism and mysticism does not need science; but man needs both. Mystical experience is necessary to understand the deepest nature of things, and science is essential for modern life. What we need, therefore, is not a synthesis but a dynamic interplay between mystical intuition and scientific analysis.

References

Bohr, N. *Atomic physics and the description of nature*. London: Cambridge University Press, 1934.

Capra, F. *The tao of physics*. London & Berkeley: Shambhala, 1975.

Chew, G. F. "Bootstrap": A scientific idea? *Science*, 1968, *161*, 762–65.

Chew, G. F. Hadron bootstrap: Triumph or frustration? *Physics Today*, 1970, *23*, 23–28.

Chew, G. F., Gell-Mann, M. & Rosenfeld, A. H. Strongly interacting particles. *Scientific American*, 1964, *210*, 74–83.

Govinda, L. A. *Foundations of Tibetan mysticism*. London & Berkeley: Shambhala, 1973.

Heisenberg, W. *Physics and philosophy*. London: Allen & Unwin, 1963.

Needham, J. *Science and civilization in China*. Vol. 2. London: Cambridge Univ. Press, 1956.

Stapp, H. P. S-matrix interpretation of quantum theory. *Physical Review*, 1971, *D3*, 1303–20.

Suzuki, D. T. Preface to *Mahayana Buddhism* by B. L. Suzuki. London: Allen and Unwin, 1959.

Suzuki, D. T. *The essence of Buddhism*. Kyoto: Hozokan, 1968a.

Suzuki, D. T. *On Indian Mahayana Buddhism*. New York: Harper & Row, 1968b.

Wheeler, J. A. The universe as home for man. *American Scientist*, 1974, *62*, 683–91.

Wilhelm, R. (Transl.) *I Ching*. London: Routledge & Kegan Paul, 1968.

2

THE NATURE OF CONSCIOUSNESS

Insofar as we are a mental process, we must expect the natural world to show similar characteristics of mentality.

GREGORY BATESON[1]

Until recently, Western psychology has largely ignored the study of consciousness. Like the proverbial fish that remains unaware of the existence of water, consciousness, as the matrix of all experience, has been given little attention by comparison with behavior. Consciousness was not a suitable subject for the tools and philosophy of Western science, which were designed to observe and measure objective material phenomena. This technical problem still remains, but recently consciousness has at last become a respectable topic for investigation.

In various Eastern pyschologies a very different situation has prevailed. Consciousness has been viewed not only as central, but as the primary constituent of reality. Clarifying one's consciousness has been regarded as the highest human goal and the path to psychological health and enlightenment. The consciousness disciplines and many of the religions of the East aim at doing just that. Transpersonal psychologists are interested in synthesizing this Eastern knowledge of consciousness with Western psychological concepts and empiricism.

The most dramatic incentive for this has been the recognition of a range of altered states of consciousness formerly unappreciated by Western psychology. With the advent of the psychedelics, and more recently the use of such consciousness-modifying technologies as meditation, yoga, and biofeedback, researchers have begun empirical investigation of altered-states phenomena. In addition, the study of the Eastern literature has revealed maps of states of consciousness that Western researchers, such as those writing in this section, are beginning to understand and to link to Western concepts and empirical data.

It appears that the range of states of consciousness is considerably broader than previously recognized, extending from psychopathology, through our usual waking state, to a number of "higher" states. "Higher" states possess all the usual capacities plus additional ones and are sometimes accompanied by experiences of transcending the usual limits of awareness, ego, and identity.

Various functions and abilities have been noted to be state-dependent, i.e., limited by the state in which they occur. For example, in state-dependent learning what is learned in one state may not necessarily be remembered or comprehended in another. Similarly, with state-dependent communication, the insights of an individual in a particular state may not be comprehensible to another in a different state. This explains why many of the non-Western psychologies, consciousness disciplines, and religions have been so problematic for the West. Psychologists did not intially recognize that they represented technologies for inducing altered states, and hence that any assessment of them required an awareness of the limitations of state-dependent communication.

A growing interest in altered states and their implications for psychological well-being has brought consciousness into the foreground of transpersonal psychology. Acknowledging the centrality of consciousness does not necessarily imply a rejection of other psychological theories and models. Rather, it represents an attempt to view them from an expanded context that includes both Eastern and Western perspectives.

Because it is so central to a transpersonal perspective, consciousness is discussed in many sections of this book. For example, meditation, a cornerstone of most advanced psychological growth, may include training in the induction of a variety of altered states. Consciousness is both the means and goal of such efforts. Similarly, transpersonal psychotherapy adds to traditional therapeutic techniques a number of approaches aimed directly at altering consciousness. The development of consciousness is therefore closely related to mental health, and in some disciplines unconsciousness is described as the only illness.

The papers included in this section provide the best maps currently available of the major states of consciousness. In "Psychologia Perennis," Ken Wilber points out that throughout history there has existed a "perennial" philosophy or psychology that has maintained that there exist states of consciousness, superior to our usual one, that allow profound insight into the nature of reality and consciousness. He suggests that states of consciousness are ranged along a spectrum, representing different levels of expression of consciousness. Each level has associated with it a unique sense of experience and identity ranging from the experience variously known as Supreme Identity, Buddhahood, Christ consciousness, cosmic consciousness or big Mind, which has been the source of the great religions and consciousness disciplines, all the way down to the drastically narrowed identity associated with egoic consciousness. Various psychologies, he suggests, have addressed different levels of this spectrum and hence should be seen as complementary rather than oppositional.

The spectrum of consciousness revealed across the centuries by the perennial psychology has found surprisingly close agreement in recent studies of psychedelics. Stanislav Grof, who has perhaps more clinical research experience with psychedelics than anyone else in the world, has found that they seem to lead through a series of experiences and states of consciousness. In "Realms of the Human Unconscious," he reports that this progression reflects the uncovering of deeper and deeper layers of the unconscious. This begins with traditional psychodynamic phenomena, progresses through Rankian-birth-trauma-like material and Jungian symbology, and finally leads to a variety of transcendental experiences. Being last to emerge, these transpersonal states are assumed to represent the deepest known levels of the unconscious. These states and accompanying experiences not only closely resemble those described by advanced practitioners of the consciousness disciplines, but once experienced, allow significant insight and understanding of these traditions. Thus this area of research suggests that the potential for attaining deep transpersonal states, which may be interpreted either religiously or psychologically as one chooses, lies latent in us all. The potential of the psychedelics as research and therapeutic tools is apparent despite current unavailability for research.

The above papers clearly point to the idea that the human unconscious is not undifferentiated and homogenous, but rather is comprised of different levels and structures. In "A Developmental Model of Consciousness,"[2] Ken Wilber examines the development of these levels and structures of the unconscious and their attendant states of consciousness. He begins with the infantile and progresses through to the adult levels described by Western psychology. What is unique, however, is that he then continues following this developmental sequence through the unfolding of the successive structures of the unconscious and attendant states of consciousness that non-Western disciplines describe in the most psychologically developed and enlightened individuals.

Another way of conceptualizing consciousness and altered states is employed by Charles Tart who adopts "A Systems Approach to States of Consciousness." He points out that a state of consciousness is a highly complex system constructed by components such as attention/awareness and identity. Different dynamic patterns of these components result in different states, and techniques for altering consciousness can be viewed as means for disrupting preexisting patterns by modifying one or more components. This systems approach provides a bridge that allows certain aspects of non-Western knowledge to be reconceptualized within a Western framework.

Notes

1. Bateson, G. *Mind and nature: A necessary unity*. New York: E. P. Dutton, 1979.

2. An expanded version of this paper is available in: Ken Wilber, *The Atman project*. Wheaton, Ill.: Theosophical Publishing House, 1980.

Psychologia Perennis:
The Spectrum of Consciousness

KEN WILBER

In the past few decades the West has witnessed an explosion of interest among psychologists, theologians, scientists, and philosophers alike in what Huxley (1970) has called *philosophia perennis*, the 'perennial philosophy,' a universal doctrine as to the nature of man and reality lying at the very heart of every major metaphysical tradition. . . . What is frequently overlooked, however, is that corresponding to the perennial philosophy there exists what I would like to call a psychologia perennis, a 'perennial psychology' — a universal view as to the nature of human consciousness, which expresses the very same insights as the perennial philosophy but in more decidedly psychological language. . . . The purpose of this paper — besides describing the fundamentals of the perennial psychology — is to outline a model of consciousness which remains faithful to the spirit of this universal doctrine yet at the same time gives ample consideration to the insights of such typically Western disciplines as ego-psychology, psychoanalysis, humanistic psychology, Jungian analysis, interpersonal psychology, and the like. At the heart of this model, the "Spectrum of Consciousness" (Wilber, 1974), lies the insight that human personality is a multi-leveled manifestation or expression of a single Consciousness, just as in physics the electro-magnetic spectrum is viewed as a multi-banded expression of a single, characteristic electro-magnetic wave. More specifically, the Spectrum of Consciousness is a pluridimensional approach to man's identity; that is to say, each level of the Spectrum is marked by a different and easily recognized sense of individual identity, which ranges from the Supreme Identity of cosmic consciousness through several gradations or bands to the drastically narrowed sense of identity associated with egoic consciousness. Out of these numerous levels or bands of consciousness, I have selected five major levels to discuss in connection with the *psychologia perennis* (see Fig. 1).

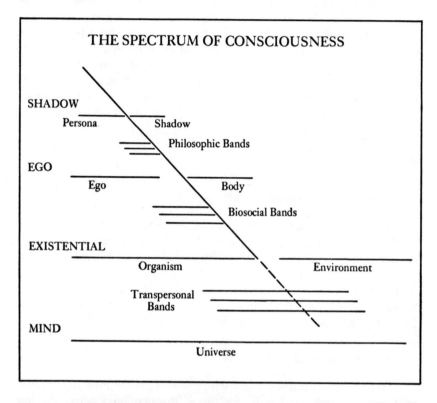

THE SPECTRUM OF CONSCIOUSNESS

SHADOW

Persona   Shadow

                 Philosophic Bands

EGO

        Ego   Body

                     Biosocial Bands

EXISTENTIAL

        Organism   Environment

        Transpersonal
        Bands

MIND

                Universe

FIGURE 1. SOME PROMINENT NODES IN THE SPECTRUM OF CONSCIOUS-NESS. The major levels of identity are indicated by broad lines, while I have arbitrarily chosen three-line groupings to represent the auxiliary bands. The diagonal slash line is representative of the self/not-self boundary, so that, for example, to an individual identified with his persona, the shadow, the body, and the environment all appear as outside of self, as foreign, external, alien, and hence potentially threatening. The self/not-self boundary breaks at the Transpersonal Bands and vanishes at the Level of Mind.

LEVELS OF THE SPECTRUM

The Level of Mind

The core insight of the *psychologia perennis* is that man's 'innermost' consciousness is identical to the absolute and ultimate reality of the universe, known variously as Brahman, Tao, Dharmakaya, Allah, the God-head—to name but a few—and which, for the sake of convenience, I will simple call 'Mind' (with a capital "M" to distinguish it from the apparent plurality of 'minds'; (*see* Watts, 1972). According to this universal tradition, Mind is what there is and all there is, spaceless and therefore infinite, timeless and therefore eternal, outside of which nothing exists.

On this level, man is identified with the universe, the All—or rather, he *is* the All. According to the *psychologia perennis*, this level is not an abnormal state of consciousness, nor even an altered state of consciousness, but rather the *only real* state of consciousness, all others being essentially illusions. . . . In short, man's innermost consciousness—known variously as the Atman, . . . the Christ, Tathagatagarbha—is identical to the ultimate reality of the universe.

This, then, is the Level of Mind, of cosmic consciousness, of man's Supreme Identity.

The Transpersonal Bands

These bands represent the area of the Spectrum that is supraindividual, where man is not conscious of his identity with the All and yet neither is his identity confined to the boundaries of the individual organism. It is on these bands that the achetypes . . . occur. In Mahayana Buddhism (Suzuki, 1968) these bands are known collectively as the . . . 'supra-individual repository consciousness'; while in Hinduism (Deutsch, 1969) they are referred to as the *karana-sarira* or 'causal body'.

The Existential Level

Here man is identified solely with his total psychophysical organism as it exists in space and time, for this is the first level where the line between self and other, organism and environment, is firmly drawn. This is also the level where man's rational thought processes, as well as his personal will, first begin to develop.

It should be mentioned that the 'upper limits' of the Existential Level contain the Biosocial Bands, the internalized matrix of cultural premises, familial relationships, and social glosses, as well as the all-pervading social institutions of language, logic, ethics, and law. . . . In effect, they act so as to profoundly color and mold the organism's basic sense of existence. As anthropologist Edward Hall (White, 1972, p. x) explains, "Selective screening of sensory data admits some things while filtering others, so that experience as it is perceived through one set of culturally patterned sensory screens is quite different from the experience perceived through another."

The Ego Level

On this level, man does not feel directly identified with his psychosomatic organism. Rather, for a variety of reasons, he identifies solely with a more-or-less accurate mental representation or picture of his total organism. In other words, he is identified with his Ego, his self-image. His total organism is thus split into a disembodied 'psyche,' the ghost in the machine, and a 'soma,' 'poor brother ass,' with man identified squarely with the psyche, the mind, the ego—a fact which he betrays by saying not "I *am* a body," but "I *have* a body." He feels that he exists *in* his body and not *as* his body. This level is identified almost exclusively with a mental picture of man's total psychophysical organism, and therefore his intellectual and symbolical processes predominate. Hence the Buddhists call this level ... the 'intellect,' while the Hindus refer to it as ... the level of the ego split from and therefore trapped in the gross body.

The Shadow Level

Under certain circumstances, man can alienate various aspects of his own psyche, dis-identify with them, and thus narrow his sphere of identity to only *parts* of the ego, which we may refer to as the persona. This level is that of the Shadow: man identified with an impoverished and inaccurate self-image (i.e., the persona), while the rest of his psychic tendencies, those deemed too painful, 'evil,' or undesirable, are alienated as the contents of the Shadow.

The above model is an extremely abbreviated description of the Spectrum. As such, it does not fully represent the flow and interaction between the various bands. Nevertheless, it should be obvious that each level of the Spectrum represents an increasingly narrowed sphere of identity, from the universe to a facet of the universe called organism, from the organism to a facet of the organism called psyche, and from the psyche to a facet of the psyche called persona. (Each major level of the Spectrum is also marked by a different mode of knowing, a different dualism or set of dualisms, a different class of unconscious processes, and so on. For this paper, I have chosen to concentrate on the pluri-dimensionality of identity. For a more detailed elaboration, *see* Wilber, 1974.)

EVOLUTION OF THE SPECTRUM

If it is true that the Level of Mind is the only reality, we might wonder just how it is that the other levels seem to exist at all. The answer is supplied by the *psychologia perennis* in the form of the doctrine of *maya*. *Maya* is any experience constituted by or stemming from dualism (specifically, the primary dualism of subject vs. object). According to Deutsch (1969, p. 28), "*Maya* is all experience that is constituted by, and follows from, the distinction between subject and object, between self and non-self." The perennial psychology declares all dualism to be not so much unreal as *illusory*. . . . Cutting of the world into seer and seen, only *apparently* and not actually divides the world, for the world always remains indistinct from itself. Dualism, in other words, is illusory: it appears to exist but remains devoid of reality. . . . In the same vein, the *psychologia perennis* declares that since the various levels of consciousness (except that of Mind itself) are the products of *maya* or dualism—as we will shortly explain—then they must exist only in an illusory fashion, with the *reality* of each level remaining always as Mind.

The *original* dualism or act of severance is mythologically referred to by the perennial philosophy as the separation of Heaven and Earth, Male and Female, Sun and Moon; epistemologically, it is the separation of subject and object, knower and known, observer and observed; ontologically, it is the separation of self and other, organism and environment. For our purposes, the most convenient labels for the two halves of this original dualism are subject and object, self and other, or simply organism and environment, for with its occurrence, man's identity apparently (not actually) shifts from the nondual All to his organism. Man's Supreme Identity becomes not lost but obscured, and thus is created "out of the Oneness of Mind" the next major level of the Spectrum: the Existential Level—man identified with his organism as against his environment. We might also mention that since this primary dualism separates the seer from the seen, the subject from the object, it simultaneously creates *space*.

As soon as man identifies exclusively with his organism, the problem of his being vs. his nullity—the problem of life vs. death—is created. . . . The creation of the dualism of life vs. death is simultaneously the creation of *time*—for in the timelessness of the eternal Mind there is neither birth nor death, beginning nor end, past nor future. . . . In other words, birth and death, past and future are one in the eternal Now, so that in separating birth from death man necessarily separates past from future, and so consequently is thrown out of the timeless Now and into historical time. And that is the Existential Level: man identified exclusively with his organism as it exists in *space* and *time*.

But the disruption of the unity of life and death—the creation of time itself—has yet another consequence. At the Existential Level, man is now in panicked flight from death, and this very flight from death results in the creation of an idealized image of himself called his 'ego,' for the ego, being essentially composed of fixed and stable symbols, *seems* to promise man something that his mere flesh will not: the everlasting escape from death embodied in static images. "The truth of the matter, according to Freud's later theory, is that the peculiar structure of the human ego results from its incapacity to accept reality, specifically the supreme reality of death" (Brown, 1959, p. 159). Man, in fleeing death, flees his mutable body and identifies with the seemingly undying idea of himself. Hence his identity shifts from his *total* psychophysical organism to his mental representation of that organism which thus creates the next major level of the Spectrum: the Ego Level, man identified with a symbolic picture of himself as against his mortal body.

Finally, in the ultimate act of dualism, man severs the unity of his egoic tendencies and identifies with only a fraction of the psychic processes that are his. He disowns, alienates, casts off the unwanted aspects of his ego (which, through the process of egoic repression, nevertheless remains his). In an attempt to make his self-image acceptable, he renders it inaccurate, thus creating the final level of the Spectrum: the Shadow Level, man identified with an inaccurate and greatly impoverished image of himself called the persona, with the unwanted aspects of himself projected as the Shadow.

Thus through successive dualisms (e.g., organism vs. environment, life vs. death, mind vs. body, persona vs. shadow) the various levels of the Spectrum of Consciousness evolve. Since time is nothing but the successive way of viewing Mind's simultaneity, the evolution of the Spectrum is not one 'in' time but 'of' time. Further, the 'level' of Mind is not actually one level among many but one without a second, and so we speak of the 'Level of Mind' only as a convenience. The levels of the Spectrum of Consciousness are thus not at all discrete but, like any spectrum, infinitely shade into one another. According to the *psychologia perennis*, these levels of the Spectrum exist, but only in an illusory fashion, much as the images seen on a television screen are unreal as actual events but exist as mere pictures. Thus the reality of each level is always nothing but Mind, and the actual levels themselves appear independently real only to those who are too enchanted to see through the illusion, who are unable to realize that the world always remains indistinct from itself despite the appearance of dualisms.

THERAPIES ADDRESSING THE VARIOUS LEVELS

Such, then, is an extremely brief description of the *psychologia perennis* and its interpretation according to the Spectrum of Consciousness. ... In a general fashion, the major fields of Western psychotherapy are each concerned with a different level of the Spectrum; that these schools need not overly concern themselves as to which is the 'correct' approach to human consciousness because each is more-or-less correct when addressing its own level; and that a truly integrated and encompassing psychology can and should make use of the complementary insight offered by each school of psychology.

Ego-Level Therapies

Common to this group of therapies is the belief that pathology results from some sort of breakdown in communication between the conscious and the unconscious processes of the psyche, from a split between the persona and the Shadow, however the latter may be conceived. Pathology, according to a popular text on ego psychotherapy (Putney, S. & Putney, G., 1966) results when a person's *self-image is distorted* and rendered inaccurate, and 'cure' consists in the establishment of an accurate and therefore acceptable self-image.

If an individual alienates certain facets of himself, he will render his self-image fraudulent. The alienated facets (i.e, the now 'unconscious' Shadow) will nevertheless remain his, but will be projected so as to appear to exist 'outside' of himself, in the environment or in others. Therapy consists in contacting the Shadow and eventually re-owning it, so that one's sense of identity expands, so to speak, to include all of the aspects of oneself which were once alienated. In this fashion, the split between the persona and Shadow is healed, and the individual consequently evolves an accurate and acceptable self-image, a more-or-less correct mental representation of his total psychophysical organism. And that is precisely the aim of Ego-level therapies.

Existential-Level Therapies

Since the Existential Level is the level of the total organism not marked by the dualism of psyche vs. soma, these therapies deal primarily with actualizing the concrete, full human being, not cut asunder into an ego vs. a body. Their aim is not so much to develop an accurate image of the total organism as to *be* that total organism. Just as the Ego-level therapies aim at 'expanding identity' to all facets of the psyche, Existential-level therapies aim at extending identity to *all facets of the total organism*. This is clearly stated by Perls et al (1951): "The aim is to extend the boundary of what you accept as yourself to include *all organic activities*." Or, as Perls later put it, "Lose your mind and come to your senses!" That is, come to the total organism.

But remember that the Existential Level is also the home of man's two root dualisms, namely, that of subject vs. object (or self vs. other) and life vs. death (or being vs. nullity). Consequently, these are a major concern of many Existential-level therapies. "Sickness unto death," "being and nothingness," "hell is others," "being-in-the-world," the "dialectic of crisis"— all are common themes for some forms of existential therapy, and accurately reflect the phenomenology of the level to which they address themselves.

Overall, then, the Existential-level therapies are concerned with the total psychophysical organism and the crises it may face as well as the incredible potentials it may display. This group of therapies would include the more noetic approaches—such as existential psychology, Gestalt therapy, logotherapy, humanistic psychology in general, and bioenergetics, as well as the more somatic approaches such as hatha yoga, structural integration, polarity therapy, and sensory awareness. Despite their many real differences, they all seek to authenticate the full and concrete human organism.

Biosocial-Band Therapies

Recall that we named the upper limits of the Existential Level 'the Biosocial Bands.' These bands represent the massive mappings of cultural patterns onto the organism itself, and they thus exert a profound and pervasive influence upon the entire organism's orientation and behavior. Among other things, they mold the structure of an individual's ego (Mead, 1964) and the pattern of his thought processes (Whorf, 1956). More importantly, as far as pathology is concerned, these bands act as a screen or filter of reality. In the words of Erich Fromm (1970, p. 98–99, 104):

> The effect of society is not only to funnel fictions into our consciousness, but also to prevent awareness of reality. . . . Every society by its own practice of living and by the mode of relatedness, of feeling and perceiving, develops a system of categories which determines the forms of awareness. This system works, as it were, like a *socially conditioned filter*. . . . Experiences which cannot be filtered through remain outside of awareness; that is, they remain unconscious. . . .

The Biosocial-band therapies are thus concerned with the very fundamental ways in which such social patterns as language and logic alter and distort awareness, and are obviously working on a 'deeper' level than that of purely individual distortions, repressions, and so on. Hence the social context of pathology most concerns these therapies, but not all so-called inter-personal therapies can be classed as Biosocial-band therapies, for many of them are more truly involved in the "the games egos play." But some forms of very fundamental social psychology, social phenomenology, basic family therapies, and semantic therapies are directly addressing themselves to this most important band of the Spectrum. (For a novel approach to the Biosocial Bands, *see* Castaneda, 1972).

Transpersonal-Band Therapies

The Transpersonal Bands represent those aspects or levels of consciousness that by their very nature are supra-individual. At this level the 'individual' is not yet completely identified with the All, and yet neither is his identity confined to the conventional boundaries of his organism. Among other things, the Transpersonal Bands are the home of the ... 'primordial images' of the 'collective unconscious' [Jung, 1960].

Now these archetypes ... exert a profound effect upon every level of the Spectrum existing 'above' the Transpersonal Bands. It is entirely possible that this is a general phenomenon seen throughout the Spectrum; the vicissitudes of *any* level can dramatically affect all of the levels above it. But the point to be emphasized here is that the Transpersonal Bands can themselves be *directly* experienced. Carl Jung (1968, p. 110) himself realized this, for he stated that "Mystics are people who have a particularly vivid experience of the processes of the collective unconscious. Mystical experience is *experience of archetypes*."

A general characteristic of the Transpersonal Bands is a suspension of all dualisms (except some form of the primary dualism). This necessarily includes the dualisms of persona vs. shadow as well as ego vs. body. In undercutting these dualisms, one simultaneously undercuts the support of individual neuroses, both egoic and existential.

To say the same thing in a slightly different fashion, in recognizing a depth of one's identity that goes beyond one's individual and separate being, a person can more easily go beyond his individual and separate neuroses. For he is no longer *exclusively* identified with just his separate-self sense and hence is no longer exclusively tied to his purely personal problems. In a sense he can start to let go of his fears and anxieties, depressions and obsessions, and begin to view them with ... impartiality.... The Transpersonal Band therapy discloses—probably for the first time— a transposition from which he can comprehensively *look at* his individual emotional and ideational complexes. But the fact that he can comprehensively *look at* them means that he has ceased using them as something *with which to look* at, and thus distort, reality. Further, the fact that he can look at them means that he is no longer exclusively identified with them. His identity begins to touch that within which is beyond.

As such, the Transpersonal Bands are sometimes experienced as the supra-individual Witness: that which is capable of observing the flow of what is — without manipulating it. The Witness simply observes the stream of events both inside and outside the mind-body in a creatively detached fashion, since, in fact, the Witness is not exclusively identified with either. In other words, *when the individual realizes that his mind and his body can be perceived objectively, he spontaneously realizes that they cannot constitute a real subjective self.* ... This position of the Witness, or we might say, this state of Witnessing, is the foundation of all beginning Buddhist practice ('mindfulness') [and] of Psychosynthesis ('disidentification and the transpersonal Self').

Further, it seems to resemble very closely what Maslow called plateau experiences, which "represent a witnessing of the world. The plateau experience is a witnessing of reality. It involves seeing the symbolic, or the mythic, the poetic, the transcendent, the miraculous. . . . It's the transcending of time and space which becomes quite normal, so to speak." It is expressly through these types of experiences that one is fully initiated into the world of metamotivations, B-values, transcendent values, mythological and supra-individual awareness — in short, the spiritual dimension of Transpersonal Bands.

Level-of-Mind Therapies

. . . This distinction between what I am calling — for lack of better terms — 'lesser' and 'true' mysticism is again the distinction between the transpersonal Witness and Mind. The transpersonal Witness is a 'position' of Witnessing reality. But notice that this state of the transpersonal Witness still contains a subtle form of the primary dualism, namely, the witness vs. what is witnessed. It is when this last trace of dualism is finally and completely shattered that one awakens to Mind, for at that moment (which is *this* moment) the witness and the witnessed are one and the same.

This is not at all to denigrate the position of the transpersonal self or Witness, for it can not only be highly therapeutic in itself, but it can frequently act as a type of springboard to Mind. Nevertheless it is not to be confused with Mind itself.

Such, then, is the major difference between the lesser mystical states of the transpersonal self, and the true mystical state which is Mind. In one, a person may witness reality; in the other he is reality. While one invariably retains some subtle form of the primary dualism, the other does not. . . . The individual goes right to the very bottom of his being to find who or what is doing the seeing, and he *ultimately* finds — instead of a transpersonal self — nothing other than what is seen, which Blyth called, "the experience by the universe of the universe."

Therapies aimed at this level — like those of any level — are trying to heal a particular dualism, in this case, the primary dualism of subject vs. object. . . . And the collapse of the dualism between subject and object is simultaneously the collapse of the dualism between past and future, life and death, so that one awakens, as if from a dream, to the spaceless and timeless world of cosmic consciousness. Therapies — and at this level we use the term 'therapies' only as a concession to language — addressing this level include Mahayana Buddhism, Taoism, Vedanta, Hinduism, Sufism, and certain forms of Christian mysticism.

CONCLUDING REMARKS

Having thus finished the above very abstract outline, a few points must at least be touched upon. First, the levels of the Spectrum of Consciousness, like any spectrum, infinitely shade and grade into one another, and in no way can they be finally separated from one another. We have merely picked out a few prominent 'nodes' in the Spectrum for discussion, so it immediately follows that the assignment of different schools of psychotherapy to one level or band is only a rough approximation. Second, when we assign a particular school to one major level of the Spectrum, this is done on the basis of a somewhat arbitrary 'deepest' level which that school recognizes. Generally speaking, the therapies of any one level recognize and even utilize the psychotherapeutic disciplines of the levels 'above' it. Thus, to place Jungian psychology on the Transpersonal Bands is not to imply that Jung had nothing to say about the Shadow Level, or the Biosocial Bands. Indeed he did have much to offer regarding those levels. . . . Third, it *is*, however, generally the case that the therapies of any one level tend to view experience of *any* level 'beneath' theirs as being pathological, and are hence quick to explain away all lower levels with a diagnostic fury, as witness the stance of orthodox psychoanalysis on mysticism. Fourth, since the descent of the Spectrum of Consciousness is, in one sense or another, an expanding of identity from the persona to the ego or the organism to the cosmos, we could just as well speak of a progressive dis-identification or a progressive *detachment* from all *exclusive* identifications. When it comes to the Level of Mind, it does not matter whether we say the individual is identified with *everything* or whether the individual is identified with *nothing*—both are logically meaningless anyway. To elucidate the former only makes the complex story of the Spectrum of Consciousness a little easier to tell. Fifth, since each level of the Spectrum is marked by a different sense of identity, each level will have more-or-less characteristic features associated with it. For instance, the different levels seem to produce different dreams, different needs, and different symptoms—to mention a few. For example, transpersonal anxiety, existential anxiety, and shadow anxiety are different beasts indeed, and simply must not be treated the same. The indiscriminate use of a single therapeutic technique for all symptoms may have the most unfortunate effects.

In this regard, the question might arise as to what effect, if any, therapeutic procedures on the upper levels (Shadow, Ego, Existential) have or might have on a person's development on or towards the lower levels (Transpersonal, Mind). Although an extended discussion of this topic is quite beyond the scope of this paper, the following may be said. The descent of the Spectrum of Consciousness can be described as a process of surrendering exclusive, narrowed, and partial identifications so as to discover broader and more encompassing ones down the Spectrum. To the extent an individual can let go of his exclusive attachments on the upper bands of the Spectrum—and this, in essence, is the aim of upper level therapies—his descent is thereby facilitated.

Theoretically, in totally healing the major dualism characteristic of any given level, the individual would be expected to necessarily, and quite spontaneously, descend to the next level. For example, in healing and wholing the split between persona and shadow, the individual—almost by definition—has descended to the Ego Level. In fully healing and wholing the split between ego and body, the individual has spontaneously descended to the Existential Level, and so on. Once on the new level, the individual will likely become more sensitive to that level's characteristics— its dreams, its dualisms, its class of 'dys-eases,' its potentials for growth, its needs. This phenomenon of spontaneous descent, which is *potentially* inherent in everyone, is an almost exact analogue of Maslow's (1968) hierarchical needs—that is, neurotic needs (Shadow Level), basic needs (Ego and Existential Levels) and meta-needs (Transpersonal Bands: Mind has no needs for there is nothing outside it). As soon as an individual clears up one set of needs, the next set spontaneously emerges, and failure to satisfy these emergent needs will result in a different set of problems.

Thus, on the Shadow Level, the basic needs are not satisfied. Through repression, alienation, or some other projective mechanism, the individual fails to recognize the nature of his basic needs. And since, as is well known, one cannot get enough of what one does not really need, a whole battery of insatiable neurotic needs develop. If, on the other hand, these neurotic needs can be understood and displaced, so that the underlying basic needs can emerge (hierarchically), the individual can begin to act on them so as to find thereby his way to a larger fulfillment. He also finds — again, almost by definition — his way to a lower level of the Spectrum. And by the time the individual reaches the Existential Level, an entirely new set of needs, the meta-needs, begin to emerge, carrying with them a call, sometimes a demand, to transcendence. Acting upon these meta-needs initiates one into the world of the Transpersonal Bands; shunning them throws one into the grips of a meta-pathology.

In light of the above, it would not be reckless to conclude that therapeutic measures on the upper levels of the Spectrum may indeed facilitate the descent to the lower levels. This does not mean that a descent to the Transpersonal Bands or the Level of Mind always *requires* upper-level therapy, even in the cases where it is indicated. It might certainly help, but may not be mandatory since lower level therapies may in a real sense reduce the work to be done on the upper levels. If this were not the case, meditation practices would probably never be useful to a neurotic unless he had undergone something akin to complete psychoanalysis.

I have only extended the *psychologia perennis* by suggesting that not only do these levels apparently exist, as maintained by the perennial psychology, but also that pathology can occur on any of these levels (except, of course, on the Level of Mind), and thus the great contribution of Western psychologies lies precisely in addressing themselves to *these* pathologies.

Thus it is possible to see the grand complementarity of Eastern and

Western approaches to consciousness and 'psychotherapy.' On the one hand, the overriding concern of the Eastern explorers of consciousness (and by 'Eastern' we really mean the *psychologia perennis* in general, geographically East or West being irrelevant) has always been with the Level of Mind, and thus they gave little, if any, attention to the pathologies that could develop on the other levels. This is understandable, for the perennial psychology maintains that *all* pathology stems from ignorance ... of Mind. Thus, although they were perfectly aware of the various levels of the Spectrum, and although they mapped them in detail, they felt that 'curing' a pathology on any of these levels was not much more than a waste of time, for the root ignorance of the subject-object dualism would still remain. The West, on the other hand, has been — at least since the seventeenth century — almost completely bereft of even the least conception of the perennial philosophy, and hence, when the study of psychopathology began to develop in this metaphysical vacuum, Western scientists had no choice but to seek out the roots of neuroses and psychoses in one or more of the 'upper' levels of the Spectrum (such as the Ego or Biosocial Levels). It is suggested that on their own levels they are *all* correct, and taken together they form a complementary approach to consciousness that spans the entire Spectrum.

References

Brown, N.O. *Life against death: The psychoanalytical meaning of history*. Middleton, O.: Wesleyan University Press, 1959.

Castaneda, C. *Journey to Ixtlan*. New York: Simon and Schuster, 1972.

Deutsch, E. *Advaita Vedanta*. Honolulu: East-West Center Press, 1969.

Fromm, E., Suzuki, D. T., & DeMartino, R. *Zen Buddhism and psychoanalysis*. New York: Harper & Row, 1970.

Huxley, A. *The perennial philosophy*. New York: Harper & Row, 1970.

Jung, C. *The structure and dynamics of the psyche*. New York: Pantheon, 1960.

Jung, C. *Analytical psychology: Its theory and practice*. New York: Vintage, 1968.

Maslow, A. H. *The farther reaches of human nature*. New York: Viking, 1971.

Maslow, A, H. *Towards a psychology of being*. New York: Van Nostrand Reinhold, 1968.

Mead, G. H. *George Herbert Mead on social psychology*. Anselm Strauss, Ed. Chicago: University of Chicago Press, 1964.

Perls, F., Hefferline, R. & Goodman, P. *Gestalt therapy*. New York: Delta, 1951.

Putney, S. & Putney, G. *The adjusted American*. New York: Harper & Row, 1966.

Suzuki, D. T. *Studies in the Lankavatara Sutra*. London: Routledge & Kegan Paul, 1968.

Watts, A. *The supreme identity*. New York: Vintage, 1972.

White, J. (Ed.). *The highest state of consciousness*. New York: Anchor, 1972.

Whorf, B. L. *Language, thought, and reality*. Cambridge: M.I.T. Press, 1956.

Wilber, K. *The spectrum of consciousness*. Main Currents, 1974, *31*, 2.

Realms of the Human Unconscious: Observations from LSD Research

STANISLAV GROF

EMPIRICAL BASIS FOR A NEW THEORETICAL FRAMEWORK

The concepts presented in this book are based on my own clinical research of LSD covering a period of seventeen years. ... My understanding of LSD and my concepts of how it should be used therapeutically underwent fundamental changes during these years of clinical experimentation. I will briefly describe the most important stages of this development.

The early years of LSD research were characterized by the so-called "model psychosis" approach. The accidental discovery of LSD and the pioneering research of its effects demonstrated that incredibly minute quantities of this substance could produce dramatic and profound changes in the mental functioning of an individual. Many researchers felt at that time that LSD could mimic the symptoms of schizophrenia and believed that the study of LSD would provide a key to the understanding of this disease as basically a biochemical deviation. ... Nevertheless, we failed to demonstrate any significant parallels between the phenomenology of the states induced by these drugs and the symptomatology of schizophrenia.

Abandoning in theory and practice the "model psychosis" approach, I found it increasingly difficult to share the opinion of the critics who considered the LSD-induced state as simply an unspecific reaction of the brain to a noxious chemical, or "toxic psychosis."

The most astonishing and puzzling aspect of the LSD sessions which I observed in the early years of experimentation was the enormous variability among individuals.

With the increasing number of sessions I observed, I became more and more aware that many of the LSD phenomena seemed to have an interesting psychodynamic meaning and could be understood in psychological terms.

Analysis indicated clearly that the LSD reaction is highly specific for the personality of the subject. Rather than causing an unspecific "toxic psychosis," LSD appeared to be a powerful catalyst of the mental processes activating unconscious material from various deep levels of the personality. Many of the phenomena in these sessions could be understood in psychological and psychodynamic terms; they had a structure not dissimilar to that of dreams. During this detailed analytical scrutiny, it soon become obvious that LSD could become an unrivaled tool for deep personality diagnostics.

At the present time, I consider LSD to be a powerful unspecific amplifier or catalyst of biochemical and physiological processes in the brain. It seems to create a situation of undifferentiated activation that facilitates the emergence of unconscious material from different levels of the personality.

We can delineate for the purpose of our discussion the following four major levels, or types, of LSD experiences and the corresponding areas of the human unconscious: (1) abstract and aesthetic experiences, (2) psychodynamic experiences, (3) perinatal experiences, and (4) transpersonal experiences.

AESTHETIC EXPERIENCES

The aesthetic experiences seem to represent the most superficial level of the LSD experience. They do not reveal the unconscious of the subject and do not have any psychodynamic significance. The most important aspects of these experiences can be explained in physiological terms as a result of chemical stimulation of the sensory organs reflecting their inner structure and functional characteristics.

The following example from an LSD session of a psychiatrist participating in the LSD training program can be used as an illustration:

> I was deeply enmeshed in an abstract world of whirling geometrical forms and exuberant colors that were brighter and more radiant than anything I have ever seen in my life. I was fascinated and mesmerized by this incredible kaleidoscopic show....

PSYCHODYNAMIC EXPERIENCES IN LSD SESSIONS

The experiences belonging to this category originate in the realm of the individual unconscious and in the areas of the personality accessible in usual states of consciousness. They are related to important memories, emotional problems, unresolved conflicts, and repressed material from various life periods of the individual. Most of the phenomena occurring on this level can be interpreted and understood in psychodynamic terms....

The least complicated psychodynamic experiences have the form of actual relivings of emotionally highly relevant events and vivid reenactments of traumatic or unusually pleasant memories from infancy, childhood, or later periods of life. More complicated phenomena in this group represent pictorial concretization of fantasies, dramatization of wishful daydreams, screen memories, and complex mixtures of fantasy and reality. In addition to these, the psychodynamic level involves a variety of experiences that contain important unconscious material appearing in the cryptic form of a symbolic disguise, defensive distortions, and metaphorical allusions.

Psychodynamic experiences are particularly common in psycholytic therapy of psychiatric patients and in unsupervised LSD sessions of individuals who have considerable emotional problems. They are much less important in the sessions of persons who are emotionally stable and whose childhood was relatively uneventful.

The phenomenology of psychodynamic experiences in LSD sessions is to a large extent in agreement with the basic concepts of classical psychoanalysis. If psychodynamic sessions were the only type of LSD experience, the observations from LSD psychotherapy could be considered to be laboratory proof of the basic Freudian premises. The psychosexual dynamics and the fundamental conflicts of the human psyche as described by Freud are manifested with unusual clarity and vividness even in sessions of naive subjects who have never been analyzed, have not read psychoanalytic books, and have not been exposed to other forms of implicit or explicit indoctrination. Under the influence of LSD, such subjects experience regression to childhood and even early infancy, relive various psychosexual traumas and complex sensations related to infantile sexuality, and are confronted with conflicts involving activities in various libidinal zones. They have to face and work through some of the basic psychological problems described by psychoanalysis, such as the Oedipus and Electra complexes, castration anxiety, and penis envy.

In spite of this far-reaching correspondence and congruence, Freudian concepts cannot explain some of the phenomena related to psychodynamic LSD sessions. For a more complete understanding of these sessions and of the consequences they have for the clinical condition of the patient, as well as for the personality structure, a new principle has to be introduced into psychoanalytical thinking. LSD phenomena on this level can be comprehended, and at times predicted, if we think in terms of specific memory constellations, for which I use the name "COEX systems" (systems of condensed experience).

COEX SYSTEMS (SYSTEMS OF CONDENSED EXPERIENCE)

A *COEX system* can be defined as a specific constellation of memories consisting of condensed experiences (and related fantasies) from different life periods of the individual. The memories belonging to a particular COEX system have a similar basic theme or contain similar elements and are associated with a strong emotional charge of the same quality. The deepest layers of this system are represented by vivid and colorful memories of experiences from infancy and early childhood. More superficial layers of such a system involve memories of similar experiences from later periods, up to the present life situation. Each COEX system has a basic theme that permeates all its layers and represents their common denominator; the nature of these themes varies considerably from one COEX constellation to another. Various layers of a particular system can, for example, contain all memories of the past exposures of an individual to humiliating and degrading situations that have damaged his self-esteem. . . . The experience of emotional deprivation and rejection in various periods of one's development is another common motif of many COEX constellations. Equally frequent are basic themes that depict sex as dangerous or disgusting, and those that involve aggression and violence. Particularly important are COEX systems that epitomize and condense the individual's encounters with situations endangering survival, health, and integrity of the body. The excessive emotional charge which is attached to COEX systems (as indicated by the often powerful abreaction accompanying the unfolding of these systems in LSD sessions) seems to be a summation of the emotions belonging to all the constituent memories of a particular kind.

Individual COEX systems have fixed relations to certain defense mechanisms and are connected with specific clinical symptoms. The detailed interrelations between the individual parts and aspects of COEX systems are in most instances in basic agreement with Freudian thinking; the new element from the theoretical point of view is the concept of the organizing dynamic system integrating the components into a distinct functional unit. The personality structure usually contains a greater number of COEX systems. Their character, total number, extent, and intensity varies considerably from one individual to another.

According to the basic quality of the emotional charge, we can differentiate *negative COEX systems* (condensing unpleasant emotional experiences) and *positive COEX systems* (condensing pleasant emotional experiences and positive aspects of an individual's past life.) Although there are certain interdependencies and overlappings, separate COEX systems can function relatively autonomously. In a complicated interaction with the environment, they influence selectively the subject's perception of himself and of the world, his feelings and ideation, and even many somatic processes.

Reliving of experiences constituting different levels of the COEX systems is one of the most frequently and constantly observed phenomena in LSD psychotherapy of psychiatric patients. This reliving is rather realistic, vivid, and complex; it is characterized by various convincing indications of regression of the subject to the age when he originally experienced the event in question.

The list of characteristic traumatic experiences that occur as core elements of negative COEX systems covers a wide range of situations that interfere with the security and satisfaction of the child. The oldest core experiences are related to the earliest stage of infancy, the suckling period. Quite frequent is the reliving of oral frustrations related to a rigid feeding schedule, to lack of milk, or to tension, anxiety, nervousness, and lack of love on the part of the nursing mother and her inability to create an emotionally warm, peaceful, and protective atmosphere. Equally frequent seem to be other traumatic experiences from infancy.

The reliving of traumatic childhood experiences is often followed by far-reaching changes in the clinical symptomatology, behavior patterns, values, and attitudes. The powerful transforming effect of the reliving and integration of such memories suggests that a more general dynamic principle is involved.

The most important part of the COEX system seems to be the core experience. It was the first experience of a particular kind that was registered in the brain and laid the foundations for a specific COEX system. The core experience, thus, represents a prototype, a matrix pattern, for the recording of subsequent events of a similar kind in the memory banks. It is not easy to explain why certain kinds of events have such a powerful traumatic effect on the child that they influence his psychodynamic development for many years or decades. Psychoanalysts have usually thought in this connection about constitutional and hereditary factors of an unknown nature. LSD research seems to indicate that this specific sensitivity can have important determinants in deeper levels of the unconscious, in functional dynamic matrices that are inborn and transpersonal in nature.

Another important fact might be the dynamiceimilarity between a particular traumatic incident in childhood and a certain facet of the birth trauma (or perinatal traumatization). In this case, the traumatic impact of a later situation would actually be due to the reactivation of a certain aspect of the psychobiological memory of the birth.

However, whatever the time or number of sessions required, sooner or later the elements of the individual unconscious tend to disappear from the LSD experience and each individual undergoing psycholytic therapy enters the realm of the perinatal and transpersonal phenomena.

PERINATAL EXPERIENCES IN LSD SESSIONS

The basic characteristics of perinatal experiences and their central focus are the problems of biological birth, physical pain and agony, aging, disease and decrepitude, and dying and death. Inevitably, the shattering encounter with these critical aspects of human existence and the deep realization of the frailty and impermanence of man as a biological creature is accompanied by an agonizing existentialist crisis. The individual comes to realize, through these experiences, that no matter what he does in his life, he cannot escape the inevitable: he will have to leave this world bereft of everything that he has accumulated and achieved and to which he has been emotionally attached. The similarity between birth and death — the startling realization that the beginning of life is the same as its end — is the major philosophical issue that accompanies the perinatal experiences. The other important consequence of the shocking emotional and physical encounter with the phenomenon of death is the opening up of areas of spiritual and religious experiences that appear to be an intrinsic part of the human personality and are independent of the individual's cultural and religious background and programming. In my experience, everyone who has reached these levels develops convincing insights into the utmost relevance of the spiritual and religious dimensions in the universal scheme of things. Even hard-core materialists, positivistically oriented scientists, skeptics and cynics, and uncompromising atheists and antireligous crusaders such as the Marxist philosophers suddenly became interested in a spiritual search after they confronted these levels in themselves.

In a way that is not quite clear at the present stage of research, the above experiences seem to be related to the circumstances of the biological birth. LSD subjects frequently refer to them quite explicitly as reliving of their own birth trauma. Those who do not make this link and conceptualize their encounter with death and the death-rebirth experience in a purely philosophical and spiritual framework quite regularly show the cluster of physical symptoms described earlier that can best be interpreted as a derivative of the biological birth. They also assume postures and move in complex sequences that bear a striking similarity to those of a child during the various stages of delivery. In addition, these subjects frequently report visions of or identification with embryos, fetuses, and newborn children. Equally common are various authentic neonatal feelings as well as behavior, and visions of female genitals and breasts.

Because of these observations and other clinical evidence, I have labeled the above pheonomena *perinatal experiences*. A causal nexus between the actual biological birth and the unconscious matrices for these experiences still remains to be established. It appears appropriate, however, to refer to this level of the unconscious as Rankian; with some modification, Otto Rank's conceptual framework is useful for the understanding of the phenomena in question.[1]

Perinatal experiences are a manifestation of a deep level of the unconscious that is clearly beyond the reach of classical Freudian techniques. The phenomena belonging to this category have been neither described in psychoanalytic literature nor taken into consideration in the theoretical speculations of Freudian analysts. Moreover, classical Freudian analysis does not allow for explanation of such experiences and does not offer an adequate conceptual framework for their interpretation.

Perinatal experiences represent a very important intersection between individual psychology and transpersonal psychology or, for that matter, between psychology and psychopathology, on one hand, and religion, on the other. If we think about them as related to the individual birth, they would seem to belong to the framework of individual psychology. Some other aspects, however, give them a very definite transpersonal flavor.

The intensity of these experiences transcends anything usually considered to be the experiential limit of the individual. They are frequently accompanied by identification with other persons or with struggling and suffering mankind. Moreover, other types of clearly transpersonal experiences, such as evolutionary memories, elements of the collective unconscious, and certain Jungian archetypes, frequently form an integral part of the perinatal matrices.

Elements of the rich and complex content of LSD sessions reflecting this level of the unconscious seem to appear in four typical clusters, matrices, or experiential patterns. Searching for a simple, logical, and natural conceptualization of this fact, I was struck by the deep parallels between these patterns and the clinical stages of delivery. It proved to be a very useful principle for both theoretical considerations and the practice of LSD psychotherapy to relate the above four categories of phenomena to consecutive stages of the biological birth process and to the experiences of the child in the perinatal period. Therefore, for the sake of brevity, I usually refer to the four major experiential matrices of the Rankian level as *Basic Perinatal Matrices (BPM I–IV)*. It must be re-emphasized that this should be considered at the present stage of knowledge only as a very useful model, not necessarily implying a causal nexus.

The Basic Perinatal Matrices are hypothetical dynamic governing systems that have a function on the Rankian level of the unconscious similar to that of the COEX systems on the Freudian psychodynamic level. They have a specific content of their own, namely, the perinatal phenomena. The latter have two important facets or components: biological and spiritual. The biological aspect of perinatal experiences consists of concrete and rather realistic experiences related to the individual stages of the biological delivery. Each stage of biological birth appears to have a specific spiritual counterpart: for the undisturbed intrauterine existence it is the experience of cosmic unity; the onset of the delivery is paralleled by feelings of universal engulfment; the first clinical stage of delivery, the contractions in a closed uterine system, corresponds with the experience of "no exit" or hell; the propulsion through the birth canal in the second clinical stage of the delivery has its spiritual analogue in the death-rebirth struggle; and the metaphysical equivalent of the termination of the birth process and of the events in the third clinical stage of the delivery is the experience of ego death and rebirth. In addition to this specific content, the basic perinatal matrices function also as organizing principles for the material from other levels of the unconscious, namely for the COEX systems, as well as for some types of transpersonal experiences that occasionally occur simultaneously with perinatal phenomena.

The deep parallel between the physiological activities in the consecutive stages of biological delivery and the pattern of activities in various erogenic zones, in particular that of the genital orgasm, seems to be of great theoretical significance. It makes it possible to shift the etiological emphasis in the psychogenesis of emotional disorders from sexuality to perinatal matrices, without denying or negating the validity of many basic Freudian principles. Even within such an extended framework, psychoanalytic observations and concepts remain useful for the understanding of occurrences on the psychodynamic level and their mutual interrelations.

TRANSPERSONAL EXPERIENCES IN LSD SESSIONS

Transpersonal experiences occur only rarely in early sessions of psycholytic therapy; they become quite common in advanced sessions after the subject has worked through and integrated the material on the psychodynamic and perinatal levels. After the final experience of ego death and rebirth, transpersonal elements dominate all subsequent LSD sessions of the individual.

The common denominator of this otherwise rich and ramified group of phenomena is the feeling of the individual that his consciousness expanded beyond the usual ego boundaries and limitations of time and space.

TRANSPERSONAL EXPERIENCES

I. Experiential extension within the framework of "objective reality"

A. Temporal expansion of consciousness
1. Embryonal and fetal experiences
2. Ancestral experiences
3. Collective and racial experiences
4. Phylogenetic (evolutionary) experiences
5. Past-incarnation experiences
6. Precognition, clairvoyance, clairaudience, and "time travels"

B. Spatial expansion of consciousness
1. Ego transcendence in interpersonal relations and the experience of dual unity
2. Identification with other persons
3. Group identification and group consciousness
4. Animal identification
5. Plant identification
6. Oneness with life and with all creation
7. Consciousness of inorganic matter
8. Planetary consciousness
9. Extraplanetary consciousness
10. Out-of-body experiences, traveling clairvoyance and clairaudience, "space travels," and telepathy

C. Spatial constriction of consciousness
    1. Organ, tissue, and cellular consciousness
II. Experiential extension beyond the framework of "objective reality"
    1. Spiritistic and mediumistic experiences
    2. Experiences of encounters with suprahuman spiritual entities
    3. Experiences of other universes and encounters with their inhabitants
    4. Archetypal experiences and complex mythological sequences
    5. Experiences of encounters with various deities
    6. Intuitive understanding of universal symbols
    7. Activation of the chakras and arousal of the serpent power (Kundalini)
    8. Consciousness of the universal mind
    9. The supracosmic and metacosmic void

Embryonal and Fetal Experiences

Vivid, concrete episodes that appear to be memories of specific events from an individual's intrauterine development are rather common.

As in the case of the reliving of childhood and birth memories, the authenticity of recaptured intrauterine events is an open question. It seems, therefore, more appropriate to refer to them as experiences rather than memories. ... However, on several occasions, I was able to get surprising confirmations by independently questioning the mother or other persons involved.

A researcher studying transpersonal phenomena occurring in LSD sessions has to be prepared for many baffling observations and coincidences that can put to a serious test the existing scientific beliefs and instigate doubts about the validity of some widely accepted and shared basic premises.

Archetypal Experiences and Complex Mythological Sequences

An important group of transpersonal experiences in LSD sessions are phenomena for which C. G. Jung has used the terms primordial images, dominants of the collective unconscious, or archetypes.

In some of the most universal archetypes, the subject can identify with the roles of the Mother, Father, Child, Woman, Man, or Lover. Many highly universalized roles are felt as sacred, as exemplified by the archetypes of the Great Mother, the Terrible Mother, the Earth Mother,

Mother Nature, the Great Hermaphrodite, or Cosmic Man. Archetypes representing certain aspects of the subject's personality, such as the Shadow, Animus and Anima, or Persona, are also rather common in advanced LSD sessions.

Not infrequently, unsophisticated subjects have reported stories that strongly resemble ancient mythological themes from Mesopotamia, India, Egypt, Greece, Central America, and other countries of the world. These observations closely parallel C. G. Jung's descriptions of the appearance of relatively unknown but distinctly archetypal themes in the dreams of children and unsophisticated patients, as well as in the manifest symptomatology of some schizophrenics.

We have mentioned elsewhere that as a result of LSD sessions some subjects have developed insights into entire systems of esoteric thought. Thus, individuals unfamilar with the cabbala have had experiences described in the Zohar and Sepher Yetzirah and have demonstrated a surprising familiarity with cabbalistic symbols. . . . Such new understanding was also observed in regard to various ancient forms of divination, such as the I Ching and Tarot.

Activation of the Chakras and Arousal of the Serpent Power (Kundalini)

Many experiences from transpersonal LSD sessions bear a striking resemblance to phenomena described in various schools of Kundalini yoga as signs of the activation and opening of individual chakras. These parallels do not exist only for experiences of a positive nature; the phenomenology and consequences of mishandled or poorly integrated LSD sessions is very similar to the complications occurring in the course of unsupervised and amateurish Kundalini practices. . . . In general, the chakra system seems to provide very useful maps of consciousness that are of great help in understanding and conceptualizing many unusual experiences in LSD sessions.

Of all the systems of yoga, Kundalini yoga bears the closest resemblance to LSD psychotherapy. Both techniques mediate an instant and enormous release of energy, produce profound and dramatic experiences, and can bring impressive results in a relatively short time. On the other hand, they involve the greatest risk and can be quite dangerous if they are not practiced under careful supervision and responsible guidance.

Consciousness of the Universal Mind

This is one of the most profound and total experiences observed in LSD sessions. Identifying with the consciousness of the Universal Mind, the individual senses that he has experientially encompassed the totality of existence. He feels that he has reached the reality underlying all realities and is confronted with the supreme and ultimate principle that represents all Being. The illusions of matter, space, and time, as well as an infinite number of other subjective realities, have been completely transcended and finally reduced to this one mode of consciousness which is their common source and denominator. This experience is boundless, unfathomable, and ineffable; it is existence itself. Verbal communication and the symbolic structure of our everyday language seem to be a ridiculously inadequate means to capture and convey its nature and quality. The experience of the phenomenal world and what we call usual states of consciousness appear in this context to be only very limited, idiosyncratic, and partial aspects of the over-all consciousness of the Universal Mind. . . .

Discussing experiences of this nature, subjects have frequently commented on the fact that the language of poets, although still highly imperfect, seems to be a more adequate and appropriate tool for this purpose. One understands why so many great seers, prophets, and religious teachers have resorted to poetry, parable, and metaphor in order to share their transcendental visions.

The experience of consciousness of the Universal Mind is closely related to that of cosmic unity but not identical with it. Its important concomitants are intuitive insights into the process of creation of the phenomenal world as we know it and into the Buddhist concept of the wheel of death and rebirth. These can result in a temporary or enduring feeling that the individual has achieved a global, nonrational, and transrational understanding of the basic ontological and cosmological problems that beset existence.

The Supracosmic and Metacosmic Void

The last and most paradoxical transpersonal phenomenon to be discussed in this context is the experience of the supracosmic and metacosmic Void, of the primordial emptiness, nothingness, and silence, which is the ultimate source and cradle of all existence and the "uncreated and ineffable Supreme." The terms supra- and metacosmic used by sophisticated LSD subjects in this context refer to the fact that this Void appears to be both supraordinated to and underlying the phenomenal world. It is beyond time and space, beyond form or any experiential differentiation, and beyond polarities such as good and evil, light and darkness, stability and motion, and agony and ecstasy.

No matter how paradoxical it might seem, the Void and the Universal Mind are perceived as identical and freely interchangeable; they are two different aspects of the same phenomenon. The Void appears to be emptiness pregnant with form, and the subtle forms of the Universal Mind are experienced as absolutely empty.

Profound transcendental experiences, such as the activation of the Kundalini or consciousness of the Universal Mind or of the Void, in addition to having a very beneficial effect on the subject's physical and emotional well-being, are usually central in creating in him a keen interest in religious, mystical, and philosophical issues, and a strong need to incorporate the spiritual dimension into his way of life.

TRANSPERSONAL EXPERIENCES AND CONTEMPORARY PSYCHIATRY

It certainly is not the first time behavioral scientists and mental health professionals have been confronted with transpersonal experiences, nor is the use of psychedelic substances the only framework in which they can be observed. Many of these experiences have been known for centuries or millennia. Descriptions of them can be found in the holy scriptures of all the great religions of the world, as well as in written documents of countless minor sects, factions, and religious movements. They have also played a crucial role in the visionary stages of individual saints, mystics, and religious teachers. Ethnologists and anthropolgists have observed and described them in aboriginal sacred rituals, ecstatic and mystery religions, indigenous healing practices, and rites of passage of various cultures. Psychiatrists and psychologists have been seeing transpersonal phenomena, without identifying and labeling them as such, in their everyday practice in many psychotic patients, especially schizophrenics. Historians, religionists, anthropologists, and experimental psychiatrists and psychologists have been aware of the existence of a variety of ancient as well as modern techniques that facilitate the occurrence of transpersonal experiences; they are the same procedures that were described earlier as conducive to the emergence of the perinatal elements.

In spite of the frequency of these phenomena and their obvious relevance for many areas of human life, surprisingly few serious attempts have been made in the past to incorporate them into the theory and practice of contemporary psychiatry and psychology. The attitude of most professionals has oscillated among several distinct approaches to these phenomena. Some professionals have been only marginally acquainted with various transpersonal experiences and have more or less ignored them.

For another large group of professionals, transpersonal phenomena are clearly too bizarre to be considered within the framework of variations of normal mental functioning. Any manifestation of this sort is then readily labeled psychotic.

Yet another group of professionals has manifested definite interest in various aspects of the transpersonal realm and made serious attempts at theoretical explanations and conceptualizations. They have not, however, acknowledged the uniqueness of this category or the specific characteristics of such phenomena. In their approach, transpersonal experiences have been explained in terms of old and widely accepted paradigms; in most instances, they are reduced to biographically determined psychodynamic phenomena. Thus, intrauterine experiences (as well as the perinatal elements) appearing in dreams and free associations of many patients are usually treated as mere fantasies; various religious thoughts and feelings are explained from unresolved conflicts with parental authority; experiences of cosmic unity are interpreted as indications of primary infantile narcissism.

At present, there is little doubt in my mind that they represent phenomena *sui generis* which originate in the deep unconscious, in areas that have been unrecognized and unacknowledged by classical Freudian psychoanalysis. I am convinced that they cannot be reduced to the psychodynamic level and adequately explained within the Freudian conceptual framework.

In psycholytic LSD sessions, all my subjects sooner or later transcended the narrow psychodynamic framework and moved into perinatal and transpersonal realms.

Notes

1. The Viennese psychiatrist Otto Rank, a renegade from the mainstream of orthodox psychoanalysis, emphasized in his book *The Trauma of Birth* (1927) the paramount significance of perinatal experiences.

A Developmental Model of Consciousness

KEN WILBER

Everywhere we look in nature, said the philosopher Jan Smuts, we see nothing but *wholes*.[1] And not just simple wholes, but hierarchical ones: each whole is a part of a larger whole which is itself a part of a larger whole. ... Further, said Smuts, the universe [tends] to produce higher- and higher-level wholes, ever more inclusive and organized. This overall cosmic process ... is nothing other than *evolution*. ... Because the human mind or psyche is an aspect of the cosmos, we would expect to find, in the psyche itself, the same hierarchical arrangement of wholes within wholes, reaching from the simplest and most rudimentary to the most complex and inclusive (cf. Welwood).[2] In general, such is exactly the discovery of modern psychology. . . . As a general approximation, then, we may conclude that the psyche — like the cosmos at large — is many-layered (pluridimensional), composed of successively higher-order wholes and unities and integrations.

Now in psychological development, the *whole* of any level becomes merely a *part* of the whole of the next level, which in turn becomes a part of the next whole, and so on throughout the evolution of consciousness. . . . Modern developmental psychology has [generally] devoted itself to the exploration and explanation of the various levels, stages, and strata of the human condition — mind, personality, psychosexuality, character, consciousness. The cognitive studies of Piaget and Werner, the works of Loevinger[3] and Arieti[4] and Maslow,[5] the moral development studies of Kohlberg[6] — all subscribe, in whole or part, to the concept of stratified stages of increasing complexity, integration, and unity. . . . We are [then] entitled to ask, "What is the *highest* stage of unity to which one may aspire?" Or perhaps . . . "What is the nature of some of the higher . . . stages of development? What forms of unity are disclosed in the most developed human? "

The problem with that type of question lies in *finding* examples of truly higher-order personalities — and in deciding exactly *what* constitutes a higher-order personality in the first place. . . . Those . . . who have . . . look[ed] at this problem have suggested that the world's greatest mystics and sages [e.g., Buddha, Lao Tse, Socrates, Aurobindo] represent some of the very highest . . . stages of human development. Bergson said exactly such; and so did Toynbee — and Tolstoy and James and Schopenhauer and Nietzsche and Maslow. . . . Let us, then, simply *assume* that the authentic mystic-sage represents the very highest stages of human development. . . . This, in effect, would give us a sample which approximates the "highest state of consciousness. "

If we take these higher stages and add them to the lower and middle stages/levels which have so carefully been described and studied by Western psychology, we would then arrive at a fairly well-balanced and comprehensive model of the spectrum of consciousness. . . . As a very general and simplistic outline, here is what we find:

THE LOWER REALMS

It is generally agreed, by Eastern and Western psychology alike, that the lowest levels of development involve simple biological functions and processes. That is, the lowest levels involve somatic processes, instincts, simple sensations and perceptions, and emotional-sexual impulses. . . . All of this simply goes to point up one of Freud's major ideas: "The ego," he said, "is first and foremost a body-ego."[7]

Now the bodyego or bodyself tends to develop in the following way:

It is generally agreed that the infant initially cannot distinguish self from not-self, subject from object, body from environment. That is, the self at this earliest of stages is literally one with the physical world. . . . In Freud's words, "The ego-feeling we are aware of now is thus only a shrunken vestige of a far more extensive feeling — a feeling which embraced the universe and expressed an inseparable connection of the ego with the external world."

That initial stage of *material oneness* . . . expresses Atman-consciousness as potential, although in terms of actualization it is the lowest of all stages.

It is out of this primordial fusion state, or . . . the "ground unconscious," that the separate self emerges, and, as Freud said, the self emerges first and foremost as a body, a bodyself. The infant bites a blanket and it does not hurt; he bites his thumb, and it hurts. . . . The infant *identifies* with the newly emergent body, with its sensations and emotions, and gradually learns to differentiate them from the material cosmos at large.

Notice that the bodyego, by differentiating itself from the material environment, actually *transcends* that primitive state of fusion and embeddedness. The bodyego transcends the material environment, and thus can perform physical *operations* upon that environment. . . . Let us note that triad: by *differentiating* the self from an object, the self *transcends* that object and thus can *operate* upon it (using the tools that constitute the self at that level — at this stage, the sensorimotor body).

At this bodyego stage(s), then, the self no longer is bound to the . . . environment — but it *is* bound to, or identified with, the biological body. The self, as bodyego, is dominated by instinctual urges, impulsiveness, the pleasure principle, involuntary urges and discharges — all the id-like primary processes and drives described so well by Freud *et al*.

Eventually, however, true *mental* or conceptual functions begin to emerge out of, and differentiate from, the bodyego. As language develops, the child is ushered into the world of symbols and ideas and concepts, and thus is gradually raised above the fluctuations of the simple, instinctual, immediate, and impulsive bodyego.

As the mental-self emerges and differentiates from the body (with the help of language), it *transcends* the body and thus can *operate* upon it using its own mental structures as tools (it can delay the body's immediate discharges and postpone its instinctual gratifications using verbal insertions). At the same time, this allows a sublimation of the body's emotional-sexual energies into more subtle, complex, and evolved activities.

By the time of adolescence, another extraordinary differentiation begins to occur. In essence, the self simply starts to differentiate *from* the representational thought process. And because the self starts to differentiate itself from the representational thought process, it can to a certain degree *transcend* the thought process and therefore *operate* upon it. Piaget calls this—his highest stage—"formal operational," because one can operate on one's own formal thought (i.e., work with linguistic objects as well as physical ones). . . . This can occur because consciousness differentiates itself from syntaxical-thought, thus transcends it, and hence can operate upon it (something that it could not do when it *was* it). Actually, this process is just beginning at this stage—it intensifies at the higher stages—but the overall point seems fairly clear: consciousness, or the self, is *starting* to transcend the verbal ego-mind. It is starting to go trans-verbal.

Now as consciousness begins to transcend the verbal ego-mind, it can integrate the ego-mind with all the lower levels. That is, because consciousness is no longer identified with any of these elements to the exclusion of any others, all of them can be integrated: the body and mind can be brought into a higher-order holistic integration. This stage is referred to as the "integration of all lower levels" (Sullivan, Grant, & Grant),[8] "integrated" (Loevinger),[9] "self-actualized" (Maslow), "autonomous" (Fromm, Reisman).[10, 11]

THE INTERMEDIATE REALMS

With the exception of transpersonal psychology, the [ego mind] is the highest level of consciousness [studied] by Western psychology. . . . Western psychiatrists and psychologists either deny the existence of any sort of higher-order unity, or . . . pathologize its existence, explaining it by diagnosis. Thus, for indications as to the nature of any higher levels of consciousness, beyond the ego and [bodymind], we have to turn to the great mystic-sages, Eastern and Western, Hindu and Buddhist, Christian and Islamic. It is somewhat surprising, but absolutely significant, that all of these otherwise divergent schools of thought agree rather unanimously as to the nature of the "farthest reaches of human nature." There are indeed, these traditions tell us, higher levels of consciousness.

Beginning with (to use the terms of yogic chakra-psychology) the sixth chakra, . . . consciousness *starts* to go trans-personal. Consciousness is now going trans-verbal *and* trans-personal. It begins to enter what is called the "subtle sphere." This process quickens and intensifies as it reaches the highest chakra . . . and then goes supra-mental as it enters the seven higher stages of consciousness beyond. . . . The sixth and seventh chakras, and the seven higher levels are, on the whole, referred to as the subtle realm.

For convenience sake, however, we speak of the "low-subtle" and the "high-subtle." The low-subtle is epitomized by the [sixth] chakra — the "third eye," which is said to include and dominate both astral and psychic events. That is, the low-subtle is "composed" of the astral and psychic planes of consciousness. Whether one believes in these levels or not, *this* is where they are said to exist.

The whole point of the low-subtle — the astral-psychic — is that consciousness, by further differentiating itself from the mind and body, is able in some ways to *transcend* the normal capacities of the gross bodymind and therefore *operate* upon the world and the organism in ways that appear, to the ordinary mind, to be quite fantastic and farfetched. For my own part, I find them a natural extension of the transcendent function of consciousness.

The high-subtle begins at the [seventh chakra] and extends into seven more levels of extraordinarily high-order transcendence, differentiation, and integration. This is, on the whole, the realm of high religious intuition and inspiration.

Aspects of this subtle realm have been called the "over-self" or "over-mind" or "supra-mind" — as in Aurobindo and Emerson. The point is simply that consciousness, in a rapid ascent, is differentiating itself entirely from the ordinary mind and self, and thus can be called an "over-self" or "over-mind" or "supra-mind." It embodies a transcendence of all mental forms, and discloses, at its summit, the intuition of that which is above and prior to mind, self, world, and body—something which, as Aquinas would have said, all men and women would call God.

But this is not God as an ontological other, set apart from the cosmos, from humans, and from creation at large. Rather, it is God as an Archetypal summit of one's own Consciousness. In this way only could St. Clement say that he who knows himself knows God. We could now say, he who knows his over-self knows God. They are one and the same.

THE ULTIMATE REALMS

As the process of transcendence and integration continues, it discloses even higher-order units, leading, consumately, to Unity itself. Beyond the high-subtle lies the causal region, which for convenience we divide into the low-causal and the high-causal.

The low-causal . . . is revealed in a state of consciousness [that] represents the pinnacle of God-consciousness . . . At this point, all the preceding subtle-realm manifestations [are recognized as] modifications of Consciousness itself, so that one . . . becomes all that previously appeared as objective visions, lights, sounds, colors (this process begins at the high-subtle, but culminates here). . . . One dissolves into Deity, as Deity—that Deity which, from the beginning, has been one's own Self or highest Archetype.

Beyond that point, into the high-causal, all forms are so radically transcended that they no longer need even appear or arise in Consciousness. This is total and utter transcendence into Formless Consciousness, Boundless Being. There is here no self, no God, no objects, no subjects, and no thingness, apart from or other than Consciousness as Such. Note the overall progression: in the high-subtle and low-causal, the self dissolves into Deity;

here, the Deity-Self dissolves into Formlessness. . . . Consciousness totally awakens as its Original Condition and Suchness . . . which is, at the same time, the condition and suchness of all that is, gross, subtle, or causal. That which witnesses, and that which is witnessed, are only one and the same. The entire World Processes then arises, moment to moment, as one's own Being, outside of which, and prior to which, nothing exists. That Being is totally beyond and prior to anything that arises, and yet no part of that Being is other than what arises.

And so, as the center of the self was shown to be God, and as the center of God was shown to be Formlessness, so the center of Formlessness is shown to be not other than the entire world of Form. "Form is not other than Void, Void is not other than Form," says the Heart Sutra. At that point, the extraordinary and the ordinary, the supernatural and the mundane, are precisely one and the same.

This is also sahaja samadhi, the Turiya state—the ultimate Unity, wherein all things and events, while remaining perfectly separate and discrete, are only One. Therefore, this is not itself a state apart from other states; it is not an altered state;[12] it is not a special state—it is rather the suchness of all states, the water that forms itself in each and every wave of experience, as all experience. It cannot be seen, because it is everything which is seen; it cannot be heard, because it is hearing itself; it cannot be remembered because it only *is*. By the same token, this is the radically perfect integration of all prior levels—gross, subtle, and causal, which, now of themselves . . . continue to arise moment to moment in an iridescent play of mutual interpenetration. This is the final differentiation of Consciousness from all forms in Consciousness, whereupon Consciousness as Such is released in Perfect Transcendence, which is not a transcendence from the world but a final transcendence into the world. Consciousness henceforth *operates*, not on the world, but only as the entire world process, integrating and interpenetrating all levels, realms, and planes, high or low, sacred or profane.

This, finally, is the ultimate Unity towards which all evolution, human as well as cosmic, drives. And, it might be said, cosmic evolution— that holistic pattern—is completed in and as human evolution, which in reaching ultimate unity consciousness . . . completes that absolute Gestalt towards which all manifestation moves. Not only does "phylogeny recapitulate cosmogeny," it completes it.

THE FORM OF DEVELOPMENT

Overall, the process of psychological development—which is the operation, in humans, of cosmic evolution—proceeds in a most articulate fashion. At each stage, a higher-order structure—more complex and therefore more unified—emerges through a differentiation of the preceding, lower-order level. This higher-order structure is introduced to consciousness, and eventually (it can be almost instantaneous, or can take a prolonged time) the self *identifies* with that emergent structure.

As evolution proceeds, however, each level in turn is differentiated *from* the self sense, or "peeled off" so to speak. The self, that is, eventually *dis-identifies* with that structure so as to identify with the next higher-order emergent structure. Or we might say that the self detaches itself from its *exclusive* identification with that structure. The point is that because the self is differentiated from the lower structure, it *transcends* that structure and thus can *operate* on that lower structure by using the tools of the newly emergent structure.

Thus, at each point in psychological growth, we find: (1) a higher-order structure emerges in consciousness; (2) the self identifies its being with that structure; (3) the next higher-order structure then eventually emerges, the self disidentifies [from] the lower structure and shifts its essential identity to the higher structure; (4) consciousness thereby transcends the lower structure and becomes capable of operating on that lower structure from the higher-order level; (5) all preceding levels can then be integrated in consciousness, and ultimately as consciousness. We noted that each successively higher-order structure is more complex, more organized, and more unified — and evolution continues until there is only Unity.

A few technical points: using the terms of linguistics, we say that each level of consciousness consists of a *deep structure* and a *surface structure*. The deep structure consists of all the basic limiting principles embedded at that level. The deep structure is the defining *form* of a level, which embodies all of the potentials and limitations of that level. Surface structure is simply a *particular* manifestation of the deep structure. The surface structure is constrained by the form of the deep structure, but within that form it is free to select various contents.

A deep structure is like a paradigm, and contains within it all the basic limited principles in terms of which all surface structures are realized. To use a simple example, take a ten-story building: each of the floors is a deep structure, whereas the various rooms and objects on each floor are surface structures. All bodyselves are on the second floor; all verbal ego-minds are on the fifth floor. . . . The point is that although all verbal egos are quite different, they are all on the fifth floor: they all share the same deep structure.

Now the movement of surface structures we call *translation*; the movement of deep structures we call *transformation*. Thus, if we [make changes or] move furniture around on the fourth floor, that is a translation; but if we move up to the seventh floor, that is a transformation. Many egos try to think about Buddha, which is translation rather than transformation.

Each transformation upward marks the emergence in consciousness of a new and higher level, with a new deep structure, within which new translations or surface structures can unfold and operate. And we say that evolution is a series of such transformations, or changes in deep structure, mediated by symbols, or forms in consciousness (the lowest form being the body, the next being the mind, then the subtle, etc.). And most importantly, we say that *all* deep structures are *remembered*, . . . whereas all surface structures are *learned*, in the sense studied by Western psychologists. A deep structure emerges in consciousness when it is remembered; a surface structure emerges when it is taught.

Every time one remembers a higher-order deep structure, the lower-order structure is subsumed under it. That is, at each point in evolution, what is the whole of one level becomes merely a part of the higher-order whole of the next level.

In precisely the same way, we can say that at each point in evolution or remembrance, a *mode* of self becomes merely a *component* of a higher-order self (e.g., the body was *the* mode of the self before the mind emerged, whereupon it becomes merely a component of self). This can be put in several different ways, each of which tells us something important about development, evolution, and transcendence: (1) what is *identification* becomes *detachment*; (2) what is *context* becomes *content*, that is, the context of cognition and experience of one level becomes simply a content of the experience of the next; (3) what is *ground* becomes *figure* which releases higher-order ground; (4) what is *subjective* becomes *objective* until both of these terms become meaningless; (5) what is *condition* becomes *element*, e.g., the mind, which is the a priori condition of egoic experience, becomes merely an element of experience in the higher-order realms. . . .

Each of those points is, in effect, a definition of *transcendence*. Yet each is also a definition of a stage of *development*. It follows that the two are essentially identical, and that evolution, as has been said, is actually "self-realization through self-transcendence."

TYPES OF THE UNCONSCIOUS

Many accounts of "the unconscious" simply assume that it is there, either as process or as content, from the start, and then proceed to describe its layers, levels, grounds, modes or contents. But I believe that approach must be supplemented by developmental or evolutionary concerns on the one hand, and dynamic factors on the other.

Clearly, what exists in "the" unconscious depends in large measure on developmental concerns—*all* of the unconscious, in all its forms, is not just given at the start. Yet, to continue the story, many writers seem to assume that there is a "transpersonal unconscious" that is present but repressed from the beginning, whereas—if it is like . . . abstract thinking and higher structures in general . . . it is not yet repressed from awareness because it has not yet even tentatively emerged in awareness in the first place.

With this developmental and dynamic, as opposed to static and given, viewpoint in mind, I will now outline five basic types of unconscious processes. These are types of unconscious processes, not levels of the unconscious (although we will mention these as well). This outline is meant to be neither exhaustive nor definitive, but only indicative of concerns that I feel transpersonal psychology must address.

The Ground-Unconscious

By "ground" I intend an essentially neutral meaning; it is not to be confused with "Ground of Being" or "Open Ground" or "Primal Ground." Although in a certain sense it is "all-encompassing," it is basically a developmental concept. The fetus "possesses" the ground-unconscious; in essence, it is *all the deep structures existing as potentials ready to emerge, via remembrance, at some future point*. All the deep structures given to a collective humanity—pertaining to every level of consciousness from the body to mind to soul to spirit, gross, subtle, and causal—are enfolded or enwrapped in the ground unconscious. All of these structures are unconscious, but they are *not* repressed because they have not yet entered consciousness.

Development — or evolution — consists of a series of hierarchical transformations or *unfoldings* of the deep structures out of the ground-unconscious, starting with the lowest (the body) and ending with the highest (God). When — and if — *all* of the ground-unconscious has emerged, then there is *only* consciousness: all is conscious *as* the All. As Aristotle put it, when all potential has been actualized, the result is God.

Finally, let us note that the closer a deep structure is to emergence, the more profoundly it affects the already emerged consciousness. This fact turns out to be of the utmost significance.

Now, all of the following four types of the unconscious can be defined *in relation* to the ground-unconscious. This gives us a concept of unconscious processes that is at once structural and dynamic, layered and developmental.

The Archaic-Unconscious

Freud's initial pioneering efforts in psychoanalysis led him to postulate two basically distinct psychic systems: the system-unconscious, as he called it, and the system-conscious. The unconscious was, he felt, *generated* by repression: certain impulses, because they were dynamically resisted by the system-conscious, were forcefully expelled from awareness.

"The unconscious" and "the repressed" were basically one and the same.

Eventually, however, Freud came to see that not all that is unconscious is repressed. . . .[13] Some of the unconscious simply finds itself unconscious from the start — it is not first a personal experience which is then repressed, but something that, as it were, *begins* in the unconscious as a common phylogenetic heritage.[14]

For Jung . . . the "phylogenetic heritage" consisted of the instincts and the mental-forms or images associated with the instincts, which he eventually termed the "archetypes." Such is the archaic-unconscious, which is simply the most primitive and least developed structures of the ground-unconscious. . . . The archaic-unconscious is not the product of personal experience; it is initially unconscious but not repressed; it contains the earliest and the most primitive structures to unfold from the ground-unconscious, and, even when unfolded they tend to remain unconscious, never clearly unfolded in awareness except as rudimentary deep structures with little or no surface content.

The Submergent-Unconscious

Once a deep structure has emerged from the ground unconscious and taken on some sort of surface structure, it can for various reasons be returned to a state of unconsciousness. That is, once a structure has emerged, it can be submerged, and the total of such structures we call the submergent-unconscious. The submergent-unconscious is that which was once conscious, in the lifetime of the individual, but is now screened out of awareness.

Now the submergent-unconscious can include, in principle, every structure that has emerged, whether collective, personal, archaic, subtle, etc. . . . Jung has written extensively on just that subject, and . . . even Freud was aware of the difference between the archaic-unconscious id and the submergent-unconscious id, even if it was difficult to differentiate them.[15]

The submergent-unconscious becomes unconscious for various reasons, and these reasons lie along a *continuum of inattention*. This continuum ranges from simple forgetting through selective forgetting to forceful/dynamic forgetting (the latter alone being repression proper). Of the *personal* submergent-unconscious, Jung states: "The personal unconscious . . . includes all those psychic contents which have been forgotten during the course of the individual's life . . . all subliminal impressions or perceptions . . . all psychic contents that are incompatible with the conscious attitude."[16]

Simple forgetting and lack of threshold response constitutes the subliminal submergent-unconscious. Dynamic or forceful forgetting, however, is repression proper, Freud's great discovery. The repressed submergent-unconscious is that aspect of the ground-unconscious which, upon emerging and picking up surface structures, is then forcefully repressed or returned to unconsciousness due to an incompatibility with conscious structures.

The Embedded-Unconscious

Besides the archaic-unconscious, which was unconscious but unrepressed, Freud found that "it is certain that much of the ego is itself unconscious."[17] At the same time, he began to locate the origin of repression in the ego, because "we can say that the patient's resistance arises from his ego."[18]

The point was this: repression *originates* in some part of the ego; it is some aspect of the ego that represses the shadow-id. But Freud then discovered that part of the ego was itself unconscious, *yet it was not repressed*. He simply put two and two together and concluded that the *unrepressed* part of the ego was the *repressing* part. This part he called the super-ego: it was unconscious, unrepressed, but repressing. "We may say that repression is the work of this super-ego and that it is carried out either by itself or by the ego in obedience to its orders . . . portions of the both of them, the ego and the super-ego themselves, are unconscious,"[19] but *not* repressed.

Before we try to make sense of this unrepressed but repressing structure, I must briefly outline the general theory of repression presented in the *Atman Project*, a theory based on the works of Piaget, Freud, Sullivan, Jung and Loevinger. In essence, we have this: the process of *translation*, by its very nature, tends to screen out all perceptions and experiences which do not conform to the basic limiting principles of the translation itself. This . . . forms the basis of "necessary and normal defense mechanisms"— it prevents the self-system from being overwhelmed by its surroundings, internal or external. . . . The essential point is that the individual is now selectively inattentive or forcefully restrictive of his awareness. He no longer simply translates his self and world, he translates *out*, or edits, any aspects of his self and world which are threatening. This mis-translation results in both a symptom and a symbol, and the job of the therapist is to help the individual re-translate ("the interpretation") his symbolic symptoms back into their original forms by suggesting "meanings" for the symptom-symbols ("Your feelings of depression are *really* feelings of masked rage"). Repression is simply a form of mis-translation, but a mis-translation that is not just a mistake but an *intentional* (even if unconscious) editing, a dynamic repression with vested interests. The individual does not just forget: he doesn't want to remember.

We saw that at each level of development, the self-sense *identifies* with the newly emergent structures of that level. . . . Further, it is the nature of

an exclusive identification that one does not and cannot realize that identification without *breaking* that identification. In other words, all exclusive
identification is unconscious identification.... At the point the adult
realizes he had a mind, he is no longer just a mind — he is actually
perceiving it from the subtle regions.

In other words, at each level of development, one cannot totally see
the seer. One uses the structures of that level as something with which to
perceive and translate the world — but one cannot perceive and translate
those structures *themselves*, not totally. That can occur only from a higher
level. The point is that each translation process sees but is not seen; it
translates, but is not itself translated; *and it can repress, but is not itself
repressed*.

The Freudian super-ego, with the defenses and the character structure, are those aspects of the ego level with which the self is unconsciously
identified, so much so that they cannot be *objectively* perceived (as can the
rest of the ego). They translate without being translated—they are repressing but unrepressed. This fits very well with Freud's own thoughts on
the matter, because he himself felt that (1) the super-ego is created by an
identification, an unconscious identification ("identifications replace
object-choices"), and (2) one of the aims of therapy is to make the super-
ego conscious — to see it (mis)translate the world. This is simply an instance of the overall evolution process we earlier described, where one
becomes free of a level by dis-identifying from it, later to integrate it in a
higher-order unity.

The super-ego is an instance of what we can call the embedded-
unconscious: because it is embedded *as* the self, the self cannot totally or
accurately see it. It is unconscious, but *not* repressed. It is that aspect of
the ground-unconscious which, upon emergence, emerges *as* the self-
system and so remains essentially unconscious, possessing the power to
send other elements to the repressed-unconscious. Again, it is unrepressed
but repressing. This can occur at any level of consciousness, although the
specifics naturally vary considerably, because the tools of resistance are
simply the structures of the given level, and each level has different structures. For example, when the bodyego is the embedded-unconscious, it
uses not repression but introjection and projection as the modes of mis-
translations.

The Emergent-Unconscious

Let us now examine someone who has evolved from the bodyself to
the ego-mind. There still remains in the ground-unconscious the deep
structures of the subtle and causal realms.

Since the higher structures encompass the lower ones, the higher
have to unfold last. At any rate, it is . . . ridiculous to speak of realizing the

trans-personal until the personal has been formed. The trans-personal (the subtle and the causal) realms are not yet repressed—They are not screened out of awareness, they are not filtered out—they have simply not yet had the opportunity to emerge.

At any point on the developmental cycle, those deep structures which have not yet emerged from the ground-unconscious are referred to as the emergent-unconscious. For someone at the ego level, the low-subtle, the high-subtle, the low-causal, and the high-causal are emergent-unconscious. They are unconscious, *but not repressed*.

Notice that the subtle-causal emergent-unconscious shares several characteristics with the archaic-unconscious, namely: they have never (or never yet) been conscious within the lifetime of the individual, and thus are not repressed, and yet find themselves in the unconscious from the start. The difference, other than the fact that one is low and primitive and the other is high and transcendent, is that the archaic-unconscious is humanity's past; the emergent unconscious is humanity's future.

Now supposing that development is not arrested at the ego-realm — which is usually the case at this point in history—the subtle may begin to emerge from the ground-unconscious sometime after adolescence, but rarely before. And for all sorts of reasons, the emergence of the subtle can be resisted and even, in a sense, repressed. For the ego is strong enough to repress not only the lower realms but also the higher realms—it can seal off the superconscious as well as the subconscious.

That part of the ground-unconscious whose emergence is resisted or repressed we call, naturally enough, the emergent-repressed unconscious. It is that part of the ground-unconscious which —*excluding developmental arrest* — remains unconscious *past* the point at which it could just as well become conscious. We are then justified in looking for reasons for this lack of emergence, and we find them in a whole set of defenses ... against Deity, transcendence, and bliss. They include rationalization ("Transcendence is impossible or pathological"); isolation or avoidance of relationship ("My consciousness is supposed to be skin-bounded!"); death-terror ("I'm afraid to die to my ego, what would be left?")' desacralizing (Maslow's term for refusing to see transcendent values anywhere); substitution (a lower structure is substituted for the intuited higher structure, with the pretense that the lower *is* the higher); contraction (into forms of knowledge or experience). Any or all of these simply become part of the ego's translation processes, such that the ego merely continues to translate whereas it should in fact begin transformation.

Because psychoanalysis and orthodox psychology have never truly understood the nature of the emergent-unconscious in its higher forms, then as soon as the subtle or causal begins to emerge in awareness — perhaps as a peak experience or as subtle lights and bliss—it is explained ... as a breakthrough of some archaic material or some past repressed impulses. Where the emergent-unconscious is not recognized, it is explained in terms of the *submergent*-unconscious seen not as a higher structure emerging but a lower one remerging.

With an understanding of these [various aspects] of the unconscious, as well as of translation/transformation and the stages of development presented in the first part of this paper, we can now turn to a study of meditation and the unconscious.

MEDITATION AND THE UNCONSCIOUS

Most of the accounts of meditation and the unconscious . . . tend simply to assume that the unconscious is *only* the submergent-unconscious (subliminal, filtered, screened, or repressed or automated), and thus they see meditation as a way to *reverse* a nasty state of affairs. . . . Meditation is pictured as a way to lift the repression, halt the filtering, de-automate the automating or de-focalize the focalizing. It is my own opinion that those issues, however significant, are . . . secondary aspects of . . . meditation. Transformation into the subtle or causal realms demands that egoic-translation wind down and be surrendered (not destroyed). These egoic-translations are usually composed of verbal-thoughts and concepts (and emotional reactions to those thoughts). Therefore, meditation consists, *in the beginning*, of a way to *break conceptual translating* in order to open the way to subtle transformation. In essence, this means *frustrate* the present translation and encourage the new transformation. . . . The individual is taught to begin translating his reality according to one of the major characteristics of the desired realms, and thus is open to *transformation* instead of mere translation.

In principle, this is no different than asking a child to put into words something he would rather act-out. . . . We are asking the ego to put into subtle forms that which [it] would rather think about conceptually. Growth occurs by adopting higher translations until one can actually transform to that higher realm itself. Since major characteristics of the higher realms include timelessness, love, no avoidances, total acceptance, and subject-object unity, these are most often the special conditions of meditation ("Stay in the Now always; recognize your avoidances; be only as love in all conditions; become one with your meditation and your world; accept everything since everything is Buddha").

As the present egoic-translation begins to loosen, . . . the individual is first exposed to the subliminal-submergent unconscious (the non-repressed submergent-unconscious in general). . . . As meditation progresses, however, the truly resistant aspects of the egoic-translation are slowly undermined and dismantled in their exclusiveness. That is, the embedded-unconscious is jarred loose from its unconscious identification with the Self and thus tends either to emerge as an actual object of awareness or to at least lose it hold on awareness.

Now recall that the embedded-unconscious translations were the unrepressed but repressing aspects of the self-system of a given level. Naturally, then, as the repressor is relaxed, ... the repressed-submergent-unconscious now tends to float — or sometimes erupt — into awareness. The individual confronts the shadow.

What has happened, up to this stage in meditation, is that the individual — through the loosening of the egoic-translation and embedded-unconscious — has "relived" his life up to that point. He has opened himself to all the traumas, the fixations, the complexes, ... and the shadows of all of the prior levels of consciousness which have so far emerged in his life. ... Up to this point in meditation, he has seen his past, and perhaps humanity's past. From this point on, he sees his future — which is perhaps humanity's future as well.

Meditation is, if anything, a sustained instrumental path of transcendence. And since — as we saw — transcendence and development are synonymous, it follows that meditation is simply *sustained development* or growth. It is not primarily a way to reverse things but a way to carry them on until all potential is actual, until all the ground-unconscious is unfolded as Consciousness.

Meditation thus occurs in the same way all the other growth-emergences did: one translation winds down and fails to exclusively dominate consciousness, and transformation to a higher-order translation occurs (a higher-order deep structure is remembered, which then underlies and creates new surface structures). There is differentiation, dis-identification, transcendence, and integration. Meditation *is* evolution; it *is* transformation — there is nothing really special about it. It seems mysterious and convoluted to the ego because it is a development beyond the ego.

My first point is that most accounts of meditation assume that the transpersonal realms — the subtle and causal — are parts of the submergent unconscious or repressed-submergent-unconscious, and that meditation means lifting the repression. And I am suggesting that the transpersonal realms are really part of the emergent-unconscious and meditation is a way of speeding up the emergence.

To begin with, we note that every transformation in development necessitates the surrendering of the particular translation (or rather, the exclusiveness of that translation). ... "The new threshold, the new translation that is established in this way can itself be reduced or transformed by continued meditation, and this one too, and so on. In each case a new spectrum of lower-intensity, subtler objects becomes accessible to the meditator's inner sight."[20]

If meditation continues into the causal realm, all prior objects, subtle or gross, are reduced to gestures of Consciousness as Such, until even the transcendent Witness or I-ness of the causal realm is broken in the Great Death of Emptiness, and the unparalleled final state is resurrected. ... At this final transformation, there are no longer any exclusive translations occuring anywhere; the mirror and the reflections are one and the same... until each and every soul remembers Buddha, as Buddha, in Buddha — whereupon there is then no Buddha, and no soul. And that is the final transformation.

Notes

1. Smuts, J. *Holism and evolution*. New York: Macmillan, 1926.

2. Welwood, J. Meditation and the unconscious. *J. Transpersonal Psychol.*, 1977, *9*, 1, 1–26.

3. Loevinger, J. *Ego development*. San Francisco: Jossey-Bass, 1976.

4. Arieti, S. *The intra-psychic self*. New York: Basic Books, 1967.

5. Maslow, A. *The farther reaches of human nature*. New York: Viking Compass, 1971.

6. Kohlberg, L. Development of moral character and moral ideology. In M. L. Hoffman & L. W. Hoffman, (Eds.), *Review of child development research* (Vol. 1), New York: Russell Sage Foundation, 1964.

7. Freud, S. *The ego and the id*. (Stand. Ed., Vol. 19). London: Hogarth Press.

8. Sullivan, C., Grant, M. Q., & Grant, J. D. The development of interpersonal maturity: Applications to delinquency. *Psychiatry*, 1957, *20*, 373–385.

10. Fromm, E. *Escape from freedom*. New York: Farrar, Straus & Giroux, 1941.

11. Riesman, D. *The lonely crowd*. New York: Doubleday, 1954.

12. Wilber, K. The ultimate state of consciousness. *J. Altered States of Consciousness*, 1975–1976, *2*, 3.

13. Freud, S. *op cit.*

14. Freud, S. *From the history of an infantile neurosis* (Stand. Ed., Vol. 17).

15. Freud, S. *Outline of psychoanalysis* (Stand. Ed., Vol. 23).

16. Jung, C. The psychological foundations of belief in spirits. *Complete Works*, (Vol. 8).

17. Freud, S. *Beyond the pleasure principle* (Stand. Ed., Vol. 18).

18. Ibid.

19. Freud, S. *New introductory lectures* (Stand. Ed., Vol. 22).

20. Washburn, M. Observations relevant to a unified theory of meditation. *J. Transpersonal Psychol.*, 1978, *10*, 1.

The Systems Approach
to Consciousness

CHARLES TART

Our ordinary state of consciousness is not something natural or given, but a highly complex construction, a specialized tool for coping with our environment and the people in it, a tool that is useful for doing some things but not very useful, and even dangerous, for doing other things. As we look at consciousness closely, we see that it can be analyzed into many parts. Yet these parts function together in a pattern: they form a system. While the components of consciousness can be studied in isolation, they exist as parts of a complex system, consciousness, and can be fully understood only when we see this function in the overall system. Similarly, understanding the complexity of consciousness requires seeing it as a system and understanding the parts. For this reason, I refer to my approach to states of consciousness as a systems approach.

To understand the constructed system we call a state of consciousness, we begin with some theoretical postulates based on human experience. The first postulate is the existence of a basic awareness. Because some volitional control of the focus of awareness is possible, we generally refer to it as *attention/awareness*. We must also recognize the existence of *self-awareness*, the awareness of being aware.

Further basic postulates deal with *structures*, those relatively permanent structures/functions/subsystems of the mind/brain that act on information to transform it in various ways. Arithmetical skills, for example, constitute a (set of related) structure(s). The structures of particular interest to us are those that require some amount of attention/awareness to activate them. Attention/awareness acts as *psychological energy* in this sense. Most techniques for controlling the mind are ways of deploying attention/awareness energy and other kinds of energies so as to activate desired structures (traits, skills, attitudes) and deactivate undesired structures.

Psychological structures have individual characteristics that limit and shape the ways in which they can interact with one another. Thus the possibilities of any system built of psychological structures are shaped and limited both by the deployment of attention/awareness and other energies and by the characteristics of the structures comprising the system. The human biocomputer, in other words, has a large but limited number of possible modes of functioning.

Because we are creatures with a certain kind of body and nervous system, a large number of human potentials are in principle available to us. But each of us is born into a particular culture that selects and develops a small number of these potentials, rejects others, and is ignorant of many. The small number of experiential potentials selected by our culture, plus some random factors, constitute the structural elements from which our ordinary state of consciousness is constructed. We are at once the beneficiaries and the victims of our culture's particular selection. The possibility of tapping and developing latent potentials, which lie outside the cultural norm, by entering an altered state of consciousness, by temporarily *restructuring* consciousness, is the basis of the great interest in such states.

The terms *state of consciousness* and *altered state of consciousness* have come to be used too loosely, to mean whatever is on one's mind at the moment. The new term *discrete state of consciousness* (d-SoC) is proposed for greater precision. A d-SoC is a unique, dynamic pattern or configuration of psychological structures, an active system of psychological subsystems. Although the component structures/subsystems show some variation within a d-SoC, the overall pattern, the overall system properties remain recognizably the same. If, as you sit reading, you think, "I am dreaming," instead of "I am awake," you have changed a small cognitive element in your consciousness but not affected at all the basic pattern we call your waking state. In spite of subsystem variation and environmental variation, a d-SoC is stabilized by a number of processes so that it retains its identity and function. By analogy, an automobile remains an automobile whether on a road or in a garage (environmental change), whether you change the brand of spark plugs or the color of the seat covers (internal variation).

Examples of d-SoCs are the ordinary waking state, nondreaming sleep, dreaming sleep, hypnosis, alcohol intoxication, marijuana intoxication, and meditative states.

A *discrete altered state of consciousness* (d-ASC) refers to a d-SoC that is different from some *baseline state of consciousness* (b-SoC). Usually the ordinary state is taken as the baseline state. A d-ASC is a new system with unique properties of its own, a restructuring of consciousness. *Altered* is intended as a purely descriptive term, carrying no values.

Our current knowledge of human consciousness and d-SoC is highly fragmented and chaotic. The main purpose of the systems approach presented here is organizational: it allows us to relate what were formerly disparate bits of data and supplies numerous methodological consequences for guiding future research. It makes the general prediction that the number of d-SoCs available to human beings is definitely limited, although we do not yet know those limits. It further provides a paradigm for making more specific predictions to sharpen our knowledge of the structures and subsystems that make up human consciousness.

There are enormously important individual differences in the structure of d-SoCs. If we map the experiential space in which two people function, one person may show two discrete, separated clusters of experiential functioning (two d-SoCs), while the other may show continuous functioning throughout both regions and the connecting regions of experiential space. The first person must make a special effort to travel from one region of experiential space (one d-SoC) to the other; the second makes no special effort and does not experience the contrast of pattern and structure differences associated with the two regions (the two d-SoCs). Thus what is a special *state* of consciousness for one person may be an everyday experience for another. Great confusion results if we do not watch for these differences: unfortunately, many widely used experimental procedures are not sensitive to these individual differences.

Induction of a d-ASC involves two basic operations that, if successful, lead to the d-ASC from the b-SoC. First we apply *disruptive forces* to the b-SoC — psychological and/or physiological actions that disrupt the stabilization processes discussed above either by interfering with them or by withdrawing attention/awareness energy or other kinds of energies from them. Because a d-SoC is a complex system, with multiple stabilization processes operating simultaneously, induction may not work. A psychedelic drug, for example, may not produce a d-ASC because psychological stabilization processes hold the b-SoC stable in spite of the disrupting action of the drug on a physiological level.

If induction is proceeding successfully, the disrupting forces push various structures/subsystems to their limits of stable functioning and then beyond, destroying the integrity of the system and disrupting the stability of the b-SoC as a system. Then, in the second part of the induction process, we apply *patterning forces* during this transitional, disorganized period — psychological and/or physiological actions that pattern structures/subsystems into a new system, the desired d-ASC. The new system, the d-ASC, must develop its own stabilization process if it is to last.

Deinduction, return to the b-SoC, is the same process as induction. The d-ASC is disrupted, a transitional period occurs, and the b-SoC is reconstructed by patterning forces. The subject transits back to his customary region of experiential space.

Psychedelic drugs like marijuana or LSD do not have invariant psychological effects, even though much misguided research assumes they do. In the present approach such drugs are disrupting and patterning forces whose effects occur in combination with other psychological factors, all mediated by the operating d-SoC. Consider the so-called reverse tolerance effect of marijuana that allows new users to consume very large quantities of the drug with no feeling of being stoned (in a d-ASC) but later to use much smaller quantities of marijuana to achieve the d-ASC. This is not paradoxical in the systems approach, even though it is paradoxical in the standard pharmacological approach. The physiological action of the marijuana is not sufficient to disrupt the ordinary d-SoC until additional psychological factors disrupt enough of the stabilization processes of the b-SoC to allow transition to the d-ASC. These additional psychological forces are usually "a little help from my friends," the instructions for deployment of attention/awareness energy given by experienced users who know what functioning in the d-ASC of marijuana intoxication is like. These instructions also serve as patterning forces to shape the d-ASC, to teach the new user how to employ the physiological effects of the drug to form a new system of consciousness.

The systems approach can also be applied within the ordinary d-SoC to deal with *identity states*, those rapid shifts in the central core of a person's identity and concerns that are overlooked for many reasons, and emotional states. Similarly the systems approach indicates that latent human potential can be developed and used in various d-ASCs, so that learning to shift into the d-ASC appropriate for dealing with a particular problem is part of psychological growth. At the opposite extreme, certain kinds of psychopathology, such as multiple personality, can be treated as d-ASCs.

One of the most important consequences of the systems approach is the deduction that we need to develop *state-specific sciences*. Insofar as a "normal" d-SoC is a semi-arbitrary way of structuring consciousness, a way that loses some human potentials while developing others, the sciences we have developed are one-state sciences. They are limited in important ways. Our ordinary sciences have been very successful in dealing with the physical world, but not very successful in dealing with particularly human psychological problems. If we apply scientific method to developing sciences within various d-ASCs, we can evolve sciences based on radically different perceptions, logics, and communications, and so gain new views complementary to our current ones.

3

PSYCHOLOGICAL WELL-BEING: EAST AND WEST

Traditionally, psychologists and philosophers have tended to avoid defining the highest good for humanity, resorting to negative terms in defining health as the absence of disease and good as the absence of evil. Health by such definition is only "not sick." Such a definition involves a number of assumptions and limitations. For example, it ignores the possibility that the healthy may display ways of being, modes and depths of experiencing, interests, and motives that do not show up at all in pathology. Similarly, the very healthy might not do some things that are so widespread in the remainder of the population that they have been accepted as universal and intrinsic to human nature. This raises the interesting question of whether the extremely psychologically healthy might not at times appear mysterious or bizarre to the rest of us. In other words we must be wary of assuming that they will fit our cultural stereotypes of health or that we will easily and automatically recognize them for what they are.

How then are we to determine the characteristics of psychological well-being? Several approaches are possible. One way is to examine the major dimensions of transpersonal models of human nature and describe the positive ends of these dimensions. Another involves reviewing the suggestions and anecdotal descriptions available in the literature, and a third approach is experimental, researching those people thought to be most healthy. Research data on the transpersonal dimensions of health is very limited, so we are left for the time being with the theoretical and anecdotal approaches. In the absence of empirical support, the following descriptions must therefore be considered as preliminary hypotheses for future thinking and research rather than as established principles.

The most frequently mentioned dimension in transpersonal models of human nature is consciousness. Probably we would expect healthier individuals to have greater access to a wider range of states, especially those possessing greater numbers and degrees of state-specific capacities, i.e., higher states. The most advanced individuals might be expected to have greater degrees of voluntary control and even to be able to enter a wide number of states at will.

In the dimension of perception, attributes of health might include perceptual sensitivity, clarity, and relative freedom from distortion. "The fully realized human is one whose doors of perception have been cleansed."[1] This is the ability to see things as they are, free from the distorting influences of desire, aversion, ignorance, and fear.

The healthy person's sense of identity would be expected to extend beyond the usual ego self-sense. On one hand we would expect health to be associated with recognizing, owning, and integrating the shadow, that component of the psyche comprising attributes judged to be negative and inconsistent with one's self-image. On the other hand we might expect the very healthy to live in the presence of the numinous, "the sacred unconscious,"[1] the transpersonal self, or pure awareness, and to realize that they are that, too.

Motivation would also be a significant dimension of health. The most widely accepted transpersonal model of motivation owes a great deal to Abraham Maslow.[2] He recognized a hierarchical organization of needs in which motives emerged sequentially, i.e., as one level of needs was satisfied, the next level became apparent. The hierarchy ranged from basic survival through security, to sense of belonging to a group, self-esteem, and self-actualization, i.e., actualizing all that one is capable of being. In ascending this hierarchy, motives shift from strong to subtle and from expressions of deficiency to expressions of sufficiency. The needs at the higher end of this scale of sufficiency Maslow called *metaneeds* or *B (being) needs*.

In his later years, Maslow maintained that beyond self-actualization lay the need for self-transcendence.[2] In this Maslow saw a drive toward modes of experiencing and being that transcended the usual limits of human experience and identity, i.e., the drive toward the transpersonal realms. Similar hierarchical models with transcendent components are also found in a number of non-Western psychologies such as Sufism and Hinduism.

In general, healthier individuals appear to be motivated more by so-called higher needs. In extreme cases, self-transcendence might be the prime motive, having superceded the more common egocentric desires for self-esteem, possessions, etc.[3]

Several traditions make the suggestions that attachment (addiction) to having one's needs gratified is the source of suffering and that highly developed individuals are likely to be motivated by a desire to contribute to, and serve, others. Health might thus be associated with fewer attachments and a higher ratio of service-oriented versus egocentric behavior.

Although they do not necessarily fit neatly into any particular formal model, various other qualities have been widely assumed to be characteristic of optimal mental health. These include the recognition that one is responsible for, and the source of, one's experience and one's sense of well-being; greater sensitivity toward others as manifested by enhanced love, compassion, empathy, and generosity; an appreciation of the awesomeness and mystery of life shown by attitudes of reverence, gratitude, wonder, and ecological sensitivity; and a wholehearted participation in life, opening fully to the joys as well as the sorrows of the human condition.

At the highest levels of well-being—in the transcendent realms where we experience ourselves as pure awareness transcendent to space, form, and time—very different possibilities for describing health become apparent. This realm is clearly transcendent to any existing concept of health. Like other subjective dichotomies, the distinction between health and illness collapses in the deepest levels of being. As various consciousness disciplines have maintained for centuries, who we are behind our illusory identifications is beyond both health and illness.[3]

A number of seeming paradoxes follow. Because this essential nature of our being continues to exist behind any illusory constrictive identifications, it follows that it remains transcendent to the health/illness dichotomy at all times. Thus, a movement toward health does not entail changing what we are but rather *recognizing* what we are. Indeed, there is not even any need for movement. As the perennial psychology would have it "there is nothing to do, nothing to change, nothing to be."

It follows, then, that the transpersonal perspective on the quest for psychological well-being is very different from the traditional Western view. Changes in behavior, thought, affect, and personality are seen not only as goals in themselves but also as means to facilitate awareness of transcendent dimensions of being.

The readings included in this section include Western and Buddhist perspectives. In "A Theory of Metamotivation: The Biological Rooting of the Value-Life," Abraham Maslow lays out a number of hypotheses about the nature and experience of self-actualizers and self-transcenders. He first describes the hierarchy of needs and suggests that higher needs (metaneeds, B-Values) for truth, beauty, transcendence, etc., are just as biologically based as are the lower, more obviously physiological ones such as thirst and sex. Further, he proposes that the failure to satisfy metaneeds may result in corresponding forms of pathology (metapathology) analogous to those resulting from unsatisfied lower needs. Thus he concludes that transcendent, religious, esthetic, and philosophical facets of life are as real and intrinsic to human nature as any biological needs.

Buddhist psychology contains a particularly clear and precise description of psychological health, which is described by Daniel Goleman in "Mental Health and Classical Buddhist Psychology." The central concept involves "mental factors." These are mental components that modify perception and consciousness and that have been classified as healthy or unhealthy. Psychological development consists of cultivating healthy factors and inhibiting negative ones. The prevailing balance between the two categories is said to determine one's degree of mental health until, in the fully enlightened individual, only healthy factors occur.

Because mental health is a concept which is central to much of transpersonal psychology, it is also discussed in other readings in this book. The sections on consciousness, meditation, and psychotherapy are particularly relevant.

Notes

1. Smith, H. The sacred unconscous. In R. Walsh & D. Shapiro (Eds.), *Beyond health and normality: Explorations of extreme psychological well-being*. New York: Van Nostrand Reinhold, in press.

2. Roberts, T. Beyond self actualization. *ReVision*, 1978, *1*, 42–46.

3. Walsh, R. and Shapiro, D. (Eds.). *Beyond health and normality: Explorations of extreme psychological well-being*. New York: Van Nostrand Reinhold, in press.

A Theory of Metamotivation:
The Biological Rooting
of the Value-Life

ABRAHAM MASLOW

1

Self-actualizing individuals (more matured, more fully human), by definition, already suitably gratified in their basic needs, are now motivated in other higher ways, to be called "metamotivation."[1]

By definition, self-actualizing people are gratified in all their basic needs (of belongingness, affection, respect, and self-esteem). This is to say that they have a feeling of belongingness and rootedness, they are satisfied in their love needs, have friends and feel loved and loveworthy, they have status and place in life and respect from other people, and they have a reasonable feeling of worth and self-respect.

2 ✓

The full definition of the person or of human nature must then include intrinsic values, as part of human nature.

If we then try to define the deepest, most authentic, most constitutionally based aspects of the real self, of the identity, or of the authentic person, we find that in order to be comprehensive we must include not only the person's constitution and temperament, not only anatomy, physiology, neurology, and endocrinology, not only his capacities, his biological style, not only his basic instinctoid needs, but also the B-values, which are also *his* B-Values.

They are equally part of his "nature," or definition, or essence, along with his "lower" needs, at least in my self-actualizing subjects. They must be included in any ultimate definition of "the human being," or of full humanness, or of "a person." It is true that they are not fully evident or actualized (made real and functionally existing) in most people. And yet, so far as I can see at this time, they are not excluded as potentials in any.

3 ✓

These intrinsic values are instinctoid in nature, i.e., they are needed (a) to avoid illness and (b) to achieve fullest humanness or growth. The "illnesses" resulting from deprivation of intrinsic values (meta-needs) we may call metapathologies. The "highest" values; the spiritual life, the highest aspirations of mankind are therefore proper subjects for scientific study and research. They are in the world of nature.

I wish now to advance another thesis. . . . It is this: I have called the basic needs instinctoid or biologically necessary for many reasons, but primarily because the person *needs* the basic gratifications in order to avoid illness, to avoid diminution of humanness, and, positively stated, in order to move forward and upward toward self-actualization or full humanness. It is my strong impression that something very similar holds true for the metamotivations of self-actualizing people. They seem to me to be also biological necessities in order (a) negatively, to avoid "illness" and (b) positively, to achieve full humanness. Since these metamotivations are the intrinsic values of being, singly or in combination, then this amounts to contending that the B-Values are instinctoid in nature.

These "illnesses" (which come from deprivation of the B-Values or metaneeds or B-facts) are new and have not yet been described as such, i.e., as pathologies, except unwittingly, or by implication, or, in a very general and inclusive way, not yet teased apart into researchable form. In general, they have been discussed through the centuries by religionists, historians, and philosophers under the rubric of spiritual or religious shortcomings, rather than by physicians, scientists, or psychologists under the rubric of psychiatric or psychological or biological "illnesses" or stuntings or diminutions.

I will call these "illnesses" (or, better, diminutions of humanness) "metapathologies" and define them as the consequences of deprivation of the B-Values either in general or of specific B-Values. . . .

It is possible to form a kind of periodic table in which illnesses not yet discovered may be listed, to be looked for in the future. To the extent that they will be discovered and described, to that extent will my impressions and hypotheses be confirmed.

I suspect that reading in the literature of religious pathology, especially in the mystical tradition, would be suggestive. I would guess that leads would also be found in the realm of "chic" art, of social pathology, of homosexual subcultures, in the literature of Nay-saying existentialism. The case histories of existential psychotherapy, spiritual illness, existential vacuum, the "dryness" and "aridity" of the mystics, the dichotomizing, verbalizing, and overabstracting dissected by the general semanticists, the philistinism against which artists struggle, the mechanization, robotizing, and depersonalizing that social psychiatrists talk about, alienation, loss of identity, extrapunitiveness, whining, complaining and the feeling of helplessness, suicidal tendencies, the religious pathologies that Jung talked about, Frankl's noogenic disorders, the psychoanalyst's character disorders — these and many other value disturbances are undoubtedly relevant sources of information.

To summarize: If we agree that such disturbances, illnesses, pathologies, or diminutions (coming from deprivation of metaneed gratifications) are indeed a diminishing of full humanness or of the human potential, and if we agree that the gratification, or fulfilling, of the B-Values enhances or fulfills the human potential, then clearly these intrinsic and ultimate values may be taken as instinctoid needs in the same realm of discourse with basic needs and on the same hierarchy. These metaneeds, though having certain special characteristics which differentiate them from basic needs, are yet in the same realm of discourse and of research as, for instance, the need for vitamin C or for calcium. They fall within the realm of science, broadly conceived, and are certainly *not* the exclusive property of theologians, philosophers, or artists. The spiritual or value-life then falls well *within* the realm of nature, rather than being a different and opposed realm. It is susceptible to investigation at once by psychologists and social scientists, and in theory will eventually become also a problem for neurology, endocrinology, genetics, and biochemistry as these sciences develop suitable methods.

4

Value-starvation and value-hunger come both from external deprivation and from our inner ambivalence and counter-values.

Not only are we passively value-deprived into metapathology by the environment; we also fear the highest values, both within ourselves and outside ourselves. Not only are we attracted; we are also awed, stunned, chilled, frightened. That is to say, we tend to be ambivalent and conflicted. We defend ourselves against the B-Values. Repression, denial, reaction-formation, and probably all the Freudian defense mechanisms are available and are used against the highest within ourselves just as they are mobilized against the lowest within ourselves. Humility and a sense of unworthiness can lead to evasion of the highest values. So also can the fear of being overwhelmed by the tremendousness of these values.

It is reasonable to postulate that metapathologies will result from self-deprivation as from externally imposed deprivation.

5

The hierarchy of basic needs is prepotent to the metaneeds.

Basic needs and metaneeds ... have the same basic characteristic of being "needed" (necessary, good for the person) in the sense that their deprivation produces "illness" and diminution, and that their "ingestion" fosters growth toward full humanness.

First of all, it is clear that the whole hierarchy of the basic needs is prepotent to the metaneeds, or, to say it in another way, the metaneeds are postpotent (less urgent or demanding, weaker) to the basic needs. I intend this as a generalized statistical statement because I find some single individuals in whom a special talent or a unique sensitivity makes truth or beauty or goodness, for that single person, more important and more pressing than some basic need.

Secondly, the basic needs can be called deficiency-needs, ... while the metaneeds seem rather to have the special characteristics described for "growth motivations."

6

The metaneeds are equally potent among themselves, on the average—i.e., I cannot detect a generalized hierarchy of prepotency. But in any given individual, they may be and often are hierarchically arranged according to idiosyncratic talents and constitutional differences.

7

It looks as if any intrinsic or B-Value is fully defined by most or all of the other B-Values. Perhaps they form a unity of some sort, with each specific B-Value being simply the whole seen from another angle.

It is my (uncertain) impression that any B-Value is fully and adequately defined by the total of the other B-Values. That is, truth, to be fully and completely defined, must be beautiful, good, perfect, just, simple, orderly, lawful, alive, comprehensive, unitary, dichotomy-transcending, effortless, and amusing. (The formula, "The truth, the whole truth, and nothing but the truth," is certainly quite inadequate.) Beauty, fully defined, must be true, good, perfect, alive, simple, etc. It is as if all the B-Values have some kind of unity, with each single value being something like a facet of this whole.

8

The value-life (spiritual, religious, philosophical, axiological, etc.) is an aspect of human biology and is on the same continuum with the "lower" animal life (rather than being in separated, dichotomized, or mutually exclusive realms). It is probably therefore species-wide, supracultural even though it must be actualized by culture in order to exist.

What all of this means is that the so-called spiritual or value-life, or "higher" life, is on the same continuum (is the same *kind* or *quality* of thing) with the life of the flesh, or of the body, i.e., the animal life, the material life, the "lower" life. That is, the spiritual life is part of our biological life. It is the "highest" part of it, but yet part of it.

The spiritual life is then part of the human essence. It is a defining-characteristic of human nature, without which human nature is not full human nature. It is part of the Real Self, of one's identity, of one's inner core, of one's specieshood, of full humanness.

Depth-diagnostic and therapeutic techniques should ultimately also uncover these same metaneeds because, paradoxically, our "highest nature" is also our "deepest nature."

An expanded science must consider the eternal verities, the ultimate truths, the final values, and so on, to be "real" and natural, fact-based rather than wish-based, human rather than superhuman, legitimate scientific problems calling for research.

We must be very careful to imply only that the higher life is in principle *possible*, and never that it is probable, or likely, or easy to attain.

Culture is definitely and absolutely needed for their actualization; but also culture can fail to actualize them, and indeed this is just what most known cultures actually seem to do and to have done throughout history.   A culture can be synergic with human biological essence or it can be antagonistic to it, i.e., culture and biology are not in principle opposed to each other.

But this higher, spiritual "animality" is so timid and weak, and so easily lost, is so easily crushed by the stronger cultural forces, that it can become widely actualized *only* in a culture which approves of human nature, and therefore actively fosters its fullest growth.

It is this consideration that offers a possible resolution of many unnecessary conflicts or dichotomies. For instance, if "spirit" à la Hegel and "nature" à la Marx are in fact hierarchically integrated on the same continuum, which means also the usual versions of "idealism" and "materialism," then various solutions are given by the nature of this hierarchical continuum. For instance, lower needs (animal, nature, material) are prepotent in quite specific, empirical, operational, limited senses to so-called higher basic needs, which in turn are prepotent to metaneeds (spirit, ideals, values). This is to say that the "material" conditions of life are meaningfully prior to (have precedence over, are stronger than) high ideals and are even prepotent to ideology, philsophy, religion, culture, etc., also in definitely definable and limited ways. Yet these higher ideals and values are far from being mere epiphenomena of the lower values. They seem rather to have the same quality of biological arid psychological reality even though differing in strength, urgency, or priority. In any hierarchy of prepotency, as in the nervous system, or as in a pecking order, the higher and the lower are equally "real" and equally human.

Placing our lower-animal inheritance on the same scale as our "highest," most spiritual, axiological, valuable, "religious" (thereby saying that spirituality is *also* animal, i.e., higher-animal) helps us to transcend many other dichotomies as well. For instance, the voice of the devil, depravity, the flesh, evil, the selfish, the egocentric, self-seeking, etc., have all been dichotomized from, and opposed to, the divine, the ideal, the good, the eternal verities, our highest aspirations, etc. Sometimes the divine or the best has been conceived to be within human nature. But far more often, in the history of mankind, the good has been conceived of as external to human nature, above it, supernatural.

9

Pleasures and gratifications can be arranged in hierarchy of levels from lower to higher. So also can hedonistic theories be seen as ranging from lower to higher, i.e., metahedonism.

The B-Values, seen as gratifications of metaneeds, are then also the highest pleasures or happinesses that we know of.

I have suggested elsewhere the need for and usefulness of being conscious that there is a hierarchy of pleasures, ranging from, e.g., relief from pain, through the contentment of a hot tub, the happiness of being with good friends, the joy of great music, the bliss of having a child, the ecstasy of the highest love-experiences, on up to the fusion with the B-Values.

Such a hierarchy suggests a solution of the problem of hedonism, selfishness, duty, etc. If one includes the highest pleasures among the pleasures in general, then it becomes true in a very real sense that fully human people also seek only for pleasure, i.e., metapleasure. Perhaps we can call this "metahedonism" and then point out that at this level there is then no contradiction between pleasure and duty since the highest obligations of human beings are certainly to truth, justice, beauty, etc., which however are also the highest pleasures that the species can experience. And of course at this level of discourse the mutual exclusiveness between selfishness and unselfishness has also disappeared. What is good for us is good for everyone else.

10

Since the spiritual life is instinctoid, all the techniques of "subjective biology" apply to its education.

Since the spiritual life (B-Values, B-facts, metaneeds, etc.) is part of the Real Self, which is instinctoid, it can in principle be introspected. It has "impulse voices" or "inner signals" which, though weaker than basic needs, can yet be "heard," and which therefore come under the rubric of the "subjective biology."

In principle, therefore, all the principles and exercises which help to develop (or teach) our sensory awarenesses, our body awarenesses, our sensitivities to the inner signals (given off by our needs, capacities, constitution, temperament, body, etc.) — all these apply also, though less strongly, to our inner metaneeds, i.e., to the education of our yearnings for beauty, law, truth, perfection, etc.

It is this experiential richness which in principle should be "teachable" or recoverable at least in degree, perhaps with the proper use of psychedelic chemicals, with Esalen-type, nonverbal methods with meditation and contemplation techniques, with further study of the peak experiences, or of B-cognition, etc.

11

But B-Values seem to be the same as B-facts. Reality then is ultimately fact-values or value-facts.

The B-Values can equally be called B-facts (or ultimate reality) at the highest levels of perspicuity (of illumination, awakening, insight, B-cognition, mystical perception, etc.). When the highest levels of personality development, of cultural development, of perspicuity, of emotional freeing (from fears, inhibitions, defenses), and of noninterference all coincide, then there are now some good reasons for affirming that human-independent reality is seen most clearly in its own (human-independent) nature, least distorted by observer-intrusions. Then reality is *described* as true, good, perfect, integrated, alive, lawful, beautiful, etc. That is, the reality-describing words that are most accurate and suitable to report what is perceived are the very same words which have been traditionally called value-words. The traditional dichotimizing of *is* and *ought* turns out to be characteristic of lower levels of living, and is transcended at the highest level of living, where fact and value fuse. For obvious reasons, those words which are simultaneously descriptive and normative can be called "fusion-words."

At this fusion level "love for the intrinsic values" is the same as "love of ultimate reality." Devotion *to* the facts here implies love *for* the facts. The sternest effort at objectivity or perception, i.e., to reduce as much as possible the contaminating effect of the observer, and of his fears and wishes and selfish calculations, yields an emotional, aesthetic, and axiological result, a result pointed toward and approximated by our greatest and most perspicuous philosophers, scientists, artists, and spiritual inventors and leaders.

Contemplation of ultimate values becomes the same as contemplation of the nature of the world. Seeking the truth (fully defined) may be the same as seeking beauty, order, oneness, perfection, rightness (fully defined) and truth may then be sought *via* any other B-Value. Does science then become indistinguishable from art? love? religion? philosphy? Is a basic scientific discovery about the nature of reality also a spiritual or axiological affirmation?

If all this is so, then our attitude toward the real, or at least the reality we get glimpses of when we are at our best and when *it* is at *its* best, can no longer be only "cool," purely cognitive, rational, logical, detached, uninvolved assent. This reality calls forth also a warm and emotional response, a response of love, of devotion, of loyalty, even peak experiences. At its best, reality is not only true, lawful, orderly, integrated, etc.; it is also good and beautiful and lovable as well.

Seen from another angle, we could be said to be offering here implied answers to the great religions and philosophical questions about, e.g., the philosophical quest, the religious quest, the meaning of life, etc.

If the B-Values are identified with and become defining characteristics of one's self, does this mean that reality, the world, the cosmos are therefore identified with and become defining characteristics of the self? What can such a statement mean? Certainly this sounds like the classical mystic's fusion with the world or with his god. Also it reminds us of various Eastern versions of this meaning, e.g., that the individual self melts into the whole world and is lost.

Can we be said to be raising into meaningfulness the possibility of absolute values, at least in the same sense that reality itself may be said to be absolute? If something of the sort turned out to be meaningful, would it be merely humanistic, or might it be transhuman?

12

Not only is man part of nature, and it part of him, but also he must be at least minimally isomorphic with nature (similar to it) in order to be viable in it. It has evolved him. His communion with what transcends him therefore need not be defined as non-natural or supernatural. It may be seen as a "biological" experience.

> ... one direction in which we find increasing confidence is the conception that we are basically one with the cosmos instead of strangers to it.
> —*Gardner Murphy*

This *biological* or evolutionary version of the mystic experience or the peak experience—here perhaps no different from the spiritual or religious experience—reminds us again that we must ultimately outgrow the obsolescent usage of "highest" as the opposite of "lowest" or "deepest." Here the "highest" experience ever described, the joyful fusion with the ultimate that man can conceive, can be seen simultanously as the deepest experience of our ultimate personal animality and specieshood, as the acceptance of our profound biological nature as isomorphic with nature in general.

This kind of empirical, or at least naturalistic, phrasing seems to me also to make it less necessary or less tempting to define "that which transcends him" as nonhuman and non-natural or supernatural as Heschel does. Communion by the person with that which transcends him can be seen as a biological experience. And although the universe cannot be said to *love* the human being, it can be said at least to accept him in a nonhostile way, to permit him to endure, and to grow and, occasionally, to permit him great joy.

It is so easy to forget ultimates in the rush and hurry of daily life, especially for young people. So often we are merely responders, so to speak, simply reacting to stimuli, to rewards and punishments, to emergencies, to pains and fears, to demands of other people, to superficialities. It takes a specific, conscious, *ad hoc* effort, at least at first, to turn one's attention to intrinsic things and values, e.g., perhaps seeking actual physical aloneness, perhaps exposing oneself to great music, to good people, to natural beauty, etc. Only after practice do these strategies become easy and automatic so that one can be living in the B-realm even without wishing or trying, i.e., the "unitive life," the "metalife," the "life of being," etc.

13

Many of the ultimate religious functions are fulfilled by this theoretical structure.

From the point of view of the eternal and absolute that mankind has always sought, it may be that the B-Values could also, to some extent, serve this purpose. They are *per se*, in their own right, not dependent upon human vagaries for their existence. They are perceived, not invented. They are transhuman and transindividual. They exist beyond the life of the individual. They can be conceived to be a kind of perfection. They could conceivably satisfy the human longing for certainty.

And yet they are also human in a specifiable sense. They are not only his, but him as well. They command adoration, reverence, celebration, sacrifice. They are worth living for and dying for. Contemplating them or fusing with them gives the greatest joy that a human being is capable of.

Immortality also has a quite definite and empirical meaning in this context, for the values incorporated into the person as defining characteristics of his self live on after his death, i.e., in a certain real sense, his self transcends death.

And so for other functions that the organized religions have tried to fulfill. Apparently all, or almost all, the characteristically religious experiences that have even been described in any of the traditional religions, in their own local phrasings, whether theist or nontheist, Eastern or Western, can be assimilated to this theoretical structure.

Notes

1. The [thirteen] italicized theses listed here are presented as testable propositions.

Mental Health in Classical Buddhist Psychology

DANIEL GOLEMAN

In Abhidhamma, the classical Buddhist psychology, the factors which compose one's mental states from moment to moment determine one's mental health.[1] The list of healthy factors represents a transpersonal model for mental health, a view of what is possible for the healthy person which transcends the limits of our present-day psychological notions of health.

UNHEALTHY FACTORS

The Abhidhamma model of mental health realistically acknowledges a full range of negative, unhealthy attitudes that stand in the way of healthy psychological development. Of the fourteen basic unhealthy factors, the major perceptual factor is delusion, a perceptual cloudiness causing misperception of the object of awareness. Delusion is seen as the fundamental source of unhealthy mental states; it leads directly to a cognitive factor, 'false view' or misdiscernment, though its role in other unhealthy factors is less direct. False view entails miscategorization, and so is the natural consequence of misperception. Other unhealthy cognitive factors include: shamelessness and remorselessness—attitudes allowing one to view evil acts without compunction, disregarding both others' opinions and internalized standards—and egoism, an attitude of self-interest where objects are viewed solely in terms of fulfilling one's own desires or needs. Perplexity is the inability to decide or make a correct judgment.

The bulk of unhealthy mental factors are affective. Agitation and worry—elements in anxiety—are two primary factors in this category. Greed, avarice, and envy form a cluster characterized by grasping attachment to an object; aversion is the negative pole on the continuum of attachment. Contraction and torpor contribute to non-adaptive, rigid inflexibility and moribund inaction to unhealthy mental states.

These unhealthy factors are opposed to a set of fourteen factors which are always present in healthy states. The key principle in the Abhidhamma for achieving mental health is the reciprocal inhibition of unhealthy mental factors by healthy ones. Just as in a systematic desensitization—where tension is supplanted by its physiological opposite, relaxation—healthy mental states are antagonistic to unhealthy ones and inhibit them. In this system, the presence of a given healthy factor disallows the arising of a specific unhealthy factor, or group of factors, though not always on a one-to-one basis. The healthy and unhealthy factors shown in the table (*below*) are in a general opposition rather than in specific opposition. More elaborate explanations are found in Guenther (1974) and Narada Thera (1956).

PRIMARY MENTAL FACTORS IN CLASSICAL BUDDHIST PSYCHOLOGY

	UNHEALTHY FACTORS	HEALTHY FACTORS
PERCEPTUAL/ COGNITIVE:	Delusion	Insight
	False view	Mindfulness
	Shamelessness	Modesty
	Remorselessness	Discretion
	Egoism	Confidence
	Perplexity	Rectitude
AFFECTIVE:	Agitation	Composure
	Greed	Non-attachment
	Aversion	Non-aversion
	Envy	Impartiality
	Avarice	Buoyancy
	Worry	Pliancy
	Contraction	Efficiency
	Torpor	Proficiency

HEALTHY FACTORS

The major healthy factor of insight or understanding—'clear perception of the object as it really is'—suppresses the fundamental unhealthy factor of delusion. These two factors cannot coexist in a single mental state: where insight is, delusion cannot be. Mindfulness in healthy mental states allows continued clear comprehension of an object, and is an essential concomitant of wisdom. Insight and mindfulness are the fundamental health factors; when they are present, the other healthy factors tend to arise.

The twin cognitive factors of modesty and discretion arise only when a healthy mental state has as object an evil act; they function to inhibit committing such acts and so directly oppose shamelessness and remorselessness. These factors are supported by rectitude, a more general cognitive factor of correctness in judgment. An associated affective factor is confidence, a sureness based on correct perception or knowledge. Non-attachment, non-aversion, and impartiality together oppose the cluster of unhealthy factors formed by greed, avarice, envy, and aversion, replacing it with an evenmindedness toward whatever object may arise in awareness. The factor of composure reflects the calm and tranquil feeling tone arising from allaying strong positive and negative emotions of attachment. A final affective group of factors influence both mind and body: buoyancy, pliancy, efficiency, and proficiency, which together supplant contraction and torpor, lending attibutes of flexibility, ease, adaptability, and skillfulness to the configuration of mental health. These core healthy factors, besides supplanting unhealthy ones, further provide the foundation for a set of positive affective states which cannot arise in the presence of unhealthy factors. These include equanimity, compassion, loving-kindness, and altruistic joy, that is, a joy which arises when the happiness of another comes into awareness.

Healthy or unhealthy factors tend to arise in groups, but any mental state which has a single unhealthy factor present is seen as entirely unhealthy. Indeed, in this system the operational definition of mental disorder is the presence of any unhealthy factors in the psychic economy of the person. Mental health is thus the absence of unhealthy factors and the presence of healthy factors in the person's mental states. All of us are most likely 'unhealthy' by this criterion. Still, each of us probably experiences wholly 'healthy' mental states for greater or lesser periods as mind-moments come and go in our stream of consciousness. Very few if any of us, however, experience only healthy mental states. But this is precisely the goal of psychological development in Abhidhamma.

THE ARAHAT AS PROTOTYPE

From the Abhidhamma point of view, the *arahat*, or ideal man, embodies the essence of mental health. The *arahat* is a being in whom no unhealthy mental factors whatsoever arise in the mind. From our perspective, he can be seen as having achieved an altered trait of consciousness, whereby certain processes of consciousness are lastingly altered. The personality and behavioral concomitants of these changes in the *arahat*'s psychological economy are numerous. A partial enumeration of a traditional list includes: (1) *absence* of: greed for sense desires, anxiety, resentments, or fears of any sort; dogmatisms such as the belief that this or that is 'the Truth'; aversions to conditions such as loss, disgrace, pain or blame; feelings of lust or anger; experience of suffering; need for approval, pleasure or praise; desire for anything for oneself beyond essential and necessary items; and (2) *prevalence* of: impartiality toward others and equanimity in all circumstances; ongoing alertness and calm delight in experience, no matter how ordinary or even boring; strong feelings of compassion and loving-kindness; quick and accurate perception; composure and skill in taking action.

While the *arahat* may seem virtuous beyond belief from a Western perspective, he embodies characteristics common to the ideal type in most every Asian psychology: the *arahat* is the prototypic saint. In our contemporary psychologies this prototype is notable in the main by its absence. Such a radical transformation of being overreaches the goals and hopes of our psychotherapies, and indeed is beyond the pale of virtually every modern theory of personality. From the perspective of Western psychology the *arahat* must seem too good to exist; he lacks many characteristics which we assume intrinsic to human nature. Yet the prototype of the saint is a major tenet of Asian psychologies which have continued to thrive for two and three millennia.

References

Guenther, H. V. *Philosophy and psychology in the Abhidhamma*. Berkeley: Shambhala, 1974.
Narada, Thera. *A manual of Abhidhamma*, I & II. Colombo, Ceylon: Vajirarama, 1956.
Shultz, J. Stages on the spiritual path. A Buddhist perspective. *J. Transpersonal Psychol.*, 1975, 1, 14–28.

Notes

1. The two best sources available in English on Abhidhamma are Narada Thera (1956) and Herbert V. Guenther (1974); *see also* Shultz (1975).

4

Meditation:
Doorway to the
Transpersonal

In our modern world it has always been assumed . . . that in order to observe oneself all that is required is for a person to "look within." No one even imagines that self-observation may be a highly disciplined skill which requires longer training than any other skill we know. . . . The . . . bad reputation of "introspection" . . . results from the particular notion that all by himself and without guidance and training, a man can come to accurate and unmixed observations of his own thought and perception. In contrast to this one could very well say that the heart of the psychological disciplines in the East and the ancient Western world consists of training at self-study.

JACOB NEEDLEMAN[1]

Traditionally associated with religious or spiritual disciplines, meditation has recently become popular in the West as a tool for relaxation and personal growth. It is estimated that by 1980 over six million people in the United States alone had learned some form of meditation. The most common is Transcendental Meditation (TM), a form of Hindu practice adapted to an essentially secular practice suitable for Westerners. Other forms of meditation widely practiced in the West at this time include various forms of yoga derived from Hinduism, and a number of different types of Buddhist practice. Among the most popular of these are Zen

135

Buddhism, Tibetan Buddhism, and vipassana (insight) meditation. Other forms of meditation are associated with the Christian practice of contemplation.

For the transpersonal psychologist, meditation is of interest for several reasons. The altered states of consciousness and enhanced psychological development it elicits are both of central concern. The fact that it elicits measurable changes in behavior and physiology has made it the focus of interest for researchers who have hoped to find in meditation a way of bridging the practices of the consciousness disciplines and Western empirical science.

Basically, meditation can be described as any discipline that aims at enhancing awareness through the conscious directing of attention. Attention may be focused on a specific object, as in concentration meditation, or remain open in a choiceless awareness of all experience. The range of specific techniques is broad. In some practices one merely sits and attempts to remain aware of the ongoing flow of experience. Others involve focusing attention on specific objects such as the breath, sensations, sounds, or visual images. In others, specific emotions such as love or compassion are generated and experienced.

Beginning meditation may be difficult. Just sitting immobile for a half hour can be arduous at first and intensive practice over a period of days can be powerful and at times disconcerting. Any unresolved psychological conflicts tend to surface as soon as attention is turned inward and the restless agitated nature of the untrained mind rapidly becomes apparent. Powerful surges of arousal and emotion may alternate with deep peace and joy.

Even a few hours of intensive practice can easily demonstrate that our usual levels of awareness and perception are grossly insensitive, distorted, and outside voluntary control. Indeed, it rapidly becomes apparent that our usual degree of voluntary control of psychological processes is far less than commonly assumed. Amazingly enough, we can live a whole lifetime without recognizing the fact that these perceptual processes continuously control, create, and distort our reality as well as our ideas of who and what we are. Most people who have tried would probably agree that training the mind and bringing it under voluntary control is one of the most difficult tasks a person can undertake.

The rewards of meditative practice tend to be subtle at first. Increased calm, sensitivity, receptivity, empathy, insight, and clarity are some of the qualities that may be experienced early as a result of regular practice. Old assumptions about oneself and the world are gradually surrendered and more finely tuned, comprehensive perspectives begin to emerge.

Such immediate benefits, however, are only tastes of what is potentially a profoundly transformative process, for when practiced intensely, meditation disciplines almost invariably lead into the transpersonal realm of experience. Advanced practitioners report states of consciousness, levels of perceptual sensitivity and clarity, and degrees of insight, calm, joy, and love that far exceed those experienced by most people in daily life. A progressive sequence of altered states of consciousness can occur, which may ultimately result in the permanent, radical shift in consciousness known as enlightenment or liberation.

The papers in this section have been chosen to reflect both Western and non-Western perspectives. In "Relative Realities," Ram Dass describes the initial stages of awakening that a beginning meditator may experience. When awareness is differentiated from objects of awareness such as thoughts or sensations, one is free to put awareness wherever one chooses. The meditator is then able to penetrate deeply into the psyche, to observe the flow of psychological processes and states of mind, to see through perceptual distortions, and to uncover the quietness and wisdom that lie hidden below surface agitation.

In "A Map for Inner Space," Daniel Goleman gives a detailed description of the sequence of experiences that practitioners undertaking advanced Buddhist meditation can expect.[2] In the path of concentration, increasing refinement of the ability to direct attention is developed, resulting in a progression of increasingly subtle states and imperturbability of concentration. However, this path is viewed as only preparatory for the path of insight, which aims at developing insight, wisdom, and ultimately full enlightenment. In this path, the meditator observes the processes of mind with increasing sensitivity and clarity and in so doing undercuts the prevailing distortions and disturbances of mental and perceptual processes. Once again a progression of altered states ensues, all of which lie beyond the ken of traditional Western psychological maps.

In "Meditation: Aspects of Theory and Practice," Jack Kornfield examines the effects of practice using the same Buddhist psychological model of mental factors that Daniel Goleman employed in his discussion of "Mental Health in Classical Buddhist Psychology." However, the meditation paper focuses on the seven "Factors of Enlightenment"; the factors said to characterize the enlightened mind. The recognition that the aim of diverse consciousness disciplines and religions is the cultivation of these mental factors makes sense of a range of seemingly unrelated traditions and practices.

In "Meditation Research: The Evolution and State of the Art," Roger Walsh reviews the past and present status of empirical research and its relationship to transpersonal psychology. Meditation research is still in its infancy but has already revealed a range of phenomenological, behavioral, chemical, endocrine, and neurophysiological effects. However, to date most experiments have employed relatively gross behavioral and physiological measures. Thus, while it is clear that meditation produces experimentally verifiable effects, it is less clear how relevant the current measures are to the subtle subjective changes which are the goal of meditation.

> We must close our eyes and invoke a new manner of seeing, a wakefulness that is the birthright of us all, though few put it to use.   —*Plotinus*

Notes

1. Needleman, J. *A sense of the cosmos: The encounter of modern science and ancient truth.* New York: Doubleday, 1975.
2. The exclusive use of masculine pronouns in his article reflects the traditional language used in the ancient Buddhist texts.

Relative Realities

RAM DASS

You have at this moment many constellations of thought, each composing an identity: sexual, social, cultural, educational, economic, intellectual, historical, philosophical, spiritual, among others. One or another of these identities takes over as the situation demands. Usually you are lost into that identity when it dominates your thoughts. At the moment of being a mother, a father, a student, or a lover, the rest are lost.

If you go to a good movie, you are drawn into the story line. When the house lights go up at the end of the film, you are slightly disoriented. It takes a while to find your way back to being the person sitting in the theater. But if the film is not very good and it does not capture you, then you notice the popcorn, the technical quality of the movie, and the people in the theater. Your mind pulls back from involvement with the movie.

The quietness meditation brings your life is like pulling back from the movie. Your own life is the movie, its plot melodramatic. . . . Will I become enlightened? Will I marry, will I have children[?] . . . Will I get a new car? These are the story lines.

Another way to understand the space you approach through meditation is to consider dreams. Perhaps you have never experienced awakening from a dream within a dream. But when you awaken every morning, you awaken from a dream into what? Reality? Or perhaps another dream? The word "dream" suggests unreality. A more sophisticated way of saying it is that you awaken from one relative reality into another.

We grow up with one plane of existence we call real. We identify totally with that reality as absolute, and we discount experiences that a.. inconsistent with it as being dreams, hallucinations, insanity, or fantasy. What Einstein demonstrated in physics is equally true of all other aspects of the cosmos: all reality is relative. Each reality is true only within given limits. It is only one possible version of the way things are. There are always multiple versions of reality. To awaken from any single reality is to recognize its relative nature. Meditation is a device to do just that.

Normal waking consciousness, dream states, emotional states, and other states of consciousness are different realities, somewhat like channels of the TV receiver. As you walk down the street you can tune your "receiver" into the world on any number of channels. Each way of tuning creates a very different street. But the street doesn't change. You do.

The meditative awareness . . . allows all ways of seeing to exist in the space surrounding the event. Meditative awareness has a clarity that lays bare both the workings of your mind and the other forces at work in a situation. This clarity allows you to see the factors that determine your choices from moment to moment. Yet you don't have to think about it to grasp all this. You find that you know, you understand. In this inner stillness and clarity you are fully aware of the entire gestalt, the whole picture. With no effort your response is optimal on all levels, not just mechanically reactive on one. The response is in tune, harmonious, in the flow.

Your ego is a set of thoughts that define your universe. It's like a familiar room built of thoughts; you see the universe through its windows. You are secure on it, but to the extent that you are afraid to venture outside, it has become a prison. Your ego has you conned. You believe you need its specific thoughts to survive. The ego controls you through your fear of loss of identity. To give up these thoughts, it seems, would eliminate you, and so you cling to them.

There is an alternative. You needn't destroy the ego to escape its tyranny. You can keep this familiar room to use as you wish, and you can be free to come and go. First you need to know that you are infinitely more than the ego room by which you define yourself. Once you know this, you have the power to change the ego from prison to home base.

We need the matrix of thoughts, feelings, and sensations we call the ego for our physical and psychological survival. The ego tells us what leads to what, what to avoid, how to satisfy our desires, and what to do in each situation. It does this by labeling everything we sense or think. These labels put order in our world and give us a sense of security and well-being. With these labels, we know our world and our place in it.

Our ego renders safe an unruly world. Uncountable sense impressions and thoughts crowd in on us, so that without the ego to filter out irrelevant information, we would be inundated, overwhelmed, and ultimately destroyed by the overload. Or so it seems.

The ego has convinced us that we need it—not only that we need it, but that we are it. I am my body. I am my personality. I am my neuroses. I am angry. I am depressed. I'm a good person. I'm sincere. I seek truth. I'm a lazy slob. Definition after definition. Room after room. Some are in high-rise apartments—I'm very important. Some are on the fringe of the city—just hanging out.

Meditation raises the question: Who are we really? If we are the same as our ego, then if we open up the ego's filters and overwhelm it, we shall be drowned. If, on the other hand, we are not exclusively what the ego defines us to be, then the removal of the ego's filters may not be such a great threat. It may actually mean our liberation. But as long as the ego calls the shots, we can never become other than what it says. Like a dictator, it offers us paternalistic security at the expense of our freedom.

We may ask how we could survive without our ego. Don't worry—it doesn't disappear. We can learn to venture beyond it, though. The ego is there, as our servant. Our room is there. We can always go in and use it like an office when we need to be efficient. But the door can be left open so that we can always walk out.

Most people cannot escape. For they identify totally with their thoughts. They are unable to separate pure awareness from the thoughts that are its objects. Meditation allows you to break this identification between awareness and the objects of awareness. Your awareness is different from both your thoughts and your senses. You can be free to put your awareness where you will, instead of it being grabbed, pushed, and pulled by each sense impression and thought. Meditation frees your awareness.

The path to freedom is through detachment from your old habits of ego. Slowly you will arrive at a new and more profound integration of your experiences in a more evolved structure of the universe. That is, you will flow beyond the boundaries of your ego until ultimately you merge into the universe. At that point you have gone beyond ego. Until then you must break through old structures, develop broader structures, break through those, and develop still broader stuctures.

Up to the very end of the climb up the mountain of liberation the most subtle suffering still remains, for there is still an individual who identifies with his or her own separateness. There is still clinging. There is still a final bond to break. At the moment of scaling the highest peak or walking the narrowest ledge the climber must let go of everything, even self-consciousness, in order to become the perfect instrument of the climb. In the ultimate moments of the climb, he or she transcends even the identity of climber. As Christ said, one must truly die and be born again.

After one arrives at the summit, after going through the total transformation of being, after becoming free of fear, doubt, confusion, and self-consciousness, there is yet one more step to the completion of that journey: the return to the valley below, to the everyday world. Who it is that returns is not who began the climb in the first place. The being that comes back is quietness itself, is compassion and wisdom, is the truth of the ages. Whatever humble or elevated position that being holds within the community, he or she becomes a light for others on the way, a statement of the freedom that comes from having touched the top of the mountain.

A Map for Inner Space

DANIEL GOLEMAN

The classical Buddhist *Abhidhamma* is probably the broadest and most detailed traditional psychology of states of consciousness. In the fifth century A.D., the monk Buddhaghosa summarized the portion of Abhidhamma about meditation into the *Visuddhimagga*, the "Path to Purification."

The Visuddhimagga gives us a comprehensive picture of a single viewpoint regarding meditation. . . . [It] begins with advice on the best surroundings and attitudes for meditation. It then describes the specific ways the meditator trains his attention and the landmarks he encounters in traversing the meditative path to the nirvanic state. It ends with the psychological consequences for the meditator of his experience of nirvana.

PREPARATION FOR MEDITATION

Practice begins with *sila* (virtue or moral purity). This systematic cultivation of virtuous thought, word, and deed focuses the meditator's efforts for the alteration of consciousness in meditation. Unvirtuous thoughts, for example, sexual fantasies or anger, lead to distractedness during meditation. They are a waste of time and energy for the serious meditator. Psychological purification means paring away distracting thoughts.

The purification process is one of three major divisions of training in the Buddhist schema, the other two being *samadhi* (meditative concentration) and *puñña* (insight). Insight is understood as the special sense of "seeing things as they are." Purification, concentration, and insight are closely related. Efforts to purify the mind facilitate initial concentration, which enables sustained insight. By developing either concentration or insight, purity becomes, instead of an act of will, effortless and natural for the meditator.

Entering the Path of Concentration

Purity is the psychological base for concentration. The essence of concentration is nondistractedness; purification is the systematic pruning away of sources of distraction. Now the meditator's work is to attain unification of mind, one-pointedness. The stream of thought is normally random and scattered. The goal of concentration in meditation is to focus the thought flow by fixing the mind on a single object, the meditation topic. In the later stages of concentrative meditation, the mind is not only directed toward the object but finally penetrates it; totally absorbed in it, the mind moves to oneness with the object. When this happens, the object is the only thing in the meditator's awareness.

At the outset, the meditator's focus wanders from the object of meditation. As he notices he has wandered, he returns his awareness to the proper focus. His one-pointedness is occasional, coming in fits and starts. His mind oscillates between the object of meditation and distracting thoughts, feelings, and sensations. The first landmark in concentration comes when the meditator's mind is unaffected both by outer distractions, such as nearby sounds, and by the turbulence of his own assorted thoughts and feelings. Although sounds are heard, and his thoughts and feelings are noticed, they do not disturb the meditator.

In the next stage, his mind focuses on the object for prolonged periods. The meditator gets better at repeatedly returning his mind to the object as it wanders. His ability to return his attention gradually increases as the meditator sees the ill results of distractions (e.g., agitation) and feels the advantages of a calm one-pointedness. As this happens, the meditator is able to overcome mental habits antagonistic to calm collectedness, such as boredom due to hunger for novelty. By now, the meditator's mind can remain undistracted for long periods.

In the early stages of meditation, there is a tension between concentration on the object of meditation and distracting thoughts. The main distractions are sensual desires; ill will, despair, and anger; sloth and torpor; agitation and worry; and doubt and skepticism. With much practice, a moment comes when these hindrances are wholly subdued. There is then a noticeable quickening of concentration. At this moment, the mental attributes, such as one-pointedness and bliss, that will mature into full absorption simultaneously come into dominance. Each has been present previously to different degrees, but when they come all at once they have special power. This is the first noteworthy attainment in concentrative meditation; because it is the state verging on full absorption, it is called "access" concentration.

This state of concentration is like a child not yet able to stand steady but always trying to do so. The mental factors of full absorption are not strong at the access level; their emergence is precarious, and the mind fluctuates between them and its inner speech, the usual ruminations and wandering thoughts. The meditator is still open to his senses and remains aware of surrounding noises and his body's feelings. The meditation subject is a dominant thought but does not yet fully occupy the mind. At this access level, strong feelings of zest or rapture emerge, along with happiness, pleasure, and equanimity.

Full Absorptions or Jhana

By continually focusing on the object of meditation, there comes the first moment marking a total break with normal consciousness. This is full absorption, or *jhana*. The mind suddenly seems to sink into the object and remains fixed in it. Hindering thoughts cease totally. There is neither sensory perception nor the usual awareness of one's body; bodily pain cannot be felt. Apart from the initial and sustained attention to the primary object, consciousness is dominated by rapture, bliss, and one-pointedness. These are the mental factors that, when in simultaneous ascendance, constitute jhana.

The first taste of jhana lasts but a single moment, but with continued efforts, the jhanic state can be held for longer and longer intervals. Until the jhana is mastered, it is unstable and can be easily lost. Full mastery comes when the meditator can attain jhana whenever, wherever, as soon as, and for as long as he wishes.

Deeper Jhanas

In the course of meditation, one-pointedness becomes more and more intensified by the successive elimination of the jhanic factors. One-pointedness absorbs the energy invested in the other factors at each deeper jhanic level.

The meditator enters the first jhana by focusing on the primary object. But then he frees the mind of any thought of the object by instead turning the mind toward rapture, bliss, and one-pointedness. This level of absorption is more subtle and stable than the first. The meditator's mind is now totally free of any verbal thoughts, even that of the original primary object. Only a reflected image of the object remains as the focus of one-pointedness.

To go still deeper, the meditator masters the second jhana as he did the first. Then, when he emerges from the second jhana, he sees that rapture — a form of excitement — is gross compared to bliss and one-pointedness. He attains the third level of jhana by again contemplating the primary object and abandoning first thoughts of the object, then rapture. In the third level of absorption, there is a feeling of equanimity toward even the highest rapture. This even-mindedness emerges with the fading away of rapture. This jhana is extremely subtle, and without this newly emergent equanimity, the meditator's mind would be pulled back to rapture. If he stays in the third jhana, an exceedingly sweet bliss fills the meditator, and afterward this bliss floods his body.

To go deeper still, the meditator has to abandon all forms of mental pleasure. He has to give up all those mental states that might oppose more total stillness, even bliss and rapture. With the total cessation of bliss, equanimity and one-pointedness gain their full strength. In the fourth jhana, feelings of bodily pleasure are fully abandoned; feelings of pain ceased at the first jhana. There is not a single sensation or thought. The meditator's mind at this extremely subtle level rests with one-pointedness in equanimity.

The next step in concentration culminates in the four states called "formless." The first four jhanas are attained by concentration on a material form or some concept derived therefrom. But the meditator attains the formless states by passing beyond all perception of form. To enter the first four jhanas, the meditator had to empty his mind of mental factors. To enter each successive formless jhana, the meditator substitutes progressively more subtle objects of concentration. All the formless jhanas share the mental factors of one-pointedness and equanimity, but at each level these factors are more refined. Concentration approaches imperturbability. The meditator cannot be disturbed but emerges after a self-determined time limit set before entering this state.

The meditator reaches the first formless absorption and the fifth jhana, . . . his attention is then turned . . . toward . . . infinite space as the object of contemplation and with the full maturity of equanimity and one-pointedness, the meditator's mind now abides in a sphere in which all perceptions of form have ceased. His mind is so firmly set in this sublime consciousness that nothing can disrupt it. Still, the barest trace of the senses exists in the fifth jhana, though they are ignored. The absorption would be broken should the meditator turn his attention to them.

Once the fifth jhana is mastered, the meditator goes still deeper by first achieving an awareness of infinite space and then turning his attention to that infinite awareness. In this way, the thought of infinite space is abandoned, while objectless infinite awareness remains. This marks the sixth jhana. Having mastered the sixth, the meditator obtains the seventh jhana by first entering the sixth and then turning his awareness to the nonexistence of infinite consciousness. Thus, the seventh jhana is absorption with no-thing-ness, or the void, as its object. That is, the meditator's mind takes as its object the awareness of absence of any object.

Mastering this seventh jhana, the meditator can then review it and find any perception at all a disadvantage, its absence being more sublime. So motivated, the meditator attains the eighth jhana by first entering the seventh. He then turns his attention to the aspect of peacefulness and away from perception of the void. The delicacy of this is suggested by the stipulation that there must be no hint of desire to attain this peacefulness or to avoid perception of no-thing-ness. Attending to the peacefulness, he reaches an ultrasubtle state in which there are only residual mental processes. There is no gross perception here at all: This is a state of "no perception." There *is* ultrasubtle perception: thus, "not nonperception." The eighth jhana, therefore, is called the "sphere of neither perception nor nonperception." No mental states are decisively present: Their residuals remain, though they are nearly absent. This state approaches the ultimate limits of perception.

Each jhana rests on the one below. In entering any jhana, the meditator's mind traverses upward each level in succession by eliminating the gross elements of each one by one. With practice, the traversal of jhanic levels becomes almost instantaneous, the meditator's awareness pausing at each level on the way for but a few moments of consciousness.

THE PATH OF INSIGHT

The Visuddhimagga sees mastery of the jhanas and tasting their sublime bliss as of secondary importance to puñña, discriminating wisdom. Jhana mastery is part of a fully rounded training, but its advantages for the meditator are in making his mind wieldy and pliable, so speeding his training in puñña. Indeed, the deeper jhanas are sometimes referred to . . . as "concentration games," the play of well-advanced meditators. But the crux of his training is a path that need not include the jhanas. This path begins with mindfulness (*satipatthana*), proceeds through insight (*vipassana*), and ends in nirvana.

Mindfulness

The first phase, mindfulness, entails breaking through stereotyped perception. Our natural tendency is to become habituated to the world around us, no longer to notice the familiar. We also substitute abstract names or preconceptions for the raw evidence of our senses. In mindfulness, the meditator methodically faces the bare facts of his experience, seeing each event as though occurring for the first time. He does this by continuous attention to the first phase of perception, when his mind is *receptive* rather than reactive. He restricts his attention to the bare notice of his senses and thoughts. He attends to these as they arise in any of the five senses or in his mind, which, in the Visuddhimagga, constitutes a sixth sense. While attending to his sense impressions, the meditator keeps reaction simply to registering whatever he observes. If any further comment, judgment, or reflection arises in the meditator's mind, these are themselves made the focus of bare attention. They are neither repudiated nor pursued but simply dismissed after being noted. The essence of mindfulness is, in the words of Nyanaponika Thera, a modern Buddhist monk, "the clear and single-minded awareness of what actually happens *to* us and *in* us, at the successive moments of perception."

In mindfulness, the meditator begins to witness the random units of mind stuff from which his reality is built. From these observations emerge a series of realizations about the nature of the mind. With these realizations, mindfulness matures into insight. The practice of insight begins at the point when mindfulness continues without lag. In insight meditation, awareness fixes on its object so that the contemplating mind and its object arise together in unbroken succession. This point marks the beginning of a chain of insights — mind knowing itself — ending in the nirvanic state.

The first realization in insight is that the phenomena contemplated are distinct from mind contemplating them: Within the mind, the faculty whereby mind witnesses its own workings is different from the workings it witnesses. The meditator knows awareness is distinct from the objects it takes, but this knowledge is not at the verbal level as it is expressed here. Rather, the meditator knows this and each ensuing realization in his direct experience. He may have no words for his realizations; he understands but cannot necessarily state that understanding.

Continuing his practice of insight, after the meditator has realized the separate nature of awareness and its objects, he can, with further insight, gain a clear understanding that these dual processes are devoid of self. He sees that they arise as effects of their respective causes, not as the result of direction by any individual agent. Each moment of awareness goes according to its own nature, regardless of "one's will." It becomes certain to the meditator that nowhere in the mind can any abiding entity be detected. This is direct experience of the Buddhist doctrine of *anatta*, literally "not self," that all phenomena have no indwelling personality. This includes even "one's self." The meditator sees his past and future life as merely a conditioned cause-effect process. He no longer doubts whether the "I" really exists; he knows "I am" to be a misconception.

Continuing to practice insight, the meditator finds that his witnessing mind and its objects come and go at a frequency beyond his ken. He sees his whole field of awareness in continual flux. The meditator realizes that his world of reality is renewed every mind moment in an endless chain. With this realization, he knows the truth of impermanence (Pali: *anicca*) in the depths of his being.

Finding that these phenomena arise and pass away at every moment, the meditator comes to see them as neither pleasant nor reliable. Disenchantment sets in: What is constantly changing cannot be the basis for any lasting satisfaction. As the meditator realizes his private reality to be devoid of self and ever changing, he is led to a state of detachment from his world of experience. From this detached perspective, the impermanent and impersonal qualities of his mind lead him to see it as a source of suffering (Pali: *dukkha*).

Pseudonirvana

The meditator then continues without any further reflections. After these realizations, the meditator begins to see clearly the beginning and end of each successive moment of awareness. With this clarity of perception, there may occur:

- the vision of a *brilliant light* or luminous form
- *rapturous feelings*
- *tranquility* in mind and body
- *devotional feelings* toward and faith in the meditation teacher, the Buddha, his teachings . . . accompanied by joyous confidence in the virtues of meditation and the desire to advise friends and relatives to practice it
- *vigor* in meditating
- sublime *happiness* suffusing the meditator's body, an unprecedented bliss that seems never-ending and motivates him to tell others of this extraordinary experience
- *quick and clear perception* of each moment of awareness: Noticing is keen, strong, and lucid, and the characteristics of impermanence, nonself, and unsatisfactoriness are clearly understood at once.
- strong mindfulness
- *equanimity* toward whatever comes into awareness
- a subtle *attachment* to the lights and other factors listed here and pleasure in their contemplation.

The meditator is often elated at the emergence of these ten signs and may speak of them thinking he has attained enlightenment and finished the task of meditation. Even if he does not think they mark his liberation, he may pause to bask in their enjoyment.

Finally, the meditator, either on his own or through advice from his teacher, realizes these experiences to be a landmark along the way rather than his final destination. At this point, he turns the focus of insight on them and on his own attachment to them.

As this pseudonirvana gradually diminishes, the meditator's perception of each moment of awareness becomes clearer. He can make increasingly fine discrimination of successive moments until his perception is flawless. As his perception quickens, the ending of each moment of awareness is more clearly perceived than its arising. Finally, the meditator perceives each moment only as it vanishes. He experiences contemplating mind and its object as vanishing in pairs at every moment. The meditator's world of reality is in a constant state of dissolution. A dreadful realization flows from this; the mind becomes gripped with fear.

At this point, the meditator realizes the unsatisfactory quality of all phenomena. The slightest awareness he sees as utterly destitute of any possible satisfaction. . . . The meditator comes to feel that in all the kinds of becoming there is not a single thing that he can place his hopes in or hold onto. . . . He becomes absolutely dispassionate and adverse toward the multitude of mental stuff—to any kind of becoming, destiny, or state of consciousness.

Between the moments of noticing, it occurs to the meditator that only in the ceasing of all mental processes is relief possible.

With this strong desire for surcease from mental processes, the meditator intensifies his efforts to notice these processes for the very purpose of escaping them. Their nature — their impermanence, the element of suffering, and their voidness of self—become clearly evident.

Now the meditator's contemplation proceeds automatically, without special effort, as if borne onward of itself. Feelings of dread, despair, and misery cease. Body pains are absent entirely. The meditator's mind has abandoned both dread and delight. An exceedingly sublime clarity of mind and a pervasive equanimity emerge.

Insight is now on the verge of its culmination; the meditator's noticing of each moment of awareness is keen, strong, and lucid.

His detachment is at a peak. His noticing no longer enters into or settles down on any phenomena at all. At this moment, a consciousness arises that takes as its object the "signless, no-occurrence, no-formation": *nirvana*. Awareness of all physical and mental phenomena ceases entirely.

This moment of penetration of nirvana does not, in its first attainment, last even for a second. Immediately following this, the "fruition" moment occurs, when the meditator's mind reflects on the experience of nirvana just past. That experience is a cognitive shock of deepest psychological consequence. Because it is of a realm beyond that of the common-sense reality from which our language is generated, nirvana is a "supramundane reality," describable only in terms of what it is not. Nirvana has no phenomenology, no experiential characteristics. It is the unconditioned state.

In nirvana, desire, attachment, and self-interest are burned out. Decisive behavior changes follow from this state of consciousness, and the full realization of nirvana actuates a permanent alteration of the meditator's consciousness per se. With the meditator's realization of nirvana, aspects of his ego and of his normal consciousness are abandoned, never to arise again.

The path of insight differs significantly from the path of concentration on this point: Nirvana destroys "defiling" aspects of mental states — hatred, greed, delusion, etc. — whereas jhana merely suppresses them. The fruit of nirvana for the meditator is effortless moral purity; in fact, purity becomes his only possible behavior.

To attain effortless purity, the meditator's egoism must "die," that is, all of his desires originating from self-interest must cease to control his behavior.

When the meditator's insight deepens so that the realizations of dukkha, anatta, or anicca more fully pervade his awareness, his insight intensifies a quantum level deeper.

When the meditator's insight fully matures, he overcomes all remaining fetters to liberation. He is now an *arahant*, an "awakened being" or saint; the word arahant means "one who is worthy" of veneration. The arahant is free from his former socially conditioned identity; he sees consensual concepts of reality as illusions. He is absolutely free from suffering and from acting in a way that would further his karma. Having no feelings of "self," his acts are purely functional, either for maintenance of his body or for the good of others. The arahant does everything with physical grace. Nothing in his past can cause thoughts of greed, hatred, and the like to come to mind. His past deeds are erased as determinants of behavior, and he is free of his past conditioned habits. He lives fully in the moment; all his actions bespeak spontaneity. The last vestiges of egoism the meditator relinquishes in this final stage include: his desire to seek worldly gain, fame, pleasure, or praise; his desire for even the bliss of the material or formless jhanas; mental stiffness or agitation; covetousness of anything whatsoever. For the arahant, the least tendency toward an unvirtuous thought or deed is literally inconceivable.

With the full extinction of "unwholesome" roots — lust, aggression, and pride — as motives in the meditator's behavior, loving-kindness, altruistic joy, compassion, and equanimity emerge as bases for his actions. Behavior stemming from unwholesome motives is seen as "unskilled"; the arahant's acts are in this sense "skilled." His motives are totally pure.

One who has awakened in this way is capable of a dual perception: "Knowing how everything actually is, and how everything appears." For the arahant, normal reality is perceived simultaneously with the validity of the "noble truths" of impermanence, suffering and nonselfhood. Both these perceptual levels are evident at every moment.

Meditation: Aspects of Theory and Practice

JACK KORNFIELD

One articulation of the purpose of spiritual practice and a viewpoint that is a product of it as well, is to come to understand that we don't exist. We don't exist in the way we usually think we do as some solid unchanging entity somehow separate from the world and the changing flow of the universe around us. We are caught in a fundamental illusion that there is a separate solid unchanging self, which we have to protect, and defend, and which on some level we think won't really die. This illusion is the major underlying cause of problems of tension, of sorrow and unhappiness in life. To dissolve this view, to come to some disillusion of self, which is not just intellectual, or a religious belief structure ("It's all one," etc.) but is an integrated and deep experience of the fact that we are *not*, can uproot the difficulties that psychotherapy would like to solve. This is also the essence of religion. To say we do not exist as a separate entity can also be said in other language: that we are everything, that there is no way to set a boundary to what we are and others are not.

There are several major categories of meditation. The two most fundamental distinctions in meditation are concentration and insight. Concentration meditation is an entire range or class of meditations in which the emphasis is to train the mind by focusing it fixedly on a particular object. Concentration means to focus on the breath, a mantra, a candle flame, and so forth in such a way that it excludes other distractions, other thoughts and inputs. The mind, being energy, can be concentrated in the same way a laser can concentrate light energy. The power of concentration can serve to transcend, or to attain a whole range of states of mind that are altered, or of different perceptions from normal ones. They are often quite blissful in that they are undisturbed, or peaceful or tranquil. In addition to providing access to many altered states, the power of concentration can also be applied to the dissection of ourselves, our experiences, and to the understanding of what makes up our world of consciousness and experience.

Awareness-training, the other major class of meditation, doesn't attempt to take the mind away from ongoing experience to focus it on a single object to create different states. Rather it works with present experience, cultivating awareness and attention to the moment-to-moment flow of what make up our life — sight, sound, taste, smell, thought, and feelings. It uses them as the meditation object, as a way to see who we are.

In the process of awareness-training meditators also begin to answer the questions about how negative states arise and how to work with them in our own minds and experience. Later, when awareness becomes well-developed they can gain access to other levels of experience that transcend our normal daily consciousness.

Meditation which involves devotion or surrender can also be assigned to this second class, because to pay attention carefully is itself a devotional practice. It is a surrender to what is actually happening in each moment without trying to alter or change or put a conceptual framework around it. In that attentive meditation, the second class, one works with a realm of experiencing that lies between the suppression of feelings, impulses, and ideas—not pushing them aside at all—and the other extreme of necessarily acting on them. This cultivates a state of mind which allows us to be open, to observe and experience fully the entire range of mental and physical reality without either suppressing it or acting it out. Through the procedure of paying attention, greater awareness, concentration and new understanding can gradually develop.

I'd like to present a model which comes from . . . Buddhist psychology. It is called the Factors of Enlightenment and may be helpful in understanding the way meditation works. The Factors of Enlightenment are seven qualities of mind described in the traditional literature (Buddhaghosa, 1976) which are the definition of a healthy or enlightened mind. They are cultivated to become present in such a way that they determine one's relationship to each moment of experience. Mindfulness, central to the seven qualities, is followed by two groups of factors which must be in balance. The first group includes energy, investigation and rapture; the second set of factors is concentration, tranquility and equanimity. The first three comprise a very active quality of mind. Here energy means the effort to stay conscious or aware; investigation means looking very deeply at experience exploring the process of ourselves, while rapture means joy and interest in the mind. These three must be balanced with concentration, tranquility and equanimity. Concentration is one-pointedness, stillness, the ability to focus the mind in a powerful way; tranquility is an inner kind of silence, a silent investigation rather than thought-filled;

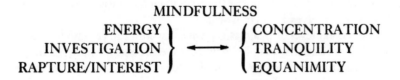

FIGURE 1. THE FACTORS OF ENLIGHTENMENT

equanimity is calm balance in relation to the changing circumstance of experience. Mindfulness when cultivated becomes the cause for the arising of all these seven qualities. It's the key meditation factor that develops the others and brings them into balance.

In Western psychology there is much emphasis on the active factors which include investigation and energy devoted to understanding of one's self. But the West has unfortunately lacked an understanding of the importance of the complementary factors of concentration and tranquility. Without cultivating concentration and tranquility, the mind's power is limited and the range of understanding that is available is rather small in scope. Conversely there is often difficulty in Eastern traditions because of too much emphasis on concentration and tranquility. They may lead to wonderful experiences of rapture, silence of mind, and trance or Jhanna states. But without the balance of investigation, and energetic observation of how things really are, such practice will not lead to a deeper understanding of self and the freedom of enlightenment.

To understand ourselves in practice is to employ the tools of focusing and concentrating the mind and then to apply them with awareness and investigation. What's interesting about this model is that it doesn't take a specific form—Sufi, Buddhist, Hindu, or psychotherapeutic. As it said in *The Lazy Man's Guide to Enlightenment* (Golas, 1972), "enlightenment doesn't care how you get there." Any method that will cultivate these qualities of mind and bring them into balance is good. Whatever techniques can bring you a place of stillness, clarity, and openness will lead to a direct understanding of the basic spiritual truths. The true nature of ourself is always here to view if we cultivate our ability to see.

When we understand spiritual practice as simply the cultivation of certain mental qualities, we can understand a wide range of seemingly diverse traditions.

There seem to be several levels of development that people go through and many ways to describe these levels. At the first level people simply realize how asleep they are, which is one of the most important insights of all. In trying to pay attention to themselves and be present as much as possible all day long, people become astonished by how much of the time they spend on automatic pilot. This insight begins to change people as they see the benefits of real wakefulness. It gives them a greater motivation in practice, and opens them up to look more realistically at how they view themselves in their world.

The second level of insights are what I would call psychodynamic or personality revelations. People begin to see more clearly patterns to their motivations and behavior. So one might see . . . for example, "My, I notice as I pay attention that I relate in a certain way to people because I am always looking for approval" or "I'm always trying to look good," or "I'm always afraid of that," etc. There's a kind of illumination in the meditation awareness process that's very much like doing therapy for oneself, simply by listening and paying attention. These insights and the acceptance that comes with a nonjudgmental awareness of our patterns promotes mental balance and understanding, so it can lessen our neurotic identification and suffering.

Beyond psychological insight in practice there are levels which are often talked about in the Eastern classical literature. Some of these are levels of the different trance or Jhanna states, very high levels of absorption or concentration. These concentration states have the drawback of leading primarily to altered state changes but not necessarily to fundamental long-term trait changes. A second array of experiences beyond the psychodynamic and awareness of personality level is a progression of insights.

This level of awareness brings an illumination of how the mind is constructed. One begins to see how the whole process of desire and motivation works in the mind, quite apart from the content of any particular desire. Further insights into the process of mind lead to seeing more deeply that everything we are is in constant change. There can arise a clear vision of the dissolution of self from moment to moment, and this often leads to a realm of fear and terror, and a kind of inner death. Later there arises from this awareness a spontaneous process of letting go of personal motivation, and with this grows an awareness of loving or 'Bodhisattva' consciousness. As the solidity of the self breaks down, there is a vision of the true connection between all of us. From this arises a spontaneous kind of warmth and compassion. Greater understanding leads to all kinds of altruistic states and eventually the highest kinds of enlightenment, in which we can see our existence as a play in the energy field that is the whole world.

In order to understand this wide range of meditation experience our meditation research must examine the various traditions and techniques from the point of view of how they are simply means to effect changes in arrays of our mental factors. Each technique alters the way that we relate to our experiences and if we look, very different practices and traditions often work to cultivate inwardly the same qualities, such as concentration, tranquility or greater awareness and balance. In particular, the seven factors of enlightenment can then also be seen as simply another model or description of mind coming into balance so that it can see more clearly the nature of our experience.

References

Buddhaghosa. *The path of purification* (2 vols.). Berkeley, Calif.: Shambhala, 1976.
Golas, T. *The lazy man's guide to enlightenment*. Palo Alto, Calif.: Seed Center, 1972.

Meditation Research: The Evolution and State of the Art

ROGER N. WALSH

INTRODUCTION

Although meditation has probably been practiced for three thousand years, scientific research on it began only some twenty years ago. Initial experiments in the 1960s were sporadic and usually involved attempts to document claims made by some yogis that they could perform certain spectacular physiological feats such as controlling heart rate. Not until the late sixties did widespread systematic research begin, and since then it has continued to expand.

At the present time meditation research is a young but vigorous field. Psychological, physiological, and chemical effects have all been demonstrated. Initial studies tended to assume that different meditation practices would have equivalent effects, but more recent research suggests that different practices may show some overlap but also some unique effects too. To date the most frequently studied practice has been Transcendental Meditation (TM).

Transpersonal psychologists have been interested in meditation research because of their hope that they could forge a link between the practices of the Eastern consciousness disciplines and Western empirical research. However, the current research tools of science are primarily aimed at measuring objective physiological, chemical, and behavioral variables. Especially intitially, the meditation variables examined have tended to be relatively gross, e.g., heart and respiration rate, by comparison with the subtle experiential shifts that are the goal of meditation. There is thus some question of the relevance of much previous research, but recent trends are toward more sensitive and refined measures.

Research in areas such as meditation tends to evolve through several stages, beginning with examining the responses that occur and their time course, then looking at the interaction of meditation with other factors such as the age, background, and personality of the practitioner, and finally looking for the mechanisms that might be involved in producing the observed effects. As might be expected of a young field, most research on meditation has focused on the earlier stages, such as its effects. Each of these stages will now be examined in detail.

RESPONSES

The responses to meditation are most easily divided into psychological, physiological, and chemical variables.

Psychological Variables

The general picture that is emerging suggests that meditation may enhance psychological well-being and perceptual sensitivity.[1, 2, 3] Many studies have reported that meditation reduces anxiety, and some have also noted enhanced confidence, self-esteem, self-actualization, and school performance. Clinical research has indicated that stress, fears, and phobias may be reduced as may drug and alcohol use and blood pressure.[2] Hospitalized psychiatric patients with a variety of disorders may benefit from daily Transcendental Meditation.[3, 4]

In summary, experimental evidence clearly shows that meditation can produce a number of psychotherapeutic benefits. However, experimental designs and control groups have often been less than ideal and it is not clear whether meditation is necessarily more effective for clinical disorders than other self-regulation strategies such as relaxation training and self-hypnosis.[1, 2, 3] On the other hand, even when psychometric tests fail to detect significant differences, meditators often report that their experiences are deeper, more meaningful, and/or more enjoyable than those resulting from other approaches.

Relatively few phenomenological studies have been performed and most have been confined to beginning meditators. Some of the more commonly reported experiences include intense and labile emotions, episodes of high arousal and deep relaxation, enhanced perceptual clarity and sensitivity to psychological processes and a range of psychological insights, increased change and fluidity in perception of objects including the body (reduced object constancy), awareness of the difficulty of controlling the mind and especially in not losing concentration or becoming lost in fantasy, altered time sense, altered states of consciousness, experience of self-transcendence and unity with others, reduced defensiveness, and greater openness to experience may all occur.[5, 6, 7, 8, 3]

The range is large and suggests that almost any experience may occur in meditation as a result of greater openness and sensitivity. Indeed, more experienced meditators note that what tends to emerge as one continues to have more and deeper experiences, is an underlying calm and nonreactive equanimity so that this greater range of experiences can be observed and allowed without disturbance, defensiveness, or interference. More and more the individual identifies him- or herself with the calm observer or witness of these experiences rather than with the experiences per se.[9]

Many meditators, including behavioral scientists, have reported that as they continued to meditate, they noticed a deepening of their intellectual understanding of the statements of more advanced practitioners. It thus appears that intellectual understanding in this area demands an experiential basis and that what was incomprehensible at one stage may subsequently become understandable once an individual has experienced some of the meditative process.

Occasionally some of the experiences that occur may be disturbing; e.g., anxiety, tension, anger, perceptual changes in sense of self and reality.[10] These may sometimes be quite intense but generally are short lived and remit spontaneously. In many cases they seem to represent the emergence and release of previously repressed psychological memories and conflicts and the discomfort of experiencing them may be a necessary price for processing and discharging them.

Experimental measures also indicate greater perceptual sensitivity. Sensory thresholds, the lowest levels at which a stimulus can be detected, are lowered, while the capacity for empathy is increased.[5, 6, 7] Thus, both phenomenological and objective studies agree with the classical literature that meditation enhances perceptual sensitivity.

Physiological Variables

The evolution of research on the physiology of meditation began with sporadic investigations of some of the more spectacular feats allegedly performed by certain yogis, such as the ability to alter heart rate. When some of these claims proved valid, more systematic investigation was begun. The introduction of better controls led to the appearance of the next phase, in which it was found that many of the physiological effects initially assumed to be unique to meditation could actually be induced by a number of other self-control strategies, such as relaxation or self-hypnosis. This has led some researchers to assume prematurely that there is little that is unique to meditation or its effects.[1, 3]

Metabolism. Thus, for example, in the field of metabolism, the initial reports of Wallace[11, 12] were met with a combination of enthusiasm and skepticism. Wallace reported marked reductions in metabolic rate as shown by reduced oxygen consumption, carbon dioxide production, and blood lactate levels and suggested that transcendental meditation led to a unique hypometabolic state. Subsequent studies did in fact confirm a reduced metabolic rate but better controls suggested that the effects were not unique to meditation.[13]

At this stage, some researchers felt that the uniqueness of meditation as a metabolic state had been disproved. However, meditation aims at very subtle shifts in awareness and perception, and the most commonly used physiological measures are probably insufficiently sensitive to detect them. Also, with rare exceptions, most studies have examined novice meditators, who may well show less marked effects. In addition, recent studies have found unique patterns of blood hormone levels and blood flow during transcendental meditation.[14] In summary, it is apparent that meditation elicits significant metabolic effects but to what extent these are unique to meditation remains unclear.

Brain Physiology. Studies of brain physiology during meditation have most frequently employed the EEG (electroencephalograph) for the measurement of brain wave electrical activity and have tentatively identified a number of patterns. With most meditative practices, the EEG patterns have slowed and displayed greater synchronization, with alpha waves (8–13 cycles per second) predominating. With more advanced practitioners even greater slowing may be evident and theta (4–7 cycles) patterns may occur.[15, 16, 4, 11] These patterns are consistent with deep relaxation. Some degree of slowing may also be evident between meditation periods.

More discrete analyses are beginning to suggest the existence of specific patterns of synchronization both between corresponding areas of the two cerebral hemispheres and within individual hemispheres.[4] These patterns appear to be different from those that occur with relaxation or biofeedback, but their significance is not yet clear. Preliminary tests indicate that meditators may exhibit enhanced ability in skills localized in the right hemisphere, e.g., ability to remember and discriminate musical tones[17], and that EEG activation may display greater flexibility in shifting from one side to the other in response to the demands of specific tasks.[18]

Once again it should not be assumed that all practices have the same effects. Zen monks, whose practice involves a continuous open receptivity to all stimuli, displayed a continued EEG responsiveness to a repeated sound, instead of habituating to it as nonmeditators would.[9] However, other subjects whose practice involved an internal focusing that reduces responsiveness to environmental stimuli, failed to show any EEG responses to repeated noises.[19]

In summary, then, both metabolic and neural responses have been clearly demonstrated to occur in meditation. Certain features of the EEG patterns appear to be unique to meditation, but whether the metabolic responses are also unique remains unclear.

TIME COURSE

Meditators vary widely in their subjective reports of how rapidly they experience effects of the practice, though almost all report that the experiences deepen with continued practice. However, as yet we have very little experimental data. Greater practice seems to produce more marked effects but the nature of the learning curve is quite unclear, and with few exceptions subjects have had amounts of experience that would be considered only beginning level by most meditation systems. On the other hand, a study of Goleman and Schwartz[20] suggested that even first-timers might show detectable effects.

THE INTERACTION OF MEDITATION WITH OTHER VARIABLES

This level of research looks at the ways in which the effects of meditation are modified by other variables. Important variables here might include the personality and background of the meditator, the combination of meditation and psychotherapy, and the identification of factors that enhance meditation effectiveness.

As might be predicted, there has as yet been little work done at this level. However, individuals who persist with the practice of transcendental meditation and appear to have a successful outcome, as compared to those who give it up, have been reported to show certain traits in common. They appear to be more interested in internal subjective experiences and more open to unusual and "unrealistic" ones. They may be less emotionally labile, possess high baseline levels of concentration and alpha wave activity, and perceive themselves as having a high degree of control over their own lives. They seem less likely to be seriously psychologically disturbed, to have little indication of psychotic tendencies, and to be more open to recognizing and acknowledging unfavorable personal characteristics.[21, 1, 3] On the other hand, some people with a past history of schizophrenia may suffer psychotic breaks if they engage in very intensive meditation practice.[10] Future research in this area may identify those subjects who will respond optimally, those at risk for negative effects, and means of enhancing favorable responses. Although there is little firm experimental data, subjective reports from both therapists and clients suggest that meditation by either the therapist or client or both may facilitate psychotherapy.[4, 6]

MECHANISMS BY WHICH THE EFFECTS OF MEDITATION ARE PRODUCED

Most effects of meditation represent the end product of a chain of reactions of mechanisms that extend from the first brain response through chemical, physiological and behavioral links. Knowledge of these mechanisms would be extremely helpful in understanding how effects of meditation are produced and how they may be influenced.[22]

At the present time the mechanisms most frequently suggested to mediate or produce meditative effects are psychological, e.g., relaxation, desensitization to formerly stressful stimuli, heightened awareness, cognitive factors, and behavioral self-control skills. At the physiological level, suggested mechanisms include reduced arousal, hemispheric-lateraliz-ation — that is, a shift in the relative activity of the two cerebral hemi-spheres — brain wave resonance and coherence, a shift in the balance between the activating and quieting components of the autonomic nervous system, and altered brain blood flow. To date few chemical mechanisms seem to have been advanced, although a number of relevant responses have been identified, e.g., reduced blood levels of lactate and of the hor-mone cortisol, which is involved in the response to stress. Precisely how any or all of these mechanisms might be involved in producing the final pattern of responses is as yet unclear. One additional mechanism which has not received the attention it may deserve is dehypnosis. Our usual state of consciousness is filled with a continuous flow of thoughts and fantasies which constrict and distort awareness to an unrecognized degree. Meditation results in the extraction of awareness from successively more subtle layers of thought, a process which may be seen as dehypnosis.

While much has been learned experimentally about meditation and its effects, this research field is still in its very early stages. As yet rela-tively little can be said about the relationships between the shifts in con-sciousness and perception that are the goals of meditation and the variables that readily lend themselves to Western empirical measures. The dream of a bridge between Eastern practice and Western research remains largely unattained, but it also remains worth seeking.

Notes

1. Shapiro, D. *Meditation: Self-regulation strategy and altered states of consciousness.* New York: Aldine, in press.

2. Shapiro, D., & Giber, D. Meditation: Self-control strategy and altered states of consciousness. *Arch. Gen. Psychiat.*, 1978, *35*, 294–302.

3. Shapiro, D., & Walsh, R. (Eds.). *The science of meditation: Research, theory, and experience.* New York: Aldine, in press.

4. Glueck, B. C., & Stroebel, C. F. Meditation in the treatment of psychiatric illness. In A. Sugarman & R. Tartar (Eds.), *Expanding dimensions of conscious-ness*, New York: Springer, 1978.

5. Kornfield, J. Intensive insight meditation: A phenomenological study. *J. Transpers. Psychol.*, 1979, *11*, 41–58.

6. Lesh, T. V. Zen meditation and the development of empathy in counselors. *J. Humanistic Psychol.*, 1970, *10*, 39–74.

7. Leung, R. Comparative effects of training in internal and external concentra-tion of counseling behaviors. *J. Couns. Psychol.*, 1973, *20*, 227–234.

8. Walsh, R. Initial meditative experiences: I. *J. Transpers. Psychol.*, 1977, *9*, 151–192.

9. Goldstein, J. *The experience of insight.* Santa Cruz, Calif.: Unity Press, 1976.

10. Walsh, R., & Roche, L. Precipitation of acute psychotic episodes by intensive meditation in individuals with a history of schizophrenia. *Amer. J. Psychiat.*, 1979, *136*, 1085–1086.

11. Wallace, R. K. Physiological effects of transcendental meditation. *Science*, 1970, *167*, 3926, 1751–1754.

12. Wallace, R. K., Benson, H., Wilson, A. F., & Garret, M. D. Decreased blood lactate during transcendental meditation. *Federation Proceedings*, 1971, *30*, 376 (Abstr.).

13. Fenwick, P. B. C., Donaldson, S., Gillis, L. Bushman, J., Fenton, G. W., Perry, I., Tilsley, C., & Serafinowicz, H. Metabolic and EEG changes during transcendental meditation: An explanation. *Biological Psychology*, 1977, *5*, 101–118.

14. Jevning, R., & O'Halloran, J. Metabolic effects of meditation. In D. Shapiro & R. Walsh (Eds.), *The science of meditation: Reseach, theory, and practice*, New York: Aldine, in press.

15. Corby, J., Roth, W., Zarcone, V., & Kopell, B. Psychophysiological correlates of the practice of tantric yoga meditation. *Arch. Gen. Psychiat.*, 1978, *35*, 571–577.

16. Kasamatsu, A., & Hirai, T. An electroencephalographic study of the Zen Meditation (Zazen). *Folia Psychiatria et Neurologica Japonica*, 1966, *20*, 315–336.

17. Pagano, R., & Frumkin, L. The effect of transcendental meditation on right hemispheric functioning, in D. Shapiro & R. Walsh (Eds.), *The art and science of meditation*. New York: Aldine, in press.

18. Bennet, J. E., & Trinder, J. Hemispheric laterality and cognitive style associated with transcendental meditation. *Psychophysiology*, 1977, *14*, 293–296.

19. Anand, B. K., China, G. S., & Singh, B. Some aspects of electroencephalographic studies in Yogis. *Electroencephalography and Clinical Neurophysiology*, 1961, *13*, 452–456.

20. Goleman, D. J., & Schwartz, G. E. Meditation as an intervention in stress reactivity. *J. Cons. Clin. Psychol.*, 1976, *44*, 456–466.

21. Smith, J. Personality correlates of continuation and outcome in meditation and quiet sitting controls. *J. Consult. Clin. Psychol.*, 1978, *46*, 272–279.

22. Walsh, R. Meditation: Theory, therapy, and research. In R. Lorsini (Ed.), *Innovative Psychotherapies*, New York: Wiley Interscience, in press.

5

Transpersonal Psychotherapy

If our science of mental health is to become more effective, psychotherapists will have to balance their knowledge of psychological concepts and techniques with a contemplative awareness.

MEDARD BOSS[1]

Transpersonal psychotherapy, as defined by therapists whose clinical practice includes transpersonal work, is the aspect of therapy that goes beyond ego goals and bridges psychological and spiritual practice. Traditionally, Western therapy has been primarily concerned with psychodynamics, behavior modification, and personal growth. A well-adjusted personality has been considered healthy, and the realm of being beyond the personality has been largely ignored. Numerous ego psychologies have developed during the past decades, aimed at helping individuals adjust to society and achieve their personal goals in life. In addition, the existential and humanistic orientations have given the search for meaning and the quest for individual identity a central place. The inner world of the psyche has also been explored in depth by Carl Jung's analytical psychology and others. However, only in the 1970s have Western therapists become interested in personally investigating meditation and other consciousness-altering technologies and begun to incorporate Eastern teachings into the practice of therapy.

Whereas the realm of the transpersonal was formerly the exclusive domain of the guru or spiritual teacher, it has become increasingly evident to therapists working with human problems involving values, meaning, and purpose, that psychological growth beyond the personality invariably

161

raises questions of a spiritual nature. Psychotherapy for the resolution of psychodynamic conflict and personal growth is often considered good preparation for spiritual disciplines that deal exclusively with transpersonal realms of being. Transpersonal therapy, however, is an attempt to facilitate clients' growth not only in attaining ego strength and existential identity, but also in going beyond ego identity into areas of transpersonal realization and transcendence.

The domain of transpersonal psychotherapy thus extends beyond traditional ego goals and adjustments. While it addresses basic ego needs and aspirations, such as the need for self-esteem and satisfying interpersonal relationships, it does not stop here. It also considers the motives, experiences, and potentials available to individuals who have already achieved a satisfactory coping level in their lives.

In his investigations of such relatively healthy people, Abraham Maslow found a variety of what he called "meta-motives," e.g., pulls toward truth, aesthetics, self-actualization, etc. The term *meta* as it is used here means something higher, beyond, or transcendent, indicating that these motives lie beyond the range of the more basic survival needs and extend to experiences of identity and modes of being not limited by customary ego boundaries. When developed, such motives and experiences are analogous to those described and sought by the great religious and spiritual disciplines, which are now becoming comprehensible in psychological terms. Maslow described the correspondence of meta-motives to transpersonal experience as follows:

> Meta-motives are, therefore, no longer *only* intra-psychic or organismic. They are equally inner and outer. ... This means that the distinction between self and not-self has broken down (or has been transcended). There is now less differentiation between the world and the person. ... He becomes an enlarged self. ... To identify one's highest self with the highest values of the world out there means, to some extent at least, a fusion with the not-self.[2]

Transpersonal psychotherapy can thus be said to encompass a wider range of human experience than that which has been the predominant concern of Western psychotherapy in the past. Transpersonal experiences, defined as those that extend awareness beyond ego boundaries, form an integral part of the therapeutic process. The pioneering work of Stanislav Grof in psychedelic therapy in the 1960s and early 1970s was one of the first indicators that transpersonal experiences seemed to be both meaningful and therapeutic and were potentially available to everyone.[3] Moreover, increasing numbers of people had transpersonal experiences outside therapeutic settings, as a result of the widespread use of psychedelics or the practice of disciplines such as yoga or meditation. Those who found such experiences disturbing frequently felt that psychotherapeutic intervention was either inappropriate or detrimental when it did not take the potential value of such experiences into account.[3]

The need for psychotherapists who were knowledgeable in these areas thus became increasingly apparent, and professionals who investigated these disciplines found useful tools for working with clients as well as themselves. Some therapists began to incorporate meditative techniques for relaxation and concentration in their regular practice. Others branched out and began suggesting the practice of disciplines such as yoga as an adjunct to therapy. An expanded appreciation of the importance of treating body, emotions, mind, and spirit as a whole coincided with the emergence of holistic medicine, which also emphasized treating the whole person rather than specific symptoms.

Although the word *psychotherapy* originally meant the nurturing or care of the breath or the spirit (soul), it has come to be associated with medical practice.[4] Transpersonal psychotherapy does not exclude "getting better" in traditional ways, but also includes a wide range of techniques for working with the body, emotions, mind, and spirit, drawn from both Eastern and Western psychology. Thus a transpersonal therapist might work with dreams and imagery, yet also suggest that diet and exercise be taken into consideration in the course of treatment. Although no single practitioner is likely to be an expert in all areas, an appreciation for the value of body work, meditation, and attention to consciousness in daily practice frequently results in recommendations that may be viewed as adjuncts to psychotherapy, but are nonetheless an integral part of the search for health and well-being. A transpersonal therapist may be eclectic in the employment of various techniques in therapy, yet claim a transpersonal orientation derived from the context within which the techniques are employed. A transpersonal context is created by the values, beliefs, attitudes, and views of human nature that the therapist espouses as givens in the practice of psychotherapy. Every transpersonal therapist may therefore be expected to examine the beliefs that determine the nature of his/her work.

A transpersonal context provides an expanded vision of the human potential for well-being. A perspective of psychotherapy based on this vision is presented by Walsh and Vaughan in their article "A Comparison of Psychotherapies." In describing some of the major dimensions of transpersonal psychotherapy and comparing them to other major schools, it places transpersonal therapy in perspective in terms of its relation to earlier attempts at approaching the perennial questions of psychological well-being. It is inconclusive insofar as it recognizes that there is more to be learned in this area, yet it provides a practical working model for current practice. Although transpersonal theory is in its infancy, this paper provides a useful starting point for the reader who is interested in understanding the relationship of transpersonal psychotherapy to other approaches.

In "The Transpersonal Stance," James Fadiman points to the spiritual traditions, Sufism in particular, and what they have to teach us about mental health, particularly with respect to treating the whole person rather than the ego or personality. By using the term *stance*, Fadiman underscores the fact that this is a particular position, context, or viewing frame, within which various methods may be employed. His perspective lays the foundation for further integration of Eastern and Western perspectives in working with consciousness.

In "Transpersonal Psychotherapy: Context, Content, and Process," Frances Vaughan spells out the difference between transpersonal context (created by the values and attitudes of the therapist) and transpersonal content (what the client works on in therapy), and examines the process of shifting from personal to transpersonal work. The article helps readers clarify these distinctions and determine whether this approach would be appropriate for their own work.

James Bugental points out in *Being Levels of Therapeutic Growth* that attaining a measure of personal sovereignty means recognizing both the enormous issues confronting human beings and the astonishing achievements that have been made. He writes: "Until men and women accept their own natures and fully realize that they are the authors, not the victims, of their destinies, all their efforts are foredoomed."[5] Bugental emphasizes the centrality of process in therapy and calls attention to the importance of the relationship between therapist and client. The passages selected for this section reflect the depth and clarity of his insight into the nature of this process, and provide a succinct and comprehensible discussion of those issues that are particularly relevant to transpersonal therapy.

In attempting to encompass a wider range of human experience, transpersonal psychotherapy adds to traditional psychological concepts of health those aspects associated with transpersonal levels of being. Each of the articles herein provides a unique perspective. Each gives the reader a different viewing frame from which to consider the options available for approaching personal transformation. The combination of theory provided by Walsh and Vaughan, process as emphasized by Bugental, and method as described by Fadiman, enables the reader to focus on different views in a rapidly expanding field of applied transpersonal psychology.

Notes

1. Boss, M. *A psychiatrist discovers India*. London: Oswald Wolff, 1965.
2. Maslow, A. H. *The farther reaches of human nature*. New York: Viking, 1971.
3. Grof, S. Realms of the human unconscious. This volume.
4. Bugental, J. *Psychotherapy and process: The fundamentals of an existential-humanistic approach*. Reading, Mass.: Addison-Wesley, 1978. p. 7.
5. Ibid, p. 131.

A Comparison of Psychotherapies

ROGER N. WALSH, FRANCES VAUGHAN

A MODEL OF PSYCHOTHERAPY

Before beginning a discussion of the principles of transpersonal psychotherapy, it may be worth considering the importance of a transpersonal perspective for therapeutic work. In acknowledging a wider spectrum and greater potential for psychological well-being and transcendence than do traditional approaches, the transpersonal perspective affords individuals who are ready to do so the opportunity of working in an expanded context. Because it recognizes the importance of transpersonal/transcendental experiences, these can be treated appropriately as valuable opportunities for growth. Individuals and systems that do not recognize the possibility of transpersonal awareness tend to interpret such experiences from an inappropriate and pathologizing perspective. This can easily lead to pathologizing interpretations and damaging suppression for healthy individuals who are beginning to move into the transpersonal realm.

The goals of transpersonal therapy include both traditional ones such as symptom relief and behavior change, and where appropriate, optimal work at the transpersonal level. This may include the provision of an adequate conceptual framework for handling transpersonal experiences, information on psychological potential, and the importance of assuming responsibility, not only for one's behavior, but also for one's experience. In addition to working through psychodynamic processes, the therapist aims to assist the client in disidentifying from and transcending psychodynamic issues. Thus the therapist may instruct the client in the possibility of using all life experience as a part of learning (karma yoga), the potentials of altered states, and the limitations and dangers of attachment to fixed models and expectations. The therapist may also intend that the therapeutic encounter be used as a karma yoga to optimize growth of both participants in a mutually facilitating manner. These goals in turn facilitate the aim of enabling the client to extract awareness from the tyranny of conditioning.

Transpersonal therapeutic techniques include both Eastern and Western methods for working with consciousness. Various forms of meditation and yoga may be added to more conventional techniques. The primary aim of these tools is not so much to change experience per se, as to alter the individual's relationship to it by heightened mindful awareness coupled with a willingness to allow it to be as it is.

Two features of the psychotherapeutic relationship that deserve special mention are modeling and karma yoga. The importance of modeling has recently been clearly recognized and acknowledged in the behavior modification literature, and recent information on its potency suggests that other therapies may have underestimated its power.[1, 2] Since modeling may be a universal, although sometimes unwitting, therapeutic process, what is distinguishing is what the therapist models rather than the process itself. For the transpersonal orientation, this is closely linked to the concept of karma yoga, which is the yoga of service and contribution to others through work.

Psychoanalytic models of psychotherapy portrayed ideal therapists as those who minimized affective involvement, offered themselves as blank projection screens, and put aside their own feelings, reactions, and personal development for the benefit of the client. The humanistic existential model, on the other hand, emphasized the importance of participation by therapists in all their humanity in the therapeutic relationship, opening themselves fully to the client's experience and to their own reactions.[3, 4]

To this participation the transpersonal orientation has added the perspective that the therapist may benefit both the client and him/herself best by using the relationship to optimize his/her own transpersonal growth through consciously serving the client. This may take many forms and may be indistinguishable externally from other therapeutic approaches, but it is always performed within the context of optimizing growth through service. Indeed, working with one's own consciousness becomes a primary responsibility. The growth of one participant in the therapeutic relationship is seen as facilitating that of the other, and by holding the relationship in the context of service and karma yoga, the therapist attempts to provide both an optimal environment and model for the client. Where the therapist is consciously serving the client there is no hierarchical status accorded to being a therapist. Rather the situation is held as one in which both therapist and client are working on themselves, each in the way that is most appropriate to their particular development. The therapist's openness and willingness to use the therapeutic process to maximize his or her own growth and commitment to service is viewed as the optimal modeling that can be provided for the client.

The means by which the therapist transforms the process into a karma yoga are several. First, and perhaps most importantly, is simply the intention to do so. Coupled with this is the intention to remain as aware and meditatively mindful as possible at all times.

In some traditional approaches the therapist is portrayed as what is called a "competent model" who is fully competent at that which he/she is trying to teach. However, the transpersonal therapist may share his or her own unresolved questions where appropriate and attempt to be as transparent as possible. The karma yogic therapist thereby combines the "competent" and the so-called "learning to cope" varieties of modeling. Interestingly, studies of modeling have demonstrated that the learning to cope model is frequently more effective than the competent one.[1, 2]

Such modeling provides a high degree of mutuality between therapist and client because both share a growth-oriented intention for therapy, are less hierarchically distanced, and function as teachers for one another. Indeed, the therapist may enhance this process by assuming responsibility for interacting with clients working at this level with complete openness and honesty, asking the client to engage in a mutually facilitating two-way feedback of any apparently withheld or incorrect communication. Such an approach demands a strong commitment by the therapist to hear the truth about him/herself and it is this which may possibly provide the optimum modeling for the client.

Transpersonal psychotherapy can be distinguished from other approaches on several dimensions that will be discussed below. However, it should be noted that such comparisons are not without dangers. All therapies share considerable areas of commonality and any comparison risks magnifying and solidifying differences without acknowledging the overlap. In addition, there are often major discrepancies between therapy as it is idealistically described and as it is practiced.[5] Furthermore, therapists of different theoretical persuasions, will exhibit selective and differing perception when viewing the same therapeutic interaction. Finally, biases are hard to eradicate no matter how objective authors attempt to be. These caveats should be born in mind during the following discussion.

A transpersonal approach may include traditional aims while incorporating further goals derived from the transpersonal model of consciousness discussed earlier. These include increasing awareness or consciousness and may include experience of altered states with the ultimate aim of attaining a true "higher" state. For example, perception and concentration may be trained, as in meditation, with the individual learning to observe mental content rather than attempting to change it. The appropriate aphorism might be "watch everything, do nothing!" As Perls observed, "Awareness per se — by and of itself — can be curative."[6] In addition to watching mental content, the individual also aims to disidentify from it, a process that explores the more fundamental question of not only *who* am I, but *what* am I?

Thus, for example, a client presenting to a traditional therapist complaining of feeling inadequate, incapable, inferior, etc., would be viewed as having low self-esteem, poor ego strength, or negative self-attributions according to the therapist's particular discipline. If a psychodynamic approach were employed, the therapist might attempt to determine the origin of these thoughts, whereas a behavioral approach might attempt to modify them directly by environmental change, differential reinforcement, or cognitive approaches.[7, 8] Whatever the approach, the effective aim would be to modify the client's belief and experience about *what type of person* he or she is. A transpersonal therapist on the other hand, might use these approaches but would also recognize that the problem represented an example of identification with negative thoughts and emotions. In addition, this problem would be viewed as only one example of the many types of identification with which the client was unwittingly involved. The distinguishing feature of the particular identification would be merely that it caused discomfort of clinical proportions. Thus, if the transpersonal therapist chose to employ a meditative approach, this would involve training awareness with the aim of disidentifying from all thoughts, thus resulting in the client's having not only a different belief about *what type of person* he or she was, but an alteration in the more fundamental perception of *what* he or she was. The relative extent to which traditional and nontraditional techniques were employed would vary with the individual client. However, the goals of meditation and transpersonal approaches extend beyond those of traditional Western psychotherapy.

For example, the transpersonal model suggests that ego identification is illusory, "only a dream." In the West, when this illusion is mistaken for reality, the therapist may help prevent the dream from becoming a nightmare, but a transpersonal approach to consciousness is aimed at awakening.

COMPARATIVE PSYCHOTHERAPY

The expanded version of psychology that the transpersonal perspective wishes to offer aims at an integration of various Western approaches with those of the East. In *The Spectrum of Consciousness*, Wilber has distinguished three primary levels of consciousness, namely the ego, the existential, and the level of Mind or pure nondualistic consciousness.[9] The ego level concerns the roles, self-images, and the analytical aspects of our mind with which we usually identify. The existential, on the other hand, concerns our basic sense of existence, the meaning of life, confrontation with death and aloneness, and the central experience of being-in-the-world. These two levels together constitute our identity as separate, self-existent individuals, and it is with these levels that most Western therapies are concerned, assuming that people are condemned by their very existence to live out their lives as isolated, alienated individuals, inherently and permanently separated from the rest of the universe. Such approaches aim at strengthening the ego.

Beyond the ego and existential levels is the level of "Mind," in which the individual experiences him/herself as pure consciousness, having let go all exclusive identification, and transcended the me/not me dichotomy, resulting in a sense of unity with the cosmos. From this perspective, the other levels are seen as illusions of identification and are accorded less importance.[9, 10, 11, 12] This process of reevaluating one state of consciousness from a new state is called subrationing.[13]

Each therapeutic approach may contribute to health and well-being in its own way at its own level. What is appropriate at one stage or in one situation may not be appropriate at another. Different approaches are simply addressed to different levels and dimensions of consciousness and growth. Ideally, the transpersonal recognizes the potential of all levels and makes optimum use of the contributions of both East and West to intervene at the appropriate level.

The following is an attempt to compare the transpersonal with the major Western traditions of psychoanalysis, analytical psychology, behaviorism, humanistic and existential psychology.

Classical Psychoanalysis

In psychoanalysis, human beings are presumed to be incessantly locked in mental conflict that can be reduced but never fully resolved.[14] The individual must therefore constantly guard against and control this conflict. A strong ego, the mediating factor between an irrational id and an overcontrolling super-ego, is considered the hallmark of health, which is defined by default as the absence of pathology. This contrasts markedly with the transpersonal perspective, in which the ego is considered as an illusory product of perceptual distortion and identification. There is no quarrel with the premise that a strong, healthy ego can be an asset in meeting the demands of life, or even that it may be a necessary prelude for more advanced work, but the transpersonal concept of health goes beyond belief in ego development as the summit of mental health. Thus, while the conflicts of the ego may indeed be unresolvable, they are transcendable via an expansion of identity beyond the ego to awareness itself. Just as from a psychoanalytic perspective the superego is recognized as an intrapsychic entity with which the individual may, but does not have to, identify, so from the transpersonal perspective the ego is viewed similarly. Such a shift in identity has the effect of greatly reducing the power of ego demands, which can now be viewed with greater detachment. Ultimately, the disidentification from ego and the discovery of one's own true nature may be considered tantamount to liberation or awakening.

Analytical Psychology

Of all the schools that have developed and departed from Freud's original work, the depth psychology of Carl Jung, also called analytical psychology, has been more concerned with transpersonal levels of experience than any other.

The in-depth exploration of the psyche in Jungian work extends beyond both the ego and existential levels in dealing with archetypes and the collective unconscious. Jung himself was the first Western psychotherapist to affirm the importance of transpersonal experience for mental health. He wrote that the main thrust of his work was not the treatment of neurosis, but the approach to the numinous dimensions of experience: ". . . The fact is that the approach to the numinous is the real therapy and inasmuch as you attain to the numinous experience you are released from the curse of pathology."[15]

Depth psychology recognizes that the psyche has within it the capacity for self-healing and self-realization, but Jungian work remains predominantly concerned with the contents of consciousness rather than with consciousness itself as the context of all experience. Thus consciousness is experienced only in relation to its objects. It remains at a dualistic level and does not encompass the potential transcendence of subject-object dualism. Analytical psychology values the mythical dimension of experience, such as in the imagery of dreams and active imagination as a powerful therapeutic agent. However, it stops short of valuing the direct imageless awareness attained in the practice of some meditative disciplines.

Behaviorism

The defining characteristics of behaviorism is its insistence on the measurability and verification of behavior and behavior change.[16,1,8] By careful, methodical, empirically based growth it has developed a technology that is often highly effective in the treatment of delimited behavioral problems. Indeed, it must be recognized that behavior modification stands alone among the literally hundreds of therapies in having clearly demonstrated its effectiveness.[17, 18]

However, its strength may also represent its weakness. The rigid demand for measurement of *observable* behavior has tended to remove subjective experience from consideration. Such dimensions as consciousness, and until recently, even thoughts and feelings, have been ignored. It is thus left unable to encompass some of the most central aspects of the human condition and has little to say about optimizing positive health and well-being. It has largely been limited to the treatment of pathologies with clearly defined overt behavioral characteristics.

At the present time, however, a major shift is becoming apparent. Cognition and cognitive mediation of behavioral manifestations are being increasingly investigated, resulting in the recognizable field of cognitive behavior modification.[19] Self-control is being increasingly emphasized and self-efficacy has been advanced as a major mediator of therapeutic change.[20, 7] Many transpersonal techniques can readily be viewed from within a behavior modification framework. Thus, for example, a variety of meditations that aim to enhance feelings of love and then use this to inhibit negative emotions such as anger are clearly based on the principle of reciprocal inhibition, which behaviorists use to replace anxiety with relaxation. Buddha gave explicit instructions for such techniques, suggesting that some of the principles of this discipline were noted over two thousand years ago.[21]

Similarly, transpersonalists have recognized the importance of modeling, and behaviorists have amassed a significant body of research data concerning it. There is, however, a major difference concerning the subtlety of the behavior and attitudes that are modeled. Behaviorism has concerned itself primarily with relatively gross, easily measured behaviors, whereas the transpersonalists have been interested in more subtle states, attitudes, experiences, and behaviors.

The field of transpersonal psychotherapy needs some of the behaviorist rigor in empirical testing and validation of many current assumptions and practices. Much work remains to be done in this area.

Humanistic Psychotherapy

The distinctions between humanistic and transpersonal psychotherapy are less apparent at first glance. Both are growth-oriented models concerned as much with health as pathology, and both are holistic, i.e., they attempt to deal with the whole person.

However, the central concepts of health are different. From a humanistic standpoint, the healthy individual is self-actualizing, and humanistic therapy addresses itself predominantly to the ego and existential levels. The development of personality and the achievement of ego goals are central, whereas from a transpersonal perspective these are accorded less importance and may sometimes be seen as obstructions to transpersonal realization. Here the human capacity for self-transcendence beyond self-actualization is brought into perspective.[22, 23]

Humanistic psychologists may not be interested in exploring transpersonal experiences, although some have clearly done so. Transpersonal therapists might be expected to have some firsthand experience of such states in order to work effectively with those who seek guidance in dealing with them. When therapists do not have such firsthand knowledge, they may unwittingly invalidate their clients' experience.[24]

Existentialism

The existential approach converges with the transpersonal and humanistic in its concern with the search for meaning and purpose, the confrontation of death and aloneness, the necessity of choice and responsibility, and the demands of authenticity.[25, 3, 4] It supports the view that we create our reality by our beliefs. For example, freedom becomes real when we believe in it. We have to know that we can have it before we can begin to exercise it. The same is true of love and other values that we can choose to make real for ourselves. If we do not believe in the reality of love it is unlikely that we will experience it. By facing these questions we can come to terms with them from an existential perspective, but more than this, we can penetrate behind the mask of our separate and alienated individuality to experience the underlying unity and interconnectedness of all life. The experience of freedom, with all its paradoxes, and the raw experience of being-in-the-world that the existentialists portray, can open the way for the personal transformation that leads to transcendence. The existentialist, however, may remain locked into his/her separate ego-defined identity and fail to make the leap beyond dualistic knowledge into the direct intuitive knowing and expansion of consciousness that characterizes transpersonal experience.

In existentialism we see a reflection of the first Noble Truth of Buddhism, namely that all life is imbued with suffering. Caught in a no-exit situation, the individual struggles continuously to confront and reconcile life with its apparent inevitabilities. However, the Buddha went further and pointed the way out of this dilemma in the remaining three truths, in which he noted that:

- The cause of all suffering is attachment.
- The relief of suffering comes from the cessation of attachment.
- The cessation of attachment comes from following the eightfold path, a prescription for ethical living and mental training aimed at attaining full enlightenment.

This path leads directly to the transpersonal realm beyond the ego and existential levels.

LIMITATIONS OF TRANSPERSONAL PSYCHOTHERAPY

If the preceding paragraphs represent a description of transpersonal psychotherapy, or at least what it seeks to become, what then are the factors that currently limit this field?

First, there is clearly an inadequate empirical foundation. Many of the concerns of the transpersonal therapist lie outside the range of interest, competence, and investigation of most researchers. Thus many assumptions, though experientially satisfying, remain experimentally untested. There has been an understandable but regrettable tendency to think that if experimenters are not interested in this area then that is their problem.

But if the transpersonal is truly to be an effective synthesis of Eastern wisdom and Western science, then its practitioners need to do all they can to ensure that their work is indeed subjected to careful scientific scrutiny. The history of psychotherapy is filled with partisan assumptions and claims of superiority that have remained intact only as long as they remained unexamined.[26, 5, 18] While there is a growing body of research on meditation, which on the whole is supportive,[27, 28] few other transpersonal areas have been examined closely.

This raises the interesting question of the applicability of traditional mechanistic scientific paradigms to the investigation of transpersonal phenomena.[28, 11] The necessity for novel approaches that are less interfering, more sensitive to subjective states, and involve the experimenter as a trained participant-observer has been frequently recognized but little used. To date, the transpersonal has not been widely integrated with other Western psychologies and therapies, but hopefully increased knowledge will correct this situation.

To anyone who has explored the transpersonal realms in depth it is apparent that intellectual comprehension demands an experiential foundation.[29, 30, 31] Experiential knowledge is clearly a limiting factor for conceptual understanding. Indeed, it is necessary to have multiple experiential recognitions of this fact before its power and implications can really be appreciated. Failure to appreciate this had led to countless misunderstandings, discounting, and superficial and pathologizing interpretation of the transpersonal. Even the most intellectually sophisticated but experientially naive mental health practitioners may make such errors, as was shown by the Group for the Advancement of Psychiatry's report on Mysticism and Psychiatry.[32] Both therapists and investigators need to be aware of this and to undertake their own personal experiential work. Since the transpersonal realm and potential for growth are so vast, far exceeding the explorations of most of us, it is probably safe to say that the limits of our personal growth represent one of the major limiting factors for this field.

Transpersonal psychotherapy places a number of stringent demands on its practitioners. This seems to reflect a principle of increasing subtlety. It seems that as one moves from working with pathology toward working with positive health, the phenomena, experiences, and barriers may become increasingly more subtle, the demands on the therapist more refined, and the appropriate techniques more fluid, more sensitive, and less interfering.

Since we are both the tools and models for what we have to offer, it is imperative that we seek to live and be that which we would offer to our clients. With few empirical guidelines, we must rely heavily on ourselves for guidance and must therefore strive for integrity, impeccability, and sensitivity. Nowhere in the field of psychotherapy is the therapist's growth and work on him/herself more important for both client and therapist.

> For what one person has to offer to another,
> is their own being, nothing more, nothing less.[33]

Notes

1. Bandura, A. *Principles of behavior modification*. New York: Holt, Rinehart and Winston, 1969.

2. Bandura, A. *Social learning theory*. Englewood Cliffs, N.J.: Prentice-Hall, 1977.

3. Bugental, J. F. T. *The search for authenticity: An existential analytic approach to psychotherapy*. New York: Holt, Rinehart and Winston, 1965.

4. Bugental, J. F. T. *The search for existential identity: Patient-therapist dialogue in humanistic psychotherapy*. San Francisco: Jossey-Bass, 1976.

5. Luborsky, L., Singer, B., & Luborsky, L. Comparative studies of psychotherapies. *Arch. Gen. Psychiat.*, 1975, *32*, 995–1008.

6. Perls, F. *Gestalt therapy verbatim*. Lafayette, Calif.: Real People Press, 1969, p. 16.

7. Thoresen, C. E., & Mahoney, M. *Behavioral self-control*. New York: Holt, Rinehart and Winston, 1974.

8. Rimm, D. C., & Masters, J. C. *Behavior therapy*. New York: Academic Press, 1975.

9. Wilber, K. *The spectrum of consciousness*. Wheaton, Ill.: Theosophical Publishing House, 1977.

10. Vaughan, F. Transpersonal perspectives in psychotherapy. *J. Humanistic Psychol.*, 1977, *17*, 69–81.

11. Wilber, K. Eye to Eye: Science and transpersonal psychology. This volume.

12. Wilber, K. *The Atman project*. Wheaton, Ill.: Theosophical Publishing House, 1980.

13. Deutsch, E. *Advaita vedanta: A philosophical reconstruction*. Honolulu: East West Centre Press, 1969.

14. Brenner, C. *An elementary textbook of psychoanalysis*. New York: Anchor, 1974.

15. Jung, C. G. *Letters* (G. Adler, Ed.). Princeton, N. J.: Princeton University Press, 1973.

16. Bandura, A. Self-efficacy: Toward a unifying theory of behavior change. *Psychol. Rev.*, 1977, *84*, 191–215.

17. Parloff, M. Twenty-five years of research in psychotherapy. New York: Albert Einstein College of Medicine, Psychiatry Department, Oct. 17, 1975.

18. Karasu, T. B. Psychotherapies: An overview. *Amer. J. Psychiat.*, 1977, *134*, 851–863.

19. Mahoney, M. *Cognition and behavior modification*. Cambridge, Mass.: Ballinger, 1974.

20. Bandura, A. *Social learning theory*. Englewood Cliffs, N. J.: Prentice-Hall, 1977.

21. Buddhagosa. P. M. Tin (Trans.). *The path of purity*. Sri Lanka: Pali Text Society, 1923.

22. Maslow, A. H. *The farther reaches of human nature*. New York: Viking, 1971.

23. Roberts, T. Beyond self-actualization. *ReVision*, 1978, *1*, 42–46.

24. Grof, S. *Realms of the human unconscious*. This volume.

25. Bugental, J. F. T. *Psychotherapy and process*. Reading, Mass.: Addison-Wesley, 1978.

26. Shapiro, D., & Giber, D. Meditation: Self-control strategy and altered states of consciousness. *Arch. Gen. Psychiat.*, 1978, *35*, 294–302.

27. Shapiro, D. N., & Walsh, R. N. (Eds.). *The science of meditation: Research, theory, and experience*. Chicago: Aldine Press, in press.

28. Shapiro, D. *Meditation: Slef-regulation strategy and altered states of consciousness*. New York: Aldine, in press.

29. Rajneesh, B. S. *The way of the white cloud*. Poona, India: Rajneesh Center, 1975.

30. Ram Dass. *Grist for the mill*. Santa Cruz, Calif.: Unity Press, 1977.

31. Deikman, A. J. Comments on the GAP report on mysticism. *J. Nerv. Men. Dis.*, 1977, *165*, 213–217.

32. Group for the Advancement of Psychiatry. *Mysticism: Spiritual quest or psychic disorder?* Washington, D.C.: Group for the Advancement of Psychiatry, 1976.

33. Ram Dass. Love, serve, remember. Audiotape produced by Hanuman Foundation, Box 61498, Santa Cruz, CA 95061, 1973.

The Transpersonal Stance

JAMES FADIMAN

[In] the emerging transpersonal orientation, [a] communality of ideas arose out of a common set of experiences with non-habitual states of consciousness and unconventional ... experiences. ... [Individuals sharing] experiences ... felt a pressing need to find some body of literature or research which could clarify, codify, interpret, and resolve the questions raised by what were emotionally important and yet [quite unfamiliar] occurrences. ... Mainstream psychology (with the exception of William James and a few others) proved to be barren. ... The search for information which would explain these experiences expanded to the older psychologies. . . . As these writings became acceptable and were read by persons trained in Western psychology, various connections were seen and the foundations for a confluence of older ideas with Western needs and values began to emerge.

THE OLDER PSYCHOLOGIES

> Western consciousness is by no means consciousness in general, but rather a historically conditioned and geographically limited factor, representative of only one part of humanity.　　　　　　　　　　　　　　　　　*—C. G. Jung*

Transpersonal psychologists draw heavily on the accumulated psychological literature outside the American mainstream. Examples of the ideas influencing current transpersonal therapists can be drawn from Buddhism, Sufism, and Yoga.

In the Yogic tradition there is the repeated suggestion that if you work to clarify the contents of your consciousness, there will be changes in how you relate to external things. What might be termed therapeutic progress proceeds from this point of view, i.e., therapeutic progress occurs not from confrontation or substitution, but from attrition or a growing disinterest in the neurotic aspects of one's life. Inappropriate habits and excessive desires seem to fade away as a person finds them to be less satisfying than the more transpersonal experiences. As one writer put it: "When does the attraction of the pleasure of the senses die away? When one realizes the consummation of all happiness and all pleasure in God — the indivisible, eternal ocean of bliss." (Ramakrishna, 1965, p. 93).

There is a considerable and sophisticated background of transpersonal theory. This extensive body of literature has encouraged the development of transpersonal therapy. The utility of a theory rests not on its internal elegance, but upon its applications. In the practice of any form of psychotherapy, the underlying theory is critical in determining the initial scope, goals, and processes that define that therapy.

PRACTICAL CONSIDERATIONS

> Stop talking about satori, but first seek and discipline yourself with your body and soul. . . .　　　　　　　　　　　　　　　　*—Zen Master Mumon*

The issue of therapeutic gains or improvement is fundamental to the practice of any form of therapy. Improvement, however, differs from therapy to therapy, and from patient to patient. A look at a few of the critical issues that concern transpersonal therapists may be the most straightforward way to explore this area.

Personality — A Subsystem of the Self

A basic assumption of transpersonal psychology is that there is more to you than your personality. Your personality is your sense of a separate, different, unique identity. Your personality is but one facet, however, of the self — the total identity — and perhaps not even a central facet. The very word "transpersonal" means through or beyond the personality. To be totally identified with one's personality may be evidence of psychopathology. One therapeutic goal is to align the personality within the total self so that it functions appropriately. These ideas fly in the face of the commonly accepted idea that the be-all and end-all of life is to improve your personality.

A goal, within the context of transpersonal therapy, is to encourage and develop those tendencies which allow an individual to disidentify from the restrictions of the personality and to apprehend their identity with the total self. (See Assagioli, 1965, and *Synthesis*, 1974, for a full discussion.

Personal Drama

When I have seriously ill patients who are obsessive — seriously ill people are obsessive by definition; they become obsessed with the significance of their internal drama, and reify it, crystallize it, stabilize it, as if the drama has no alternatives — I put them in contact with a real scenario.
—*Minuchin in Malcolm, 1978*

An alternative way to begin redefining the importance of personality is to describe it as a personal drama. . . . Personal dramas are predictable, repetitive, and complex patterns of behavior performed either with or without the presence or participation of others. Their repetitive nature is often not appreciated. . . . For example, in a therapy group one person begins: "You know what I'm feeling right now is . . ." With that opening line the group knows that the person is about to begin one of his personal dramas. . . . "I will now do 'my mother really loved my sister more than me' followed by a chorus of 'my sexual feelings are frozen up inside me' and a final riff of 'sometimes I wish I were a lesbian, but if I were, I'd kill myself.'"

Personal dramas are an unnecessary luxury and interfere with full functioning. They are part of our emotional baggage. It is usually beneficial for a person to gain some detachment from his/her own dramas, as well as to learn to become detached from the personal dramas of others.

[One therapeutic approach to dealing with] personal dramas is to let the person know that you are watching his/her personal drama and that you are not confusing the writer with the actor. With children this might take the following form: when a tantrum begins, you draw your chair closer; you say to the child that you are impressed with their temper, their violence, but you would like to see the tantrum again with more kicking or perhaps with breath holding, like last week. This deflates the child's purpose in performing the tantrum. Initially, when you confront a person with the possibility that a behavior is only a personal drama, you may find the response to be fury and excitement. This quickly passes. If you are genuine in your appreciation of the person, the drama will often end with laughter and the relief that comes from being unmasked.

How and when can a person rise to a level of detached awareness which will enable him to discard old dramas and decide on more fitting ones? One possible answer may be found in learning to use the "witness consciousness"; the "witness" is that part of us which observes our actions without either praise or blame. The experience of being the witness and various methods for training oneself are described in meditational systems, in the words of Gurdjieff and his followers, in the psychosynthesis literature, and elsewhere.

It may be realistic to encourage people to pick and choose among their behavior patterns. This may be accomplished by utilizing a strategy in therapy which views the personality as a collection of personal dramas and which treats each facet or each drama as a semiautomatic performance, which can be revised or replaced if a person wills. This strategy does not lead to the therapist empathizing with the suffering of the client. In fact, from this perspective, it appears that identifying with the suffering of the client will reinforce the suffering. Not identifying with the suffering may be the first step in eliminating it from the client's repertoire.

One Self or Many Selves

It is not appropriate to see as separate, things which cannot be distinguished.
—*Albert Einstein*

An issue in transpersonal theory reflected in differing models of transpersonal therapy is the question of the apparent unity, or diversity, of personality. The way in which an individual therapist treats this issue may predetermine the therapeutic goals. If one believes that we are fundamentally a unity and that all separation eventually falls away with the awareness of higher consciousness, then a goal of therapy is to help the client become aware of the illusory nature of the sub- or partial identifications within the self. This notion is . . . a classic position within Buddhism and well-represented in Yogic thought as well.

Since transpersonal therapy is a stance, a place from which to work, rather than a tightly defined and explicit system, transpersonal therapies differ in how they regard the self or selves. But few restrict their thinking or practices to the material or the social levels of the self.

Nobody Wants to Change

Lord, make me chaste, but not yet.   —*St. Augustine*

People who enter therapy rarely wish to change themselves. They wish to be relieved of the suffering, anxiety, pain, failure, and uncertainty in their lives. People don't want to change their personalities. To the extent they identify with a neurosis, a facial tic, inadequate sexual performance, fears of dying, lack of meaning, phobias, etc., they do not see "change" as exchange, but rather as loss. People don't willingly give up, shed, or relinquish any part of their identity.

The transpersonal stance accepts the resistance of the personality to change. No behavior can be lost, only temporarily extinguished; no childhood-based complex can be eradicated, only minimized in its effects. Traumatic situations are made conscious rather than left to remain unconscious, but they still exert their effects on habits and anticipations of future events.

A goal of transpersonal therapy is to stop dwelling on those portions of the personality which should be neglected and to allow the *entire personality* to exert less and less effect on the day-to-day activities of the individual. It is not that a person does not want to change; it is that the personality does not want to change. As one stops over-valuing the needs and opinions of the personality, the more inclusive and more extensive overall self can and does assume a more dominant position. The personality is shrunken in power and dominion but remains intact with all its essential strengths and weaknesses.

An example of this goal is to get patients to understand the difference between desire and craving. Desire is natural, normal, periodic, and inescapable. When you are tired, you desire sleep; when lonely, you desire companionship; when aroused, you desire activity. Craving occurs when you cannot satisfy the object of your desire and *persist* in desiring. Transpersonal therapy can teach people to regulate their desires so that they are not controlled by them. This does not lower the intensity of desires, but helps people discover the capacity to determine their own reactions to their desires. The self, as it is described in all transpersonal theories, does not desire; only the personality is capable of desiring. Therefore, any therapeutic intervention which decreases the centrality of the personality will in turn decrease the compulsive effects of desire and the debilitating effects of unfulfilled craving.

FUTURE ISSUES

There are other issues surfacing within transpersonal psychology which will affect the way therapy is practiced. These include:

The Mind-Body Interface

There is a growing body of research that indicates that mental and physical symptoms are so interconnected that it is unrealistic to continue the present dichotomy between mental and physical medicine. Two underlying assumptions have emerged. First, the body is a subsystem of the mind. It is sensible to approach all symptoms from asthma to cancer as if the symptom is partially generated and maintained by mental and emotional causes. Conversely, it is also assumed that the mind is a subsystem of the body. This assumption allows one to approach all mental symptoms from delusions to phobias as if the conditions are partly generated and maintained by physical (environmental, nutritional, constitutional) causes. The resolution of these two blending streams is clearly visible in the emerging reorganization within medicine termed "holistic" or "integral" medicine. It is an issue for transpersonal therapists to determine where to place themselves on the spectrum — somewhere between "it's-all-in-the-mind" and "it's-all-in-the-body." The idea of only treating the body or only treating the mind is seen as unrealistic and without empirical justification.

The Goal of Therapy

The end state of psychotherapy is the daily experience of a state known in different traditions as certainty, liberation, enlightenment, or gnosis. In psychology the term that most closely describes this level of functioning is "self-actualization."

It has been traditional (a tradition perhaps derived from Christian monasticism) to assume that people who are self-actualized or enlightened are quiet, gentle, spiritual, materially poor, sexless, dull, and righteous, and that their very presence is slightly uncomfortably for the rest of us. We cannot describe the activities of the post-transpersonal therapy clients in such pious or simplistic terms. They are as likely to be at a World Series, running a corporation, enjoying a plate of oysters, or rebuilding an old car as they are to be doing anything else. The goal of the self, unbound from the burdens and the deficiencies of the personality, seems to be to enjoy the world but not be attached to it, to be of service, but not to make a pest of oneself.

Toward a Comprehensive Psychology

It is axiomatic within the transpersonal world to recognize our need to re-introduce, study, practice, and assimilate the older and more extensively developed systems of psychology. Psychology historically has been concerned with helping individuals answer the basic questions of their existence:

Who am I?

Why am I here?

Where am I going?

Transpersonal psychology is bringing together the insights of the individualistic psychologies of the West with the spiritual psychologies of the East and Middle East. The realization that our own training has been limited and that Western ideas are not the center of the psychological universe is disturbing at first. The feeling passes when one becomes aware of the amazing amount of work that has already been accomplished, but which awaits validation with the scientific and experimental tools of Western psychology, to be fully realized.

References

Assagioli, Robert. *Psychosynthesis*. New York: Hobbs, Dorman, 1965.

Gurdjieff, George I. *All and everything, the first series: Beelzebub's tales to his grandson*. New York: Dutton, 1950.

James, Henry (Ed.). *The letters of William James* (2 vols.). Boston: Little, Brown, 1926.

Jung, C. G. *Memories, dreams, reflections* (Recorded and edited by Aniela Jaffe). New York: Pantheon, 1963.

Malcolm, Janet. The one-way mirror. *The New Yorker*, May 15, 1978, pp. 39–114.

Ramakrishna. *Sayings of Sri Ramakrishna*. Madras, India: Sri Ramakrishna Math, 1965.

Shafii, Mohammad. *Developmental stages in man in Sufism and psychoanalysis*. Unpublished manuscript, 1974.

Sirij-Ed-Din, Abu Bakr. *The book of certainty*. New York: Samuel Weiser, 1970.

Synthesis: The realization of the self. Redwood City, Calif.: Synthesis Press, 1974.

Transpersonal Psychotherapy: Context, Content, and Process

FRANCES VAUGHAN

Transpersonal psychotherapy may be conceived as an open-ended endeavor to facilitate human growth and expand awareness beyond limits implied by most traditional Western models of mental health. However, in the process of enlarging one's felt sense of identity to include transpersonal dimensions of being, the therapist may employ traditional therapeutic techniques as well as meditation and other awareness exercises derived from Eastern consciousness disciplines.

Since transpersonal psychotherapy is concerned with the attainment of levels of psychological health that surpass what is commonly accepted as normal, it is useful to define some goals of therapy. One goal is to develop the capacity for taking responsibility for oneself in the world and in one's relationships. It may also be assumed that the healthy person is capable of experiencing a full range of emotions while remaining relatively detached from the personal melodrama.[1] Another goal is to enable each person to meet physical, emotional, mental, and spiritual needs appropriately, in accordance with individual preferences and predispositions. Hence, no one path can be expected to be appropriate for everyone. In transpersonal psychotherapy, impulses toward spiritual growth are considered basic to full humanness.[2] It is assumed that in addition to basic survival needs for food, shelter, and relationship, higher needs for self-realization must be met for full functioning at optimum levels of health.

From a transpersonal viewpoint, every client is seen as having the capacity for self-healing. In other words, the therapist does not cure an ailment for a patient, but enables a client to tap inner resources and allow the natural healing or growth process to occur. Furthermore, the human organism is seen as seeking to enhance and surpass itself in the process of self-actualization. This implies that it has potential for bringing into being those qualities and capacities that may be latent or undeveloped within the person experiencing conflict or stress. Beyond this is the possibility of self-transcendence or transpersonal realization, in which the separate and isolated ego may be experienced as illusory, while the underlying oneness of existence is experienced as real.

The therapist need not share the client's views of reality in order to acknowledge them as subjectively valid. Since any point of view is necessarily relative and limited, the underlying ground of being remains indescribable. Recognizing the subjective nature of his/her own beliefs and subjecting them to closer examination may allow the client to break out of self-imposed limitations and constrictions of awareness. As partial identifications with limited views are discarded or transcended, the process of healing imaginary psychological splits, reintegrating disowned parts of the psyche, and resolving internal conflicts may be accelerated. Ideally, a transpersonal psychotherapeutic orientation supports a balanced integration of physical, emotional, mental, and spiritual aspects of well-being. Given the above orientation, it is useful to make a distinction between transpersonal *content* or experience that may emerge in psychotherapy and a transpersonal *context* within which the therapy is conducted. Since transpersonal psychotherapy may work directly on consciousness in order to alter the context in which life is experienced rather than attempting to change the contents of experience, defining these terms in relation to therapy is essential.

CONTEXT

A transpersonal context in therapy is determined entirely by the beliefs, values, and intentions of the therapist. For example, if a therapist intends to communicate attitudes that facilitate trust, and is comfortable with his/her own transpersonal experiences, the client may gain confidence in exploring these realms. What can take place in therapy is inevitably limited by the personal fears and beliefs of the therapist, just as it is limited by the readiness of the client to explore these realms. Therefore, in order to establish favorable conditions for transpersonal exploration, the therapist must be willing to handle any obstacles to self-awareness that may arise in the process. When, for example, a therapist identifies with an expanded sense of the self as the source of experience, the potential for healing in the therapeutic relationship is enhanced.

A transpersonal context also implies that the therapist is aware of the centrality of consciousness in determining the outcome of therapy. In transpersonal therapy consciousness itself is both the object and the instrument of change. Thus the process is not concerned with problem solving per se, but in creating the conditions in which problems can either be solved or transcended as appropriate. In other words, the therapist is primarily concerned with having the client learn to handle problems and situations as they arise rather than resolving a particular situation in the client's life. The metaphor of the fisherman teaching a hungry person how to fish rather than simply providing a fish is fitting, in that a transpersonal approach enables each person to tap his or her own inner resources, rather than providing insights, solutions, or predetermined goals. The therapist's assumption here is that, given the opportunity, the inner wisdom of the organism will emerge as an integrating, healing force that the client can trust. Learning to recognize and trust those inner impulses toward wholeness and transcendence is part of the process — a task that may be popularly identified as getting in touch with the inner guru, guide, or higher self. The direction of searching in transpersonal therapy, as in all enlightenment teachings, whether religious or psychological, is inward.[3]

Acknowledging the centrality of consciousness in psychotherapy implies that the state of consciousness of the therapist has a profound and far-reaching effect on the therapeutic relationship. For example, the relationship may be deepened by the therapist's awareness of the underlying oneness of all beings and his/her essential connectedness with the client. Recognizing the illusory nature of limited perceptions of reality and the infinite possibilities of expanding inner vision, the transpersonal therapist may well view therapy as a process of awakening. Attaining an expanded state of consciousness as well as an expanded sense of identity and a transformed world view is implied as a possibility, depending on the client's willingness to let go of constricting beliefs and identification. Frequently this expansion may be facilitated by reversing customary patterns, e.g. an overly assertive person may need to learn to be more compliant, whereas a very compliant person may need to learn to be more assertive. The person who believes "I have to make it on my own," may need to relinquish control and learn to accept support, whereas the person who is always seeking external support may need to come to terms with aloneness and learn to take responsibility for him/herself.

In a transpersonal context the therapist realizes that, although no particular method will necessarily lead to a transpersonal awakening or personal transformation, there is much that can be done to remove the obstacles to such experience. Clearly, if the therapist does not believe such change is possible, disbelief itself becomes an obstacle. Similarly, if the therapist believes that such a change takes years, it probably will. It seems, however, that the attainment of illumination or liberation, according to both Eastern and Western mystical teachings, can occur in an instant. It is therefore recommended that the therapist examine his/her beliefs about what is possible in order to prevent these limitations from interfering with potential awakening.

The therapist creates a transpersonal context for psychotherapy by working with open-ended beliefs about the process. One such belief is the assumption that all thoughts, beliefs, and values directly affect this process, regardless of whether they are expressed overtly or not. It is common knowledge that people in Jungian analysis have Jungian dreams, while those in Freudian analysis have Freudian dreams. Thus, people in transpersonal psychotherapy are given the opportunity to experience their own capacity for transcendence and awakening. As one psychiatrist remarked after becoming personally involved in a spiritual practice, his clients, for the first time in twenty years, began to voice their spiritual concerns, although he did not mention his interest.

Establishing a transpersonal context may thus facilitate the exploration of transpersonal *content* but does not require it. The content of therapy is determined by the client and consists of whatever problems, experiences, and concerns the client brings. The therapist may use dream work, guided imagery, inward focusing, or any number of techniques useful for evoking transpersonal content, but the techniques do not define either the context or the content as transpersonal.

CONTENT

Transpersonal content includes any experiences in which an individual transcends the limitations of identifying exclusively with the ego or personality. Transpersonal content also includes the mythical, archetypal, and symbolic realms of inner experience that can come into awareness through imagery and dreams.

Although the therapeutic value of transpersonal experience has been explicitly acknowledged by Jung[4] and other Western psychotherapists, the attainment of transpersonal experience is not the aim of therapy per se. Such experiences, though not valued as ends in themselves, are accepted as healthy and potentially valuable for human development. Such experiences are notably useful in facilitating disidentification from superficial roles and distorted self-image. When transpersonal experiences are affirmed, validated, and integrated as meaningful aspects of the totality of oneself rather than being repressed or avoided, they tend to bring up fundamental questions concerning the nature of reality and one's true identity. Belief systems may therefore be subjected to intense examination and discarded or revised as appropriate. Thus, a person who comes to therapy concerned about a relationship that is unsatisfactory may be encouraged to examine the beliefs that limit awareness of options for change within the existing structure as well as exploring the possibility of creating new forms that would allow for fuller self-expression and mutual growth. Working in depth with clients, therefore, cannot be divorced from questions of values, although transpersonal psychology does not attempt to establish the validity of any particular belief system. Indeed, the willingness to question all beliefs and assumptions concerning our essential nature is fundamental to expanding our knowledge of this field.

The content of therapy is never exclusively transpersonal, since it invariably reflects the full spectrum of the client's life experience. When defined by its content, therapy may be addressed to different levels of consciousness, according to the predominant themes. Thus therapy at the ego level addresses problems of coping with life and getting what one wants in the world, while therapy at the existential level is predominantly concerned with questions of authenticity, meaning, and purpose. At the transpersonal level, therapy approaches the possibility of transcendence.

PROCESS

From a transpersonal perspective the *process* of moving from one stage to another, although clearly not a linear progression in time, may be conceptualized as follows:[5]

Psychotherapy at the ego level may be considered a stage of development concerned with *identification*. At this stage the client is likely to be concerned with developing ego strength, raising self-esteem, and letting go of negative patterns of self-invalidation. Bugental has observed that most people operate out of unexamined ideas of their own identities. He therefore attempts to bring these self-conceptions to consciousness, and says, "... many of my interventions are designed to challenge existing self-pictures and to suggest enlarged awareness of being."[6] As one begins to identify and own feelings, thoughts, and previously rejected or projected parts of the self, one can assume responsibility for who one is and for the consequences of the choices one has made. The successful completion of this stage implies an awareness of freedom and a shift from other-directedness to self-determination.

A second stage in the process of transpersonal awakening is one of *disidentification*. As Assagioli noted, "We are dominated by everything with which our self becomes identified. We can dominate and control everything from which we disidentify."[7] Wei Wu Wei says, "As long as we are identified with an object, that is bondage."[8] Work at this stage corresponds to work at the existential level, where the individual confronts basic questions of meaning and purpose in life, and begins to disidentify from roles, possessions, activities, and relationships. At this stage success in terms of ego goals or personal gratification is often felt to be meaningless. A confrontation with the existential reality of death and aloneness may lead to despair or resignation. At this stage the self is experienced as an independent entity confronting a world devoid of meaning. Resolution of this level in transcendence involves a kind of ego death, which means further disidentification from both outer and inner definitions of oneself. While owning that one has a body, feelings, thoughts, and points of view, one recognizes that one is no-thing. When one begins to disidentify from the ego and identify instead with the transpersonal self or the detached observer of one's psychological processes, the process of inner liberation is set in motion.

When the transpersonal self is recognized as the context of all experience, a distinction can be made between consciousness and the objects or contents of consciousness. Thus, changing thoughts and emotions may be observed as contents of consciousness, and all experience may be held as the content of pure, unchanging transpersonal awareness. When this occurs, one reaches the stage of *self-transcendence*, wherein the whole personal melodrama becomes less significant. At this point, one no longer experiences oneself as totally isolated, but as part of something larger, inherently connected, and related to everything. The realization that one exists as a web of mutually conditioned relationships and that one is absolutely connected with all of existence may be, as Leonard suggests, the next step in human evolution.[9] With this realization, a significant shift in the sense of identity may take place, and this shift may be incomprehensible to one who has no experiential understanding of this phase.

This transpersonal world view is supported by both modern physics and Eastern mysticism, which describes the universe as a dynamic, intricate web of relationships in continuous change.[10] As one becomes aware of the transpersonal dimension of being, values and behavior tend to change. Problems that remain insoluble at the ego level may now be transcended. For example, inappropriate behavior motivated by fear, regardless of whether it be fear of loss, rejection, failure, or whatever, changes automatically when one begins to see such fears as founded on the illusory identification with ego as a separate self-existent entity.

Fear itself may be held as a *content* or object of consciousness. Only when one becomes identified with it does it appear insurmountable. In acknowledging the transpersonal self as *context* rather than content, any content may be perceived as acceptable and useful in the process of evolving consciousness. Thus, a client working at the transpersonal level in therapy learns to witness his/her experience and state of mind, letting it be and accepting it as part of a process in which he/she willingly participates.

Reflecting on the changes she observed as a result of her work in transpersonal therapy, after considerable experience with more traditional therapy, one client writes, "I no longer examine *every* action and its motives in order to justify it and myself. I no longer *continually* measure my worth in terms of accomplishments or defined roles. I am no longer frantically involved in changing myself. . . . I have begun to gain a sense that my life (fate) is my path and to own the choices I have made on my way. . . . Two changes are a much lowered anxiety level as I have developed a capacity for inner quiet and a loss of my obsession with death and meaninglessness, as I have realized birth and death as one." The Buddhist teaching that clinging and attachment cause pain and suffering is often relevant to such insight. The attachment to any particular experience or attempts to change one experience for another—e.g., the frantic pursuit of pleasure and avoidance of pain—invariably results in continuing frustation and disappointment.

Even when a person has succeeded in disidentifying from ego roles derived from position in the world and from various mind states, he/she may still be subject to archetypal identifications such as healer, wise man, teacher, etc. As symbols that point beyond themselves, the archetypes are the final pointers and also the final barriers to the direct, imageless awareness of transpersonal consciousness.[11] Nonetheless, the symbolization of

experience can be the vehicle for releasing the self from constricting identifications. Although such symbolization facilitates this release by increasing awareness of the transpersonal potentials of the psyche, the symbols
themselves can become obstacles if the ego mistakenly identifies with
them. Writing about his own journey from traditional medicine to transpersonal work, Brugh Joy says, "Initially, dreams, the Tarot, and the *I
Ching* are to make one more self-aware. As with any good teacher, they fall
away as one enters more deeply into the states of direct knowledge."[12]

The successful outcome of transpersonal therapy may be described as
an enlarged sense of identity, in which the self is viewed as the context of
life experience, which in turn is held as content. This shift in identity is
frequently associated with a shift in motivation from self-enhancement to
service, implying less investment in the achievement of specific ego goals
and a predominant motivation for participation and service in the world.
One is likely to be more accepting of all life experience and develop
increased tolerance for paradox and ambiguity. Inner and outer experience
becomes harmonious and congruent. There is no way of measuring increased compassion, generosity, inner peace, and the capacity for love and
relatedness in the world, yet these qualities of being tend to be manifested
as a result of transpersonal work. Once a person has awakened to the
transpersonal dimensions of existence, life itself is held in a different
perspective. A new sense of meaning may well be the content derived
from the newly experienced transpersonal self as context. Although a
transcendent experience per se is not necessarily required for the development of this awareness, it frequently accelerates the process of disidentification and awakening.

For example, one woman who was in therapy during a mid-life transition described the following experience while focusing on inner imagery:

> I am ready for the inward journey and I see myself on a country road walking
> through meadows. The weather is clear and sunny. There appears to be
> above me a sort of capsule interpenetrating the view of the country landscape
> as if two films were being simultaneously projected on a screen. I get into the
> capsule but I don't like the feeling. I feel apprehensive. It lifts me up and
> appears to pierce through a membrane, only it doesn't really pierce the
> membrane. The membrane seems to open from the other side. On the other
> side there is nothing—just clear radiant space. I am no longer in a body or a
> capsule. I am pure awareness of space.

This particular person had no previous experience of contentless consciousness, nor was she acquainted with Eastern traditions that describe
the self as emptiness or no-thing. Yet her imagery was profoundly moving
and allowed her an unexpected glimpse of transpersonal experience.

Paradoxically, the experience of disidentification and transcendence
and the awakening to the transpersonal self also tends to be accompanied
by a sense of personal freedom and a renewed sense of inner directedness

and responsibility. The actual process by which these desirable outcomes in therapy are attained flows out of the context established by the therapist, and is equally determined by the content of the sessions provided by the client. Thus, the process may be said to be mutually determined in the therapeutic relationship between therapist and client, and the therapist serves the client best by establishing the broadest possible context, allowing the client to handle any content that may emerge. The transpersonal therapist attempts to provide the optimum conditions for the client to explore as deeply as possible the wellsprings of transpersonal consciousness.

Notes

1. Fadiman, J. The transpersonal stance. This volume.

2. Sutich, A. Transpersonal therapy. *J. Transpers. Psychol.*, 1973, 5 (1), 1–6.

3. Metzner, R. *Know your type: Maps of identity*. Garden City, N.Y.: Anchor Press/Doubleday, 1979.

4. Jung, C. G. *Letters*. G. Adler (Ed.). Princeton, N.J.: Princeton University Press, 1973.

5. Vaughan Clark, F. Transpersonal perspectives in psychotherapy. *J. of Humanistic Psychol.*, *17*, Spring 1977, 69–81.

6. Bugental, J. *Psychotherapy and process: The fundamentals of an existential-humanistic approach*. Reading, Mass.: Addison-Wesley, 1978.

7. Assagioli, R. *Psychosynthesis*. New York: Hobbs Dorman, 1965.

8. Wei Wu Wei. *All else in bondage*. Hong Kong: Hong Kong University Press, 1970.

9. Leonard, G. *The silent pulse*. New York: E. P. Dutton, 1978.

10. Capra, F. *Modern physics and eastern mysticism*. This volume.

11. Wilber, K. *The spectrum of consciousness*. Evanston, Ill.: Theosophical Publishing House, 1977.

12. Joy, W. B. *Joy's way: A map for the transformational journey*. Los Angeles, Calif.: J. P. Tarcher, Inc., 1979.

Being Levels of
Therapeutic Growth

JAMES BUGENTAL

BEING LEVELS OF THERAPEUTIC GROWTH

Abraham Maslow ... repeatedly ... contrasted *deficiency motivation* and *growth motivation*, and here I'll follow his model.

Adjustment and coping counseling efforts, as well as what I have termed self-renewal therapy, are chiefly concerned with deficiency motivation. They are concerned with reducing negative experiences; essentially they seek to repair one's way of being in the world. In contrast, growth, emancipation, and transcendence are goals which are concerned with realizing more from one's being. They ... seek to ... draw one forward to richness and meaningfulness in life, greater than that person has known before.

In the process of our development from infancy to adulthood, we each work out ways of surviving in the world, of avoiding harm as much as possible, and of getting some satisfactions. These ways become the structure of our lives; they are importantly part of how we see our own identities and how we believe the world to be.

We try, unwittingly, to live out a child's view of life and, when we are adults, we find many inaccuracies and needless limitations within it.

These patterns or structures of living, when viewed as ways of holding off what seems to be unbearable anxiety are called *resistances*. ... Now it becomes evident that there are two kinds of resistances: One kind of resistance deals with issues that are no longer so potent in the client's life—for example, the feeling that estrangement from the parents is tantamount to death (which was true for the small child, but is not true for the adult); the fear that one will be eternally damned for being sexual; or the dread of being totally unproductive if not spurred by authorities. The other kind of resistances seek to stem anxieties, which are as great today as they ever have been. Generally these are what may be termed existential anxieties: the fear of death, of contingency, of responsibility, of separateness, of the emptiness of the universe.

The client may find it possible to face and work through the first type of resistances, those chiefly surviving from the past. Doing so results in relief and the release of energies long bound up in holding the repressions in place. For some clients this marks the end of a satisfactory therapeutic experience. The anxieties about which we can do nothing are shoved back into the keeping of the resistances, and therapy ends. Although this constitutes less than a complete therapeutic product, it needs to be recognized that *completeness* is always a relative matter. No form of therapy produces people truly free of resistances or repressions.

Existential Emancipation

However, for those clients who are willing, the confrontation with existential anxiety — the anxiety that arises from the conditions of life itself — is made as unblinkingly as client and therapist can endure, which is always something less than fully. Nevertheless the exposure of the resistances goes forward, and the pursuit of full and unhampered inner awareness is continued.

Slowly, if client and therapist persist, there emerges a fresh vision of how life might be with most constraints relaxed. Then there comes a time of crisis for most who venture this far. Now the client must face the possibility of genuinely relinquishing the old ways of being, ways which are integrated into the very fabric of personal identity and the world in which that identity is set. Now the client has the possibility of moving into a truly new way of being. This possible new living is, in its deepest significances, radically different from any previous level. Rather than repairing and bringing the self up to date or even developing a new self, now the possibility opens of breaking free of full identification with the self in any importantly limiting way.

Transcendence

... The self, we are coming to realize, is a construct of our consciousness. It is arbitrary, not a constitutional given. Its particular content and form are occasioned by the experience of one's life but are in no sense immutable.

Indeed, and this is the key point, one need not be identified with one particular self-configuration. One may be able to accept a way of being in the world (a self), which is appropriate to the life situation, but set it aside on occasion.

We construct, each of us, a *self* as a record of who we have been, and we mistakenly confuse that record for a prescription for who we can be. Without attention to our inward sensing, we make choices and undertake courses of action in terms of what we have done in the past, and then we often find that our choices are unsatisfying and our actions are not invested with full commitment.

Nothingness

When I begin to realize that my truest identity is as process and not as fixed substance, I am on the verge of a terrible emptiness and a miraculous freedom. The nothingness of being, the transitoriness of substance, the endless possibilities of awareness are so shocking to recognize that often the sensations are those of vertigo, anxiety, and denial. The familiar fear of death and oblivion is but one form of this most existential of confrontations. We feel lost in space without any sense of direction and bereft of all comfort so long as we persist in seeking a given identity or a preexisting form for our existence. Yet, that is exactly what we feel compelled to do over and over again.

We begin to realize that the world which has been the solid foundation of our being is equally a construction of our awareness. We have learned from infancy to see it a certain way, and although we alter that some over the years, essentially we accept what we have been taught and believe that to be the intrinsic nature of being. It is not; it is our construction. Other peoples experience the world differently. No longer can we in the West so blithely and blindly assume that these people are just less intelligent, less scientific, or less developed than we. They have built their worlds in quite other but equally valid ways.

Freedom

It is only after we begin genuinely confronting and incorporating the recognitions that our own identities are solely as processes and that world is the quite arbitrary construction of our awarenesses that we can move toward discovering and appreciating the freedom thus opened to us. If I am but the process of my being, then I can, and indeed must, remake my life each moment, and I can choose to make it quite different than it has been in the past, for the past is no longer the master of this present moment.

Each minute the choice. Freedom and trade-offs. Each possibility has something to make it inviting, but each has some costs. I weigh one against the other, and I choose. And I choose. And I choose.

THE PRIMACY OF THE SUBJECTIVE

Discovery of the Power of Presence

Presence, being here, centeredness, and immediacy—all are terms to point to a fundamental reality. Only in this moment am I alive. All else is in some measure speculative. Only now, *now*, can I make my life different. The client who experiences this fact of great power realizes that its importance goes far beyond the therapeutic office.

Most of us are truly present in the moment but rarely. Those words circle around a fact of unique and powerful significance. Our usual condition has been called *sleepwalking*, while *being truly awake* is that only occasionally achieved state in which we are in a place of power and from which we may have true governance of our lives. To truly and fully experience one's life and one's concerns in a present-tense, here-and-now, active-voice, first-person way is to bring about an evolution in those concerns. Any other posture is impotent. Only those who come to this recognition through working toward full presence fully appreciate what a fundamental truth is here available.

Searching — The Inner Vision

Many people, when they first come to therapy, are not accustomed to giving serious and continued attention to their subjectivity. Only when emotional pain or other distress enforces such awareness do they attend to their inner processes. Even then, many seek chiefly to have this distraction alleviated so they can get back to the *real world* of objective concerns. But the hidden significance of that word *concerns* is that the world of objectivity is only discovered and given meaning through the operation of subjectivity. . . . Therapy's insistence on paying attention to the subjective life is the beginning of a pervasive change. One of the results of this process is that the client may begin to experience the centering of life as being within rather than external. That is a profound transition.

Releasing Latent Potential

To be really centered in one's subjectivity with full presence is to discover conveniently at hand much that is ordinarily unavailable. Mental contents of a kind often regarded as unconscious — memories, impulses, and fantasies usually denied or represented only symbolically—are accessible. The search process has demonstrated that control and choice are greater when consciousness is open, and one now knows that undesired acts need not automatically issue from acceptance of their impulses into awareness.

Summary: Subjective Sovereignty

My own experience and that of those whom I accompany convince me that a great deal of the distress which so many people experience may be traced in no small part to our living as exiles from our own homeland, the inner world of subjective experience. Through psychotherapy, we can overcome the social conditioning which has taught us to be suspicious and guilty about living from the center out, about truly putting internal wholeness at the highest priority, and about making choices in terms of inner sensing of our own unique needs and wants. When we have gained that liberation, the whole experience of being alive can be subtly different.

We know our own individuality; we find richness within our own flow of awareness; we deal with issues and concerns with greater integrity, and we find the possibility of creative and aesthetic participation of life.

The heart of the matter is simple, fundamental, and often totally overlooked — *the true home of each of us is in inner experiencing*. Thus the true mission of psychotherapy is to affect that experiencing in ways which improve the quality of life for the person. Symptoms are superficial. Whether a particular symptom is eliminated, changed, or unaffected is secondary to whether the person having that symptom experiences more vitality, potency, and opportunity in life. Behavior changes are by-products. Whether a specific behavior pattern continues unaffected, is replaced, or is modified is trivial in contrast to whether the person having that pattern discovers more dignity, choice, and personal meaningfulness in life.

Our homeland is within, and there we are sovereign. Until we discover that ancient fact anew and uniquely for each of us as an individual, we are condemned to wander seeking solace where it cannot be found, in the outer world.

A tragic sense of life. One looks from the perspective of subjective centeredness upon human life with a sense of tragedy. . . . One cannot see the human experience in this way without feeling sadness at the great effort of so many to be as they think they should be, at the tremendous caring which somehow is manifested on every side in the midst of so much that is despairing, at the immense outpouring of hope and dedication of which so much is foredoomed because it is so unaware.

It is not that the person who has achieved a measure of subjective sovereignty feels ready to be a new Messiah; usually, quite to the contrary, there is a general feeling of humility before the enormous issues confronting human beings and the astonishing achievements that have been made. The only special perspective is the recognition that there is an absolutely essential first step which is being almost totally overlooked. Until men and women accept their own natures and fully realize that they are the authors, not the victims, of their destinies, all their efforts are foredoomed. So long as human beings mistrust themselves and found their attempts to improve their lot upon antagonism to their own natures, those attempts can be nothing but antagonistic to their creators. This is the tragedy of the human situation.

Drawing on Inner Wisdom

Our identities are as subjects, and thus they are invisible. We are most truly the seeing, not that which is seen. We are the knowing, not what is known. We are the process of being aware, not the content of the awar-ing. Awareness is not measurable in objective terms. We cannot say how much is in awareness or what its shape or dimensions. All such descriptions would make awareness into an object, which it is not. We can talk about memory and its contents, for memory is really only evidenced by its contents. So it is too with consciousness; it is evidenced by what it is we are conscious of, and thus we can talk about how much we are conscious of.

The searching process, which has been so central to what I described . . . is a means for bringing materials into consciousness. It is a way of exploring awareness, like a flashlight probing a dark attic and picking out first one item and then another. Clearly there is much more potential in awareness than we are conscious of at any time. Whether there is, in the ideal state, any limit to awareness is an unanswerable question. Indeed, it may not even be a sensible question, since awareness is not in the same dimension of being as are limits and contents.

Accepting Our God-Nature

To me, God is a word used to point to our ineffable subjectivity, to the unimaginable potential which lies within each of us, to the aspirations which well up within us for greater truth and vividness of living, to our compassion for the tragedy of the human condition, to our pride in the undestroyed but endlessly assaulted dignity of our being, and to something more—to the sense of mystery within which we always live if we are truly aware and to the dedication to explore that mystery which is the very essence of being human.

We human beings take our sense of God from our deepest intuitions as to what is ultimate in our own depths. This is a view born of my own inner searching, of course, and it has been supported by the discoveries of people with whom I've traveled toward the transcendent levels of therapeutic/growth outcomes.

6

RIPPLES OF CHANGE: IMPLICATIONS FOR OTHER DISCIPLINES

*Every response you make is determined by what you think you
are, and what you want to be is what you think you are. What
you want to be, then, must determine every response you make.*

ANONYMOUS[1]

Whatever observations a particular discipline is designed to handle, its underlying meaning cannot be divorced from the beliefs and models of reality shared by individuals involved in it. If those beliefs and models shift, then so do the purpose and meaning of the discipline. Furthermore, since "facts" are not isolated entities independent of the knower, but are actively created by observation and interpretation, then what is "fact" may also shift. Thus the development of transpersonal psychology and the spread of its ideas and models may hold implications for a variety of disciplines.

There exists a little-recognized but pervasive dynamic interplay between cultural beliefs and psychological models. Psychologies and the premises on which they are based are products of the culture from which they spring. Indeed, they are to some extent an autobiography and projection of their originators. Psychologists pose models consistent with their own beliefs and experience and these reflect the stamp of both the culture and the individual that produce them.

Thus theories of human nature in general naturally reflect culturally shared beliefs. A feedback cycle may be set up in which psychologies spring from a given cultural context, become popularized, and then permeate the culture and formalize beliefs about the nature of self, human nature, norms, potentials, and limitations. This dynamic interplay and positive feedback between culture and psychology holds immense potential for either benefit or harm. Alterations in either component could set in train self-reinforcing feedback cycles, with the possibility of producing major shifts in cultural beliefs.

Because everything we do, think, or feel stems in part from who and what we think we are, it may be that one of the most important tasks confronting us is to shift the prevailing limiting cultural beliefs about our basic nature and our relationship to the world. Let us then examine the possible effects of such shifts on a number of disciplines: science, education, philosophy, parapsychology, and social science.

Perhaps the most widely respected general discipline in Western society today is science. Science is, fundamentally, a way of knowing, a way that relies heavily on the logical analysis of sense data. As such it has largely excluded the investigation of subjective experience except inasmuch as this can be shown to correlate with sensorially observable physical effects, e.g., brain wave activity. Such an exclusion maintains the power of the scientific approach at the cost of significantly limiting its range of application.

Many have wondered about the possibility of extending this range and Charles Tart raises the question anew in "States of Consciousness and State-Specific Sciences." He suggests the training of scientists to function in altered states as participant observers to report on their experiences. Tart argues that, due to the limitations of state dependency, we may need a number of different state-dependent sciences. While knowledge gained in one particular state may complement that gained in another, it cannot directly validate or invalidate it. He also suggests the creative possibilities inherent in stimulating interactions between different state-specific sciences.

The next reading, "Different Views from Different States," consists of two letters written in response to Charles Tart's article. These must surely be among the most unusual and remarkable responses ever written to a scientific paper. For the two letters were written in two different states of consciousness and come to diametrically opposite conclusions about the validity of Tart's hypothesis. Here we have the unique situation of a professor of psychiatry, a man respected as both a researcher and philosopher of science, denying the need or usefulness of state-specific sciences while he was in his ordinary state, yet finding the suggestion appropriate while in an altered state. This is compelling support for the power of state-dependent phenomena. Interestingly, the journal *Science* declined to publish the letters.

In "Eye to Eye: Science and Transpersonal Psychology," Ken Wilber takes a different position. He points to the traditional distinctions between empirical, rational, and contemplative knowledge. What can be known by observation, says Wilber, should not be confused with what can be known by reasoning. Moreover, what can be known through contemplation is accessible neither to observation nor reason, transcending both. Knowledge gained through one of these modes of knowing cannot be adequately defined solely in terms of the other two. Science takes as its domain knowledge gained by the application of reason to empirical observation. Wilber therefore questions Tart's assumption that science can be expanded sufficiently to apply to areas of knowledge that are actually the province of contemplation. He proposes instead that transpersonal psychology is in a unique position to be able to employ all three modes in a balanced fashion, thus allowing a fuller psychology than anything heretofore.

In the next paper Roger Walsh points to "The Possible Emergence of Cross-Disciplinary Parallels" as a result of increasing sensitivity to reality. This sensitivity may be enhanced either directly by disciplines such as meditation or indirectly by instrumentation. The resultant view of the fundamental nature of reality may be similar, independent of the object observed or the mode of observation. Our usual pictures may then appear as the illusory products of limited perceptual sensitivity. Thus, with growing scientific sophistication and sensitivity, illusory distortions may be seen through and the fundamental descriptions of reality may show increasing parallels, not only between different branches of science, but also between science and the consciousness disciplines.

Our current educational systems are almost entirely addressed to the mode of reason. Training of the observational and contemplative modes and affective dimension is almost completely lacking. Even within the mode of reason, most emphasis is placed on the acquisition of data and less on actual training and developing skill in reasoning itself.

One of the goals discussed by Tom Roberts in "Education and Transpersonal Relations" is therefore the expansion of the educative process into these other dimensions. Roberts suggests that though the field is very young, a number of useful and enjoyable techniques exist for facilitating the attainment of traditional and nontraditional goals. One of the most important tasks awaiting transpersonal educators is the exploration of the optimal goals and potentials of such an expanded educational curriculum.

Although it has been described for centuries, Western philosophers and scientists have tended to forget the distinction between the two major types of knowledge, symbolic and intimate. Symbolic, map, or inferential knowledge is the knowledge about something given us by symbols such as language, as opposed to the direct knowing of an object that comes from nonsymbolic intimate knowledge. In "Two Modes of Knowledge," Ken Wilber reminds us of this distinction and points out that the failure to remember it results in forgetting that our ordinary conception of the world is only a symbolic knowledge map—a conceptual creation rather than the real world itself. Only by moving to the intimate nonsymbolic knowledge of the contemplative mode and its corresponding state of consciousness can we know the real world.

Parapsychology has traditionally generated both fascination and aversion among scientists. Willis Harman notes in "The Societal Implications and Social Impact of Psi Phenomena" that, thanks to the shifting paradigms and cultural movements of the last few years, the emotional climate has changed and the data of parapsychology is becoming increasingly acceptable. It appears that a number of so-called paranormal abilities may actually represent normal human capacities that are commonly suppressed or disregarded. By examining the premises of the scientific paradigm, Harman points to the reconciliation of science with the exploration of consciousness and psychic phenomena and notes that scientists are forced to confront questions they had previously relegated to philosophers. Harman calls attention to the fact that changing values and images of humanity must inevitably affect the whole fabric of society and wonders whether the transformation he foresees can be accomplished without severe social disruption.

The social implications of a commitment to the inner life and development of transpersonal awareness are not to be underestimated. It has frequently been suggested that the pursuit of self-knowledge is inherently a selfish one that detracts from an involvement with, and contribution to, society. However, such criticism is not valid inasmuch as the product of this work is necessarily a transcendence of limited self-interest. Concern with the general good of one's fellow beings and a desire for harmony with the broader universe is intrinsic to the work. E. F. Schumacher writes:

> It is a grave error to accuse a man who pursues self-knowledge of "turning his back on society." The opposite would be more nearly true: that a man who fails to pursue self-knowledge is and remains a danger to society, for he will tend to misunderstand everything that other people say or do, and remain blissfully unaware of the signficance of many of the things he does himself.[2]

In "The Tao of Personal and Social Transformation," Duane Elgin suggests that expanded awareness is reflected in a quality of life that seeks harmony with nature, both inner and outer, rather than domination over it. For the person working in these areas there is no question of their connection with, and responsiblity for, the larger whole of which they experience themselves to be an inseparable component. For a person beginning to experience what was formerly "other," as "self," it makes no sense not to acknowledge responsibility and the need for ethicality and service. With the attendant reduction in egocentric desires, there is less wish to impose one's will on nature and others and more interest in harmonizing with them in an ecological and Taoistic manner. Fewer desires means less need for consumerism or susceptibility to advertising pressures, resulting in a tendency toward a choiceful life of voluntary simplicity.

A new vision of social interaction and lifestyle emerges as we learn to integrate all aspects of human experience, inner and outer, Eastern and Western, personal and transpersonal. The capacity of human beings to transcend the limitations of social conditioning and to take responsiblity for designing their lives in harmony with nature and others becomes increasingly apparent to those individuals who commit themselves to the self-exploration necessary for direct experience of the deeper nature of their being.

> If life and living are experienced as an unbroken pattern of interconnection that extends from the most minute details of daily existence to the largest scale features of the cosmos, then withdrawal from worldly responsibility is not possible. If a person engages life consciously and directly, there is literally no place to go where one can escape the experiencable connection with all of life.... The task then becomes one of bringing one's life, in all of its diverse expressions, into increasingly conscious and harmonious alignment with the changing web of relationships of which one is an inseparable part.
> —*Duane Elgin*[3]

Notes

1. Anonymous. *A course in miracles*. New York: Foundation for Inner Peace, 1975.
2. Schumacher, E. F. *A guide for the perplexed*. New York: Harper & Row, 1977.
3. Elgin, D. *Voluntary simplicity*. New York: William Morrow, in press.

SCIENCE

States of Consciousness and State-Specific Sciences

CHARLES TART

An increasingly significant number of people are experimenting with ASC's in themselves, and finding the experiences thus gained of extreme importance in their philosophy and style of life. The conflict between experiences in these ASC's and the attitudes and intellectual-emotional systems that have evolved in our ordinary state of consciousness (SoC) is a major factor behind the increased alienation of many people from conventional science. Experiences of ecstasy, mystical union, other "dimensions," rapture, beauty, space-and-time transcendence, and transpersonal knowledge, all common in ASC's, are simply not treated adequately in conventional scientific approaches. These experiences will not "go away" if we crack down more on psychedelic drugs, for immense numbers of people now practice various nondrug techniques for producing ASC's, such as meditation and yoga.[1]

The purpose of this article is to show that it is possible to investigate and work with the important phenomena of ASC's in a manner which is perfectly compatible with the essence of scientific method. The conflict discussed above is not necessary.

STATES OF CONSCIOUSNESS

An ASC may be defined for the purposes of this article as a qualitative alteration in the overall pattern of mental functioning, such that the experiencer feels his consciousness is radically different from the way it functions ordinarily. An SoC is thus defined not in terms of any particular content of consciousness, or specific behavior or physiological change, but in terms of the overall patterning of psychological functioning.

An analogy with computer functioning can clarify this definition. A computer has a complex program of many subroutines. If we reprogram it quite differently, the same sorts of input data may be handled in quite different ways; we will be able to predict very little from our knowledge of the old program about the effects of varying the input, even though old and new programs have some subroutines in common. The new program with its input-output interactions must be studied in and of itself. An ASC is analogous to changing temporarily the program of a computer.

The ASC's experienced by almost all ordinary people are dreaming states and the . . . transitional states between sleeping and waking. Many other people experience another ASC, alcohol intoxication.

The relatively new (to our culture) ASC's that are now having such an impact are those produced by marijuana, more powerful psychedelic drugs such as LSD, meditative states, so-called possession states, and auto-hypnotic states.[2]

STATES OF CONSCIOUSNESS AND PARADIGMS

It is useful to compare this concept of an SoC, a qualitatively distinct organization of the patterning of mental functioning, with Kuhn's concept of paradigms in science.[3] A paradigm is an intellectual achievement that underlies normal science and attracts and guides the work of an enduring number of adherents in their scientific activity. It is a kind of "super theory," a formulation of scope wide enough to affect the organization of most or all of the major known phenomena of its field. Yet it is sufficiently open-ended that there still remain important problems to be solved within that framework. Examples of important paradigms in the history of science have been Copernican astronomy and Newtonian dynamics.

Because of their tremendous success, paradigms undergo a change which, in principle, ordinary scientific theories do not undergo. An ordinary scientific theory is always subject to further questioning and testing as it is extended. A paradigm becomes an implicit framework for most scientists working within it; it is the natural way of looking at things and doing things. It does not seriously occur to the adherents of a paradigm to question it any more (we may ignore, for the moment, the occurrence of scientific revolutions). Theories become referred to as laws: people talk of the law of gravity, not the theory of gravity, for example.

A paradigm serves to concentrate the attention of a researcher on sensible problem areas and to prevent him from wasting his time on what might be trivia. On the other hand, by implicitly defining some lines of research as trivial or nonsensical, a paradigm acts like a blinder. Kuhn has discussed this blinding function as a key factor in the lack of effective communications during paradigm clashes.

The concept of a paradigm and of an SoC are quite similar. Both constitute complex, interlocking sets of rules and theories that enable a person to interact with and interpret experiences within an environment. In both cases, the rules are largely implicit. They are not recognized as tentative working hypotheses; they operate automatically and the person feels he is doing the obvious or natural thing.

The thesis I shall now present in detail is that we can deal with the important aspects of ASC's using the essence of scientific method, even though a variety of nonessentials, unfortunately identified with current science, hinder such an effort.

THE NATURE OF KNOWLEDGE

Basically, science (from the Latin *scire*, to know) deals with knowledge. Knowledge may be defined as an immediately given experiential feeling of congruence between two different kinds of experience, a matching. One set of experiences may be regarded as perceptions of the external world, of others, of oneself; the second set may be regarded as a theory; a scheme, a system of understanding. The feeling of congruence is something immediately given in experience, although many refinements have been worked out for judging degrees of congruence.

All knowledge, then, is basically experiential knowledge. Even my knowledge of the physical world can be reduced to this: given certain sets of experiences, which I (by assumption) attribute to the external world activating my sensory apparatus, it may be possible for me to compare them with purely internal experiences (memories, previous knowledge) and predict with a high degree of reliability other kinds of experiences, which I again attribute to the external world.

Because science has been incredibly successful in dealing with the physical world, it has been historically associated with a philosophy of physicalism, the belief that reality is all reducible to certain kinds of physical entities. The vast majority of phenomena of ASC's have no known physical manifestations: thus to physicalistic philosophy they are epiphenomena, not worthy of study. But insofar as science deals with knowledge, it need not restrict itself only to physical kinds of knowlege.

THE ESSENCE OF SCIENTIFIC METHOD

I shall discuss the essence of scientific method, and show that this essence is perfectly compatible with an enlarged study of the important phenomena of ASC's. In particular, I propose that state-specific sciences (SSS) be developed.

The development of scientific method may be seen as a determined effort to systematize the process of acquiring knowledge in such a way as to minimize the various pitfalls of observation and reasoning.

I shall discuss four basic rules of scientific method to which an investigator is committed: (i) good observations; (ii) the public nature of observation; (iii) the necessity to theorize logically; and (iv) the testing of theory by observable consequences; all these constitute the scientific enterprise. I shall consider the wider application of each rule to ASC's and indicate how unnecessary physicalistic restrictions may be dropped. I will show that all these commitments or rules can be accommodated in the development of SSS's that I propose.

OBSERVATION

The scientist is committed to observe as well as possible the phenomena of interest and to search constantly for better ways of making these observations. But our paradigmatic commitments, our SoC's, make us likely to observe certain parts of reality and to ignore or observe with error certain other parts of it.

Many of the most important phenomena of ASC's have been observed poorly or not at all because of the physicalistic labeling of them as epiphenomena, so that they have been called "subjective," "ephemeral," "unreliable," or "unscientific." Observations of internal processes are probably much more difficult to make than those of external physical processes, because of their inherently greater complexity. The essence of science, however, is that we observe what there is to be observed whether it is difficult or not.

We must consider one other problem of observation. One of the traditional idols of science, the "detached observer," has no place in dealing with many internal phenomena of SoC's. Not only are the observer's perceptions selective, he may also affect the things he observes. We must try to understand the characteristics of each individual observer in order to compensate for them.

A recognition of the unreality of the detached observer in the psychological sciences is becoming widespread, under the topics of experimenter bias[4] and demand characteristics.[5] A similar recognition long ago occurred in physics when it was realized that the observed was altered by the process of observation at subatomic levels. When we deal with ASC's where the observer is the experiencer of the ASC, this factor is of paramount importance. Knowing the characteristics of the observer can also confound the process of consensual validation, which I shall now consider.

PUBLIC NATURE OF OBSERVATION

Observations must be public in that they must be replicable by any properly trained observer.

The physicalistic accretion to this rule of consensual validation is that, physical data being the only "real" data, internal phenomena must be reduced to physiological or behavioral data to become reliable or they will be ignored entirely. I believe most physical observations to be much more readily replicable by any trained observer because they are inherently simpler phenomena than internal ones. In principle, however, consensual validation of internal phenomena by a trained observer is quite possible.

Given the high complexity of the phenomena associated with ASC's, the need for replication by trained observers is exceptionally important. Since it generally takes 4 to 10 years of intensive training to produce a scientist in any of our conventional sciences, we should not be surprised that there has been very little reliability of observations by untrained observers of ASC phenomena.

Further, for the state-specific sciences that I propose should be established, we cannot specify the requirements that would constitute adequate training. These would only be determined after considerable trial and error. We should also recognize that very few people might complete the training successfully. Some people do not have the necessary innate characteristics to become physicists, and some probably do not have the innate characteristics to become, say, scientific investigators of meditative states.

Public observation, then, always refers to a limited, specially trained public. It is only by basic agreement among those specially trained people that data become accepted as a foundation for the development of a science. That laymen cannot replicate the observations is of little relevance.

A second problem in consensual validation arises from a phenomenon predicted by my concept of ASC's, but not yet empirically investigated, namely, state-specific communication. Given that an ASC is an overall qualitative and quantitative shift in the complex functioning of consciousness, such that there are new "logics" and perceptions (which would constitute a paradigm shift), it is quite reasonable to hypothesize that communication may take a different pattern. For two observers, both of whom, we assume, are fluent in communicating with each other in a given SoC, communication about some new observations may seem adequate to them, or may be improved or deteriorated in specific ways. To an outside observer, an observer in a different SoC, the communication between these two observers may seem "deteriorated."

Practically all investigations of communication by persons in ASC's have resulted in reports of deterioration of communication abilities. In designing their studies, however, these investigators have not taken into account the fact that the pattern of communication may have changed. If I am listening to two people speaking in English, and they suddenly begin to intersperse words and phrases in Polish, I, as an outside (that is, a non-Polish speaking) observer, will note a gross deterioration in communication. Adequacy of communication between people in the same SoC and across SoC's must be empirically determined.

Thus consensual validation may be restricted by the fact that only observers in the same ASC are able to communicate adequately with each other, and they may not be able to communicate adequately to someone in a different SoC, say normal consciousness.[6]

THEORIZING

A scientist may theorize about his observations as much as he wishes to, but the theory he develops must consistently account for all that he has observed, and should have a logical structure that other scientists can comprehend (but not necessarily accept).

The requirement to theorize logically and consistently with the data is not as simple as it looks, however. Any logic consists of a basic set of assumptions and a set of rules for manipulating information, based on these assumptions. Change the assumptions, or change the rules, and there may be entirely different outcomes from the same data. A paradigm, too, is a logic: it has certain assumptions and rules for working within these assumptions. By changing the paradigm, altering the SoC, the nature of theory building may change radically. Thus a person in SoC 2 might come to very different conclusions about the nature of the same events that he observed in SoC 1. An investigator in SoC 1 may comment on the comprehensibility of the second person's ideas from the point of view (paradigm) of SoC 1, but can say nothing about their inherent validity. A scientist who could enter either SoC 1 or SoC 2, however, could pronounce on the comprehensibility of the other's theory, and the adherence of that theory to the rules and logic of SoC 2. Thus, scientists trained in the same SoC may check on the logical validity of each other's theorizing. We have then the possibility of a state-specific logic underlying theorizing in various SoC's.

OBSERVABLE CONSEQUENCES

Any theory a scientist develops must have observable consequences, and from that theory it must be possible to make predictions that can be verified by observation. If such verification is not possible, the theory must be considered invalid, regardless of its elegance, logic, or other appeal.

Ordinarily we think of empirical validation, of validation in terms of testable consequences that produce physical effects, but this is misleading. Any effect, whether interpreted as physical or nonphysical, is ultimately an experience in the observer's mind. All that is essentially required to validate a theory is that it predict that "When a certain experience (observed condition) has occurred, another (predicted) kind of experience will follow, under specified experiential conditions." Thus a perfectly scientific theory may be based on data that have no physical existence.

STATE-SPECIFIC SCIENCES

We tend to envision the practice of science like this: centered around interest in some particular range of subject matter, a small number of highly selected, talented, and rigorously trained people spent considerable time making detailed observations on the subject matter of interest. They may or may not have special places (laboratories) or instruments or methods to assist them in making finer observations. They speak to one another in a special language which they feel conveys precisely the important facts of their field. Using this language, they confirm and extend each other's knowledge of certain data basic to the field. They theorize about their basic data and construct elaborate systems. They validate these by recourse to further observation. These trained people all have a long-term commitment to the constant refinement of observation and extension of theory. Their activity is frequently incomprehensible to laymen.

This general description is equally applicable to a variety of sciences, or areas that could become sciences, whether we called such areas biology, physics, chemistry, psychology, understanding of mystical states, or drug-induced enhancement of cognitive processes. The particulars of research would look very different, but the basic scientific method running through all is the same.

More formally, I now propose the creation of various state-specific sciences. If such sciences could be created, we would have a group of highly skilled, dedicated, and trained practitioners able to achieve certain SoC's, and able to agree with one another that they have attained a common state. While in that SoC, they might then investigate other areas of interest, whether these be totally internal phenomena of that given state, the interaction of that state with external, physical reality, or people in other SoC's.

The fact that the experimenter should be able to function skillfully in the SoC itself for a state-specific science does not necessarily mean that he would always be the subject. While he might often be the subject, observer, and experimenter simultaneously, it would be quite possible for him to collect data from experimental manipulations of other subjects in the SoC, and either be in that SoC himself at the time of data collection or be in that SoC himself for data reduction and theorizing.

Examples of some observations made and theorizing done by a scientist in a specific ASC would illustrate the nature of a proposed state-specific science. But this is not possible because no state-specific sciences have yet been established.[7] Also, any example that would make good sense to the readers of this article (who are, presumably, all in a normal SoC) would not really illustrate the uniqueness of a state-specific science. If it did make sense, it would be an example of a problem that could be approached adequately from both the ASC and normal SoC's, and thus it would be too easy to see the entire problem in terms of accepted scientific procedures for normal SoC's, and miss the point about the necessity for developing state-specific sciences.

STATE-SPECIFIC SCIENCES AND RELIGION

Some aspects of organized religion appear to resemble state-specific sciences. There are techniques that allow the believer to enter an ASC and then have religious experiences in that ASC which are proof of his religious belief. People who have had such experiences usually describe them as ineffable in important ways—that is, as not fully comprehensible in an ordinary SoC. Conversions at revivalistic meetings are the most common example of religious experiences occurring in various ASC's induced by an intensely emotional atmosphere.

In examining the esoteric training systems of some religions, there seems to be even more resemblance between such mystical ways and state-specific sciences, for here we often have the picture of devoted specialists, complex techniques, and repeated experiencing of the ASC's in order to further religious knowledge.

Nevertheless the proposed state-specific sciences are not simply religion in a new guise. The use of ASC's in religion may involve the kind of commitment to searching for truth that is needed for developing a state-specific science, but practically all the religions we know might be defined as state-specific technologies, operated in the service of a priori belief systems. The experiencers of ASC's in most religious contexts have already been thoroughly indoctrinated in a particular belief system. This belief system may then mold the content of the ASC's to create specific experiences which reinforce or validate the belief system.

The crucial distinction between a religion utilizing ASC's and a state-specific science is the commitment of the scientist to reexamine constantly his own belief system and to question the obvious in spite of its intellectual or emotional appeal to him. Investigators of ASC's would certainly encounter an immense variety of phenomena labeled religious experience or mystical revelation during the development of state-specific sciences, but they would have to remain committed to examining these phenomena more carefully, sharing their observations and techniques with colleagues, and subjecting the beliefs (hypotheses, theories) that result from such experiences to the requirement of leading to testable predictions. In practice, because we are aware of the immense emotional power of mystical experiences, that would be a difficult task, but it is one that will have to be undertaken by disciplined investigators if we are to understand various ASC's.

RELATIONSHIP BETWEEN STATE-SPECIFIC SCIENCES

Any state-specific science may be considered as consisting of two parts, observations and theorizations. The observations are what can be experienced relatively directly; the theories are the *inferences* about what sort of non-observable factors account for the observations. For example, the phenomena of synesthesia (seeing colors as a result of hearing sounds) is a theoretical proposition for me in my ordinary SoC: I do not experience it, and can only generate theories about what other people report about it. If I were under the influence of a psychedelic drug such as LSD or marijuana I could probably experience synesthesia directly, and my descriptions of the experience would become data. [8]

It would be naively reductionistic to say that the work in one state-specific science *validates* or *invalidates* the work in a second state-specific science; I prefer to say that two different state-specific sciences, where they overlap, provide quite different points of view with respect to certain kinds of theories and data, and thus complement each other.[9] The proposed creation of state-specific sciences neither validates nor invalidates the activities of normal consciousness sciences (NCS). The possibility of developing certain state-specific sciences means only that certain kinds of phenomena may be handled more adequately within these potential new sciences.

The possibility of stimulating interactions between different state-specific sciences is very real. Creative breakthroughs in NCS have frequently been made by scientists temporarily going into an ASC.[10] In such instances, the scientists concerned saw quite different views of their problems and performed different kinds of reasoning, conscious or nonconscious, which led to results that could be tested within their NCS.

A current example of such interaction is the finding that in Zen meditation (a highly developed discipline in Japan) there are physiological correlates of meditative experiences, such as decreased frequency of alpha-rhythm, which can also be produced by means of instrumentally aided feedback-learning techniques.[11] This finding might elucidate some of the processes peculiar to each discipline.

INDIVIDUAL DIFFERENCES

A widespread and misleading assumption that hinders the development of state-specific sciences and confuses their interrelationships is the assumption that because two people are normal (not certified insane), their ordinary SoC's are essentially the same. In reality I suspect that there are enormous differences between the SoC's of some normal people. Because societies train people to behave and communicate along socially approved lines, these differences are covered up.

For example, some people think in images, others in words. Some can voluntarily anesthetize parts of their body, most cannot. Some recall past events by imaging the scene and looking at the relevant details; others use complex verbal processes with no images.

This means that person A may be able to observe certain kinds of experiential data that person B cannot experience in his ordinary SoC, no matter how hard B tries. There may be several consequences. Person B may think that A is insane, too imaginative, or a liar, or he may feel inferior to A. Person A may also feel himself odd, if he takes B as a standard of normality.

Another important source of individual differences, little understood at present, is the degree to which an individual may first make a particular observation or form a concept in one SoC and then be able to reexperience or comprehend it in another SoC. That is, many items of information which were state-specific when observed initially may be learned and somehow transferred (fully or partially) to another SoC. Differences across individuals, various combinations of SoC's, and types of experience will probably be enormous.

I have only outlined the complexities created by individual differences in normal SoC's and have used the normal SoC as a baseline for comparison with ASC's; but it is evident that every SoC must eventually be compared against every other SoC.

The first important problem in the proposed development of state-specific sciences is the obvious perception of truth. In many ASC's, one's experience is that one is obviously and lucidly experiencing truth directly, without question. An immediate result of this may be an extinction of the desire for further questioning. Further, this experience of obvious truth, while not necessarily preventing the individual investigator from further examining his data, may not arouse his desire for consensual validation. Since one of the greatest strengths of science is its insistence on consensual validation of basic data, this can be a serious drawback. Investigators attempting to develop state-specific sciences will have to learn to distrust the obvious.

A second major problem in developing state-specific sciences is that in some ASC's one's abilities to visualize and imagine are immensely enhanced, so that whatever one imagines seems perfectly real. Thus one can imagine that something is being observed and experience it as datum. If one can essentially conjure up anything one wishes, how can we ever get at truth?

One way of looking at this problem is to consider any such vivid imaginings as potential effects: they are data, in the sense that what can be vividly imagined in a given SoC is important to know. It may not be the case that anything can be imagined with equal facility, and the relationships between what can be imagined may show a lawful pattern.

The effects of this enhanced vividness of the imagination in some ASC's will be complicated further by two other important problems, namely, experimenter bias,[4, 5] and the fact that one person's illusion in a given ASC can sometimes be communicated to another person in the same ASC so that a kind of false consensual validation results. Again, the only long-term solution to this would be the requirement that predictions based on concepts arising from various experiences be verified experimentally.

A third major problem is that state-specific sciences probably cannot be developed for all ASC's: some ASC's may depend on or result from genuine deterioration of observational and reasoning abilities, or a deterioration of volition. Those SoC's for which state-specified sciences might well be developed will be discussed later, but it should be made clear that the development of each science should result from trial and error and not from a priori decisions based on reasoning in our ordinary SoC's.

A fourth major problem is that of ineffability. Some experiences are ineffable in the sense that: (i) a person may experience them, but be unable to express or conceptualize them adequately to himself; (ii) while a person may be able to conceptualize **an** experience to himself he may not be able to communicate it adequately to anyone else. Certain phenomena of the first type may simply be inaccessible to scientific investigation. Phenomena of the second type may be accessible to scientific investigation only insofar as we are willing to recognize that a science, in the sense of following most of the basic rules, may exist only for a single person. Insofar as such a solitary science would lack all the advantages gained by consensual validation, we could not expect it to have as much power and rigor as conventional scientific endeavor.

Many phenomena which are now considered ineffable may not be so in reality. This may be a matter of our general lack of experience with ASC's and the lack of an adequate language for communicating about ASC phenomena. In most well-developed languages the major part of the vocabulary was developed primarily in adaptation to survival in the physical world.

Finally, we should recognize the possibility that various phenomena of ASC's may be too complex for human beings to understand. The phenomena may depend on or be affected by so many variables that we shall never understand them. In the history of science, however, many phenomena which appeared too complex at first were eventually comprehensible.

PROSPECTS

I believe that an examination of human history and our current situation provides the strongest argument for the necessity of developing state-specific sciences. Throughout history man has been influenced by the spiritual and mystical factors that are expressed (usually in watered-down form) in the religions that attract the masses of people. Spiritual and mystical experiences are primary phenomena of various ASC's: because of such experiences, untold numbers of both the noblest and most horrible acts of which people are capable have been committed. Yet in all the time that Western science has existed, no concerted attempt has been made to understand these ASC phenomena in scientific terms.

It was the hope of many that religions were simply a form of superstition that would be left behind in our "rational" age. Not only has this hope failed, but our own understanding of the nature of reasoning now makes it clear that it can never be fulfilled. Reason is a tool, and a tool that is wielded in the service of assumptions, beliefs, and needs which are not themselves subject to reason. The irrational, or, better yet, the *a*rational, will not disappear from the human situation. Our immense success in the development of the physical sciences has not been particularly successful in formulating better philosophies of life, or increasing our real knowledge of ourselves. The sciences we have developed to date are not very human sciences. They tell us how to do things, but give us no scientific insights on questions of what to do, what not to do, or why to do things.

The youth of today and mature scientists in increasing numbers are turning to meditation, oriental religions, and personal use of psychedelic drugs. The phenomena encountered in these ASC's provide more satisfaction and are more relevant to the formulation of philosophies of life and deciding upon appropriate ways of living, than "pure reason."[12] My own impressions are that very large numbers of scientists are now personally exploring ASC's, but few have begun to connect with their scientific activities.

It is difficult to predict what the chances are of developing state-specific sciences. Our knowledge is still too diffuse and dependent on our normal SoC's. Yet I think it is probable that state-specific sciences can be developed for such SoC's as auto-hypnosis, meditative states, lucid dreaming, marijuana intoxication, LSD intoxication, self-remembering, reverie, and biofeedback-induced states.[13] In all of these SoC's, volition seems to be retained, so that the observer can indeed carry out experiments on himself or others or both. Some SoC's, in which the volition to experiment during the state may disappear, but in which some experimentation can be carried out if special conditions are prepared before the state is entered, might be alcohol intoxication, ordinary dreaming, hypnogogic and hypnopompic states, and high dreams. It is not clear whether other ASC's would be suitable for developing state-specific sciences or whether mental deterioration would be too great. Such questions will only be answered by experiment.

I have nothing against religious and mystical groups. Yet I suspect that the vast majority of them have developed compelling belief systems rather than state-specific sciences. Will scientific method be extended to the development of state-specific sciences so as to improve our human situation? Or will the immense power of ASC's be left in the hands of many cults and sects? I hope that the development of state-specific sciences will be our goal.

Notes

1. Naranjo, C. and Ornstein, R. *On the psychology of meditation.* New York: Viking, 1971.
2. Note that an SoC is defined by the stable parameters of the pattern that constitutes it, not only by the particular technique of inducing that pattern, for some ASC's can be induced by a variety of induction methods. By analogy, to understand the altered computer program you must study what it does, not study the programmer who originally set it up.

3. Kuhn, T. *The structure of scientific revolutions*. Chicago: University of Chicago Press, 1962.

4. Rosenthal, R. *Experimenter effects in behavioral research*. New York: Appleton-Century-Croft, 1966.

5. Orne, M. *Amer. Psychol*, 1962, *17*, 775

6. A state-specific scientist might find his own work somewhat incomprehensible when he was not in that SoC because of the phenomenon of state-specific memory—that is not enough of his work would transfer to his ordinary SoC to make it comprehensible, even though it would make perfect sense when he was again in the ASC in which he did his scientific work.

7. "Ordinary consciousness science" is not a good example of a "pure" state-specific science because many important discoveries have occurred during ASC's, such as reverie, dreaming, and meditative-like states.

8. An attempt to describe the phenomena of marijuana intoxication in terms that make sense to the user, as well as the investigator, has been presented elsewhere. See Tart, C. *On being stoned: A psychological study of marijuana intoxication*. Palo Alto: Science and Behavior Books, 1971.

9. Bohr, N. in *Essays*, 1958–1962, on *Atomic physics and human knowledge*. New York: Wiley, 1963.

10. Ghiselin, B. *The creative process*. New York: New American Library, 1963.

11. Green, E., Green, A., Walters, E. *J. Transpers. Psychol.*, 1970, *2*, 1.

12. Needleman, J. *The new religions*. New York: Doubleday, 1970.

13. Tart, C. *Altered states of consciousness: A book of readings*. New York: Wiley, 1969.

Different Views from Different States

GORDON GLOBUS

June 30, 1972

Editors of Science
Science
American Association for the Advancement of Science
1515 Massachusetts Avenue, N.W.
Washington, D.C. 20005

Dear Sirs:

It is commendable that *Science* has published Tart's controversial article, "States of Consciousness and State-Specific Sciences." Tart rightfully has emphasized the importance of scientific investigation into altered states of consciousness (ASC's). It is hard to imagine a moment in scientific history when science has lagged so far behind the culture at large that even otherwise ordinary students recognize the irrelevance of the few behavorial studies on psychedelic drugs. Unfortunately, Tart's philosophy of science perspective is so narrow, and his views on the relations among "state-specific sciences" so radical, that his discussion is liable to be dismissed by those toward whom it is directed, i.e., the "straight" scientific establishment reading the paper in an ordinary state of consciouness.

The discussion of the "public nature of observation" as one basic rule of the scientific method is quite beside the issue. Tart is correct in indicating that "observations must be public in that they must be replicable by any properly trained observer." However, in addition to replicability, the observations must be equally accessible to all observers. The methodological problem with respect to ASC's is precisely that the subject has a special access to his own consciousness that no other observer has.

This is the fundamental problem in investigating ASC's and is aside from difficulties in describing complex ASC's, the training of the observer, or his "innate characteristics."

Until empirical investigation proves otherwise, it would seem most justifiable and parsimonious to develop one science for all states of consciousness—ordinary and extraordinary—rather than following the dubious path of a science (and scientists) for each state of consciousness.

Gordon G. Globus, M.D.
Department of Psychiatry & Human Behavior
University of California Irvine

July 10, 1972

Editors of Science
Science
American Association for the Advancement of Science
1515 Massachusetts Avenue, N.W.
Washington, D.C. 20005

Dear Sirs:

This letter is in response to my previous letter, which was critical of Tart's recent discussion on altered states of consciousness (ASC's). I happened to recall Tart's paper while in an ASC and — to my great amazement — his proposal that a science specific to a given ASC may be independent of sciences specific to other ASCs now seems quite correct to me. *I therefore immediately drafted this letter while remaining in the ASC.*

It is quite apparent to me at this moment that I do not appreciate in the ordinary state of consciousness just what the ASC is like. The peak of the ASC takes me quite by surprise as I forget what a unique experience it is until I am in it again. It seems clear to me that if I were to talk with a person in an ordinary state, he could not appreciate my unique experience at this moment; nor, I now predict, will I fully appreciate it when I again regain the ordinary state.

I am struck, then, by the extraordinary paradox that Tart's proposal for state-specific sciences seems absurd to me in an ordinary state but quite correct in terms of my "incorrigible experience" while in an ASC. I have retained my critical stance toward all other issues in Tart's paper with which I previously disagreed.

ADDED IN PROOF: Again in an ordinary state, I would argue in favor of one science for all states of consciousness and trust that there is an explanation for my experience that while in an ASC, the ASC seems clearly incomprehensible to an ordinary state. It seems obvious to me that I can remember what occurred in the ASC, but I can't remember it in the way I experienced it at that time, i.e., the memory is not veridical. There seems no way to retrieve completely the experience in the ASC without entering again the ASC, which supports Tart's thesis. But available scientific data on "state-dependent learning" easily can explain this phenomenon.

It seems to me, then, that at an experiential level Tart may have a sound point in favor of state-specific science, but that at a conceptual level a single science still can encompass all states of consciousness. In any case, the difference in my letters, written in both ordinary and altered states of consciousness, supports scientific interest in these intriguing phenomena.

Gordon G. Globus, M.D.
Department of Psychiatry & Human Behavior
University of California Irvine

Eye to Eye: Science and Transpersonal Psychology

KEN WILBER

It is probably true that the single greatest issue today facing transpersonal psychology is its relation to empirical science. The burning issue is *not* the scope of transpersonal psychology, not its subject matter, not its methodology — not its premises, not its conclusions, and not its sources — because, according to modern thinking, *all* of those are purely secondary issues compared with whether or not transpersonal psychology itself is *valid* in the first place. That is, whether it is an *empirical science*. For, the argument goes, if transpersonal psychology is not an empirical science, then it has no valid epistemology, no valid means of acquiring knowledge. There is no use trying to figure out the range or scope or methods of knowledge of the new and "higher" field of transpersonal psychology until you can demonstrate that you *have* actual knowledge of any sort to begin with.

I would like, then, to examine briefly the nature of science, the nature of transpersonal psychology, and the relationship between them.

THREE EYES OF THE SOUL

St. Bonaventure, a favorite philosopher of the mystics, taught that men and women have at least three modes of attaining knowledge — "three eyes," as he put it: the *eye of flesh*, by which we perceive the external world of space, time, and objects; the *eye of reason*, by which we attain a knowledge of philosophy, logic, and the mind itself; and the *eye of contemplation*, by which we rise to a knowledge of transcendent realities.

Now that particular wording — eye of flesh, mind, and contemplation — is Christian; but similar ideas can be found in every major school of traditional psychology, philosophy, and religion. The "three eyes" of a human being correspond, in fact, to the three major realms of being described by the perennial philosophy, which are the gross (flesh and material), the subtle (mental and animic), and the causal (transcendent and contemplative). These realms have been described extensively elsewhere, and I wish here only to point to their unanimity among traditional psychologists and philosophers.[1, 2, 3]

To extend on Bonaventure's insights, we moderns might say that the eye of flesh participates in a select world of shared sensory experience, which it partially creates and partially discloses. This is the "gross realm," the realm of space, time, and matter. It is the realm *shared* by all those possessing a similar eye of flesh. ... This is basic sensorimotor intelligence—object constancy—the eye of flesh. It is the *empirical eye*, the eye of sensory experience. It should be said, at the start, that I am using the term "empirical" as it is employed in philosophy: capable of detection by the five human senses or their extensions.

The eye of reason, or, more generally, the eye of mind, participates in a world of ideas, images, logic, and concepts. ... Because so much of modern thought is based solely on the empirical eye, the eye of flesh, it is important to remember that the mental eye *cannot* be reduced to the fleshy eye. The mental field includes but transcends the sensory field. ... Although the eye of mind relies upon the eye of flesh for much of its information, not all mental knowledge comes strictly from fleshy knowledge, nor does it deal solely with objects of the flesh. Our knowledge is *not* entirely empirical and fleshy. The truth of a logical deduction is based on internal consistency, it is not based on its relation to sensory objects.

The eye of contemplation is to the eye of reason as the eye of reason is to the eye of flesh. Just as reason transcends flesh, so contemplation transcends reason. Just as reason cannot be reduced to, nor derived from, fleshy knowledge, so contemplation cannot be reduced to nor derived from reason. Where the eye of reason is trans-empirical, the eye of contemplation is trans-rational, trans-logical, and trans-mental.

Let us simply assume that all men and women possess an eye of flesh, an eye of reason, and an eye of contemplation; that each eye has its own objects of knowledge (sensory, mental, and transcendental); that a higher eye cannot be reduced to nor explained in terms of a lower eye; that each eye is valid and useful in its own field, but commits a fallacy when it attempts, by itself, to fully grasp higher or lower realms.

The only point I wish here to emphasize is that when one eye tries to usurp the role of any of the other eyes, a category mistake occurs. And it can occur in any direction: the eye of contemplation is as ill-equipped to disclose the facts of the eye of flesh as the eye of flesh is incapable of grasping the truths of the eye of contemplation. Sensation, reason, and contemplation disclose their own truths in their own realms, and any time one eye tries to see for another eye, blurred vision results.

Now that type of category error has been *the* great problem for almost every major religion.

The point is that Buddhism and Christianity and other religions contained, at their summit, ultimate insights into ultimate reality, but these trans-verbal insights were invariably all mixed up with rational truths and empirical facts. Mankind had not, as it were, yet learned to differentiate and separate the eyes of flesh, reason, and contemplation. And because (for example) revelation was confused with logic and with empirical fact, and all three were presented as *one truth*, then two things happened: the philosophers came in and destroyed the rational side of religion, and science came in and destroyed the empirical side. . . . From that point on, spirituality in the West was dismantled, and only philosophy and science remained.

Within a century, however, philosophy as a rational system — a system based on the eye of mind — was in its own turn decimated, and decimated by the new scientific empiricism. At that point, human knowledge was *reduced* to only the eye of flesh. Gone was the contemplative eye; gone the mental eye — and mankind restricted its means of valid knowledge to the eye of flesh.

For science became scientism. It did not just speak for the eye of flesh, but for the eye of mind and for the eye of contemplation as well. In so doing, it fell prey to precisely the same category mistakes that it discovered in dogmatic theology, and for which it made religion dearly pay. The scienticians tried to force science, with its eye of flesh, to work for all three eyes. And that is a category error. And for that not only science but the world has paid dearly.

Thus, in effect, the sole criterion of truth came to be the scientific criterion, that is to say, a sensorimotor test by the eye of flesh based on measurement. . . . And yet here is the real point: "This position on the part of the scientists was . . . pure bluff"[4] of the part playing the whole. The eye of flesh came to say, what it can't see does not exist; whereas what it should have said was, what it can't see it can't see.

A "HIGHER" SCIENCE

Is it not possible that scientists themselves have defined the scientific method in a too narrow fashion? Could a more expanded science be applied to the realm of the mind's eye and the realm of the eye of flesh? Is science *tied* to the eye of flesh, or can it expand into the eye of mind and contemplation? Is state-specific science — science occurring on higher states of consciousness — a possibility or a well-intentioned mistake?

Charles Tart believes that the scientific method has been unnecessarily and arbitrarily limited to the eye of flesh by a "physicalistic bias,"[5, 6] the assumption that only material entities are worth studying. The scientific method itself, he feels, can be freed from its materialistic accretions and applied to higher states of consciousness and being (and that is the concept of state-specific sciences). He thus concludes that "the essence of scientific method is perfectly compatible with the study of various altered states of consciousness."

My opinion is twofold: first, Tart has defined science in such a broad fashion that it can apply to all sorts of endeavors. And, second, the tighter and firmer we make his propositions, in order to avoid that difficulty, then the less they apply to higher states of consciousness and the more they return to the old physicalistic science.

If this is so, then it seems that the scientific method is not well suited to the higher states of being and consciousness, but rather must remain basically what it has always been: the best method yet devised to discover the facts of the realm of the eye of flesh. My own opinion is that Tart, in his pioneering attempts to legitimize the *existence* of higher states of consciousness, has inadvertently applied lower-state-specific criteria to the higher states in general.

Empirical/physical research conducted by the eye of flesh or its extensions will always be important *adjuncts* to transpersonal psychology, but they will never form its core, which alone is concerned with the eye of contemplation. Transpersonal psychology is a state-specific enterprise (not science), which—because it transcends the eye of flesh and the eye of reason—is free to use both; the former in scientific-empiric studies, the latter in philosophical/psychological inquiry. But it cannot be grasped or defined by either.

THE PROBLEM OF PROOF

It is important to realize that scientific knowledge is not the only form of knowledge; it is simply a refined eye of flesh, and there exists beyond it mental knowledge and contemplative knowledge. Thus, the fact that transpersonal psychology is not a science doesn't mean that it is invalid, emotional, nonverifiable, antireason, noncognitive, and meaningless. Transpersonal psychologists tend to panic when it is said that transpersonal psychology is not a science, because the scienticians have taught us that "nonscientific" means "not verifiable." But if transpersonal psychology is nonscientific, how *can* it be verified?

This seems to be a problem because we do not see that all knowledge is essentially similar in structure. That is, all knowledge consists of three basic components:

1. *An instrumental or injunctive wing:* This is a set of instructions, simple or complex, internal or external. All have the form: "If you want to see this, do this."

2. *An illuminative wing:* This is an illuminative *seeing* by the particular eye of knowledge evoked by the injunctive wing. Besides being self-illuminative, it leads to the possibility of:

3. *A communal wing:* This is the actual sharing of the illuminative seeing with others who are using the same eye. If the shared vision is agreed upon by others, this constitutes a communal proof of true seeing.

Those are the basic wings of any type of true knowledge using any eye. Knowledge does become more complicated when one eye tries to match its knowledge with a higher or lower eye, but these basic wings underlie even that complication. ... In other words, the injunctive strand demands that, for whatever type of knowledge, *the appropriate eye must be trained until it can be adequate to its illumination*. This is true in art, in science, in philosophy, in contemplation. It is true, in fact, for all valid forms of knowledge.

Now, if a person refuses to train a particular eye (flesh, mental, contemplative), then it is equivalent to refusing to look, and we are justified in disregarding this person's opinions and excluding him from our vote as to communal proof. Someone who refuses to learn geometry cannot be allowed to vote on the truth of the Pythagorean theorem; someone who refuses to learn contemplation cannot be allowed to vote on the truth of Buddha-nature.

It is my own feeling that the most important thing transpersonal psychology can do is try to avoid the category errors: confusing the eye of flesh with the eye of mind with the eye of contemplation (or, in the more detailed models, such as the Vedanta, avoid confusing any of the six levels). When someone asks, "Where is your empirical proof for transcendence?" we need not panic. We explain the instrumental methods for our knowledge and invite him or her to check it out personally. Should that person accept, and complete the injunctive wing, then that person is capable of becoming part of the community of those whose eye is adequate to the transcendent realm. Prior to that time, that person is inadequate to form an opinion about transpersonal concerns. We are then no more obliged to account to that person than is a physicist to one who refuses to learn mathematics.

In the meantime, the transpersonal psychologist should attempt to avoid category mistakes. He or she should not present transcendent insights as if they were empirical scientific facts, because those facts *cannot be scientifically verified*, and therefore the entire field will quickly gain the reputation of being full of nonsensical statements. A transpersonal psychologist is free to use the eye of flesh (scientifically) in gathering adjunct data; and a transpersonal psychologist is free to use the mind's eye to coordinate, clarify, criticize, and synthesize. But none of these realms should be confused with each other, and especially none of them should be confused with the realm of contemplation. Especially the eyes of flesh and reason should not think they have "proven" the Transcendent, circumscribed the Transcendent, or even adequately described the Transcendent. To the extent the transpersonal psychologist commits those errors, then the more the entire field faces the fate of the medieval theologian: it becomes psuedo-science and pseudo-philosophy, and is thereby destroyed by real scientists and real philosophers—and rightly so.

Transpersonal psychology is in an extraordinarily favorable position: it can preserve for itself the utterly unique position of possessing a balanced yet complete approach to reality—one which can include the eye of flesh and the eye of reason and the eye of contemplation. And I think that the history of thought will eventually prove that to do more than that is impossible, to do less than that, disastrous.

Notes

1. Wilber, K. *The Atman project*. Wheaton, Ill.: Quest, 1980.
2. Smith, H. *Forgotten truth*. New York: Harper & Row, 1976.
3. Schuon, F. *The transcendent unity of religions*. New York: Harper & Row, 1976.
4. Whitehead, A. N. *Science and the modern world*. New York: Macmillan, 1967.
5. Tart, C. *States of consciousness*. New York: E. P. Dutton, 1975.
6. Tart, C. (Ed.). *Transpersonal psychologies*. New York: Harper & Row, 1975.

The Possible Emergence of Cross-Disciplinary Parallels

ROGER N. WALSH

BASIC HYPOTHESIS

The basic hypothesis of this paper is that as human perceptual sensitivity increases beyond a certain threshold we penetrate beyond the realm of our ordinary experience of the world and its concomitant "reality" and obtain a fundamentally different view of nature. This view may be obtained through any of the epistemological modes of acquiring knowledge: sensory perception, intellectual conceptual analysis, or contemplation.... The heightened sensitivity may be obtained either through direct training of awareness, as in meditation or other consciousness disciplines, through refinement of conceptual analysis, or by augmentation and systematization of sensory perception through instrumentation and experiment as in advance science. But no matter how it is obtained, enhancement of sufficient degree will reveal a different order of reality from that to which we are accustomed. Furthermore, the properties so revealed will be essentially more fundamental and veridical than the usual, and will display a greater degree of commonality across disciplines. Thus, as empirical disciplines evolve and become more sensitive they might be expected to uncover phenomena and properties that point toward underlying commonalities and parallels between disciplines and across levels.

Thus, what this paper suggests is that we may be witnessing a paradigm transition in which one of our most fundamental paradigms, the bedrock of Western science, the classical Greek concept of the universe as essentially atomistic, divisible, isolatable, static, nonrelatavistic, and comprehensible by reductionism, is in the process of replacement, not just for physics, where evidence for such a shift was first obtained, but for all sciences. In physics this image of the universe is increasingly, though far from unanimously, recognized.[1, 2, 3, 4, 5] What is being suggested here is that much of this new paradigm may also be applicable to the neurosciences in particular and ultimately to all science, and that as the individual branches of science evolve we may witness increasing degrees of cross-disciplinary parallels, not only between sciences, but between science and the consciousness disciplines, as each discovers the same fundamental underlying properties of nature.

Epistemological Limitations

Both modern science and the consciousness disciplines point out that our usual perception is limited and distorted to an unrecognized degree. For millennia the meditative and yogic disciplines have devoted themselves specifically to this problem and have stated that it is only when we begin to increase our perceptual sensitivity and accuracy that we begin to appreciate the existence and magnitude of the problem.[6, 7, 8]

The aim of modern science is similar: namely to transcend our usual perceptual limitations in order to obtain more accurate and sensitive knowledge of the universe. Western psychology has long recognized and explored perceptual limitations, but in recent years certain data derived from physics have begun to confirm certain aspects of the picture of underlying reality described by the consciousness disciplines and the limitations of perception. They suggest that our usual perceptual limitations tend to produce consistent yet unrecognized distortions no matter where we look. These distortions include tendencies to solidify, dichotomize, separate, oversimplify, concretize, and to underappreciate the extent of continous flux, impermanence, interconnectedness, and holistic consistency of the universe. Both the consciousness disciplines and modern physics, and now perhaps also the neurosciences, suggest that these distortions are so pervasive and unrecognized that our usual picture of the universe, i.e., reality, is fundamentally erroneous or illusory. The word illusory has often been misunderstood to imply that the world does not really exist. Rather, it simply implies that our perception of it is coloured and distorted to an unrecognized degree.

THE EVOLUTION OF SCIENTIFIC INVESTIGATION

The preceding sections have suggested that the evolution of science along lines of increasing perceptual sensitivity may reveal increasing cross-disciplinary parallels and that the neurosciences may be at the threshold of such a stage. Let us now examine the general evolution of scientific research within a field in order to suggest how the nature and evolution of research designs may interact with and determine scientific models of nature, and ultimately result in the holistic model described above.

Scientific investigation in any field usually begins with the study of simplified isolated systems. Usually the effects of one or a small number of selected independent variables are tested and all others are excluded or ignored, as are interactions with other systems and dynamic processes. These few selected variables are usually those which account for the greatest portion of the variance.

With increasing experimental sophistication and sensitivity the effects of formerly excluded variables intrude more and more and must eventually be taken into consideration. Yesterday's confounding variable becomes today's independent variable. The total amount of variance accounted for continues to increase, though usually at asymptotic rates, since independent variables tend to be investigated in decreasing order of potency. With increasing numbers of variables, interactions and interdependencies become increasingly apparent, until eventually it is recognized that all variables, including the state of the observer, exert multiple effects.[9] A complete understanding requires no less than a consideration of all variables, i.e., of the entire universe.

At this stage, the original model of an isolatable limited system breaks down and is recognized as an illusory artifact. The scientific model has led to its own annihilating edge and the inherently holistic, indivisible, interconnected, interdependent, infinitely overdetermined and dynamic nature of the world is recognized. Such a perspective as this obviously transcends traditional models of causality, resulting in an omnideterminism in which all components are seen to mutually determine all others. The state of any part reflects the state of the whole. However, it should be noted that this does not necessarily point to a holographic model in which the whole is implicated *in* each part, as certain models of physics and the consciousness disciplines propose.

Having examined the general principles of the hypothesis presented in this paper and of the evolution of scientific investigation, let us now turn to the specific evidence from the neurosciences that appears to lend support to these general principles and to certain claims of the consciousness disciplines and modern physics.

To summarize a long . . . neuroscientific story, it is now apparent that the brain is a plastic organ whose structure and function mirror its ecology.[10, 11, 12, 13] Moreover, this structure and function are largely dynamic, continuously adapting to changing functional demands. ....[14, 15] Neural components show complex interconnections and interdependence; changes in any one part of the brain are likely to affect many if not all other parts. For the most part, environmentally induced changes cannot be predicted with absolute certainty but rather tend to be probabilistic, i.e., predictable only within certain limits. Furthermore, no one single mechanism can account for observed changes. No one chemical reaction, physiological principle, psychological property, is sufficient ... to precisely circumscribe neural events.

Rather, any one change reflects the totality of responses of all parts, dimensions, and levels of the brain. There is thus no one fundamental mechanism to which neural responses can be reduced and by which they can be explained. At the more fundamental levels, all effects reflect and are consistent with the state of the whole brain. Neural causality is thus not fully describable by reductionism but rather must be sought in the state of the whole brain — and ultimately, at a level which transcends traditional concepts of causality, in the state of the brain plus its environment.

On the other hand, the environment can only be known through the brain. The brain and the remainder of the universe thus constitute a coherent whole; they cannot be separated and studied independently without constituting an artificial and distorting duality that hides their underlying unity and interconnectedness. The structure and function of the brain are a function of the whole and of the brain-nonbrain (environment) interaction. The record of their interaction is dynamically engraved in chemical and anatomical script in the neural pathways. The universe comes to know itself through the brain and, within its limits, the brain appears to modify and adapt itself so as to better know the universe.

The evolution of the study of brain ecology thus begins to suggest a number of features of holism, interconnection and interdependence, dynamism, probablism, complexity, and acausal self-determininism, which are reminiscent of parallels in both modern physics and the consciousness disciplines.

CROSS-DISCIPLINARY PARALLELS

When perceptual limitations are overcome, the reality which is revealed appears strikingly different from the everyday one. In general, the following characteristics are descriptive of the reality described by the consciousness disciplines, certain models of physics, and suggestions from some areas of the neurosciences. The universe appears to be:

nondualistic as opposed to dichotomous

a *unitive whole* as opposed to unrelated parts

interconnected as opposed to comprised of separate and isolated components

dynamic and in continous motion or flux as opposed to static

impermanent and ephemeral as opposed to lasting and permanent

empty, (largely constituted by non-solid empty space), rather than solid

acausal (but not anticausal), i.e., transcendent to traditional models of causality, since every component enters into the determination of every event (omnideterminism)

foundationless and self-consistent, in that since all components and mechanisms are interconnected and interdependent none are ultimately more fundamental than any other. Hence the universe is inexplicable in terms of a limited number of fundamental mechanisms

statistical and probabilistic instead of certain

paradoxical rather than ultimately intellectually comprehensible, codifiable, and communicable

inextricably linked with the observer

What can be known is the interaction between observer and observed and never the independent properties of the observed alone. All observation is a function of the consciousness of the observer and thus the known universe is inextricably linked with consciousness rather than being separable into consciousness and objects of consciousness: "The world may be called physical or mental or both or neither as we please; in fact the words serve no purpose" (Bertrand Russell).[4]

Thus the fundamental ontology that is being revealed is largely dynamic, fluid, impermanent, holistic, interconnected, interdependent, foundationless, self-consistent, empty, paradoxical, probabilistic, infinitely over-determined, and inextricably linked to the consciousness of the observer.

It might be hypothesized that since the above-mentioned description refers to fundamental properties common to all phenomena, then perception of sufficient sensitivity and veridicality will begin to recognize these properties no matter what the perceptual mode and no matter what the object of perception. Thus, any object, if examined by any perceptual mode with a sensitivity enhanced to sufficient degree either by direct training or scientific instrumentation, might be expected to present a picture of its inherent nature as described above.

But at this level of greater sensitivity another factor enters, namely the consciousness of the observer. Since ultimately we can know only the properties of the interaction between observer and observed, any discipline will begin to detect fundamental properties of both the objects under investigation as described above, plus the observational system, including the consciousness of the observer.

Thus, the common properties of all objects plus the involvement of consciousness in all observations may both provide a basis for cross-disciplinary parallels.

LIMITATIONS TO THESE PARALLELS

In pointing to these parallels I do *not* wish to suggest that physics, the consciousness disciplines, and the neurosciences are converging on a common level of reality. . . . There has been much overly simplistic and wishful thinking about this, as Ken Wilber[16, 17] has clearly described, and the following discussion owes much to him.

For example, the microworld of quantum physics is very different from the macroworld that we observe with our unaided physical senses. So different, in fact, that it is not fully communicable in language but only in mathematics. Indeed, it is not even fully imaginable within our physical senses and macroworld-oriented imagination. . . . [18] In addition, while the neurosciences may be beginning to suggest a holistic model, the perennial philosphies and certain schools of quantum physics propose models that are both holistic and holographic (each part not only influences every other part but actually contains it).

Just as physics describes limits on the equivalence of properties across size scales, the perennial philosophies describe limits to the equivalence of properties across an ontological scale, which they range from consciousness at one end to inanimate physical matter at the other. Levels are held to be interdependent and interpenetrating, but it is also held that the properties of consciousness cannot be reduced to those of physical matter and must be known by a different epistemological mode, i.e., contemplation as opposed to sensory perception and conceptual reasoning.[16, 17]

Note that the size levels of the physicist and neuroscientist are encompassed within the physical matter level and sensory perception — conceptual modes of the perennial philosophy. The physicist is thus describing holism and perhaps holography within one size level — the findings of neurosciences reflect parallels across size levels — while the perennial philosophy is describing holism *and holography* within *and across* all size and ontological levels and epistemological modes.

Popularizing extrapolations from holographic interpretations of quantum physics has recently become fashionable, except among some physicists who are by no means unanimous or happy with some of these interpretations.[19]

It has frequently been claimed that quantum physics is finding proof of the claims of the perennial philosophy. Not so! One interpretation of quantum physics suggests a holographic reality at this ontological and size level. It can say little about other size levels and nothing about other ontological levels. At the present time we can only point to parallels.

CONCLUSION

In general, we might hypothesize that the more mature a discipline or branch of science, the more it will begin to unearth and point toward underlying phenomena and properties that parallel those found by other disciplines. This will not be instead of, but in addition to, the unique properties of the specific objects that it studies. Perhaps the same principles will be re-discoverable at many levels, with many degrees of subtlety and pervasiveness. The more sensitive the discipline, the more these underlying principles may be recognized. Beneath the initial appearance of infinite diversity may perhaps be found a complementary, underlying essential commonality pervading all of nature, transcending traditional disciplinary boundaries, and ultimately representing a function of our own consciousness.

Notes

1. Beynam, L. M. The emergent paradigm in science. *ReVision*, 1978, *1*, 56–72.

2. Bohm, D. The enfolding-unfolding universe. *ReVision*, 1978, *1*, 24–51.

3. Capra, F. Modern physics and eastern mysticism. This volume.

4. Wilber, K. *The spectrum of consciousness*. Wheaton, Ill.: Theosophical Publishing House, 1977.

5. Zukav, G. *The dancing Wu Li masters: An overview of the new physics*. New York: William Morrow, 1979.

6. Goldstein, J. *The experience of insight*. Santa Cruz, Calif.: Unity Press, 1976.

7. Goleman, D. A map for inner space. This volume.

8. Kornfield, J. Meditation theory and practice. This volume.

9. Walsh, R. N. & Cummins, R. A. The open field test: A critical review. *Psychol. Bull.*, 1976, *83*, 482–504.

10. Greenough, W. T. Enduring brain effects of differential experience and training. In M. Rosenzweig & E. Bennett (Eds.), *Neural mechanisms of memory and learning*, Cambridge, Mass.: MIT Press, 1976.

11. Rosenzweig, M.R., and Bennett, E. L. Effects of environmental enrichment or impoverishment on learning, and on brain values in rodents. In A. Oliverio (Ed.), *Genetics, environment, and intelligence*, Holland: Elsevier, 1977, pp. 163–196.

12. Walsh, R. *Towards an ecology of brain*. Jamaica, N.Y.: Plenum Press, in press.

13. Walsh, R. N. & Greenough, W. T. (Eds.). *Environments as therapy for brain dysfunction*. New York: Plenum Press, 1976.

14. Beck, E. C., Dustman, R., & Sakai, M. Electrophysiological correlates of selective attention. In C. Evans and T. Mulholland (Eds.), *Attention in neurophysiology*, London: Butterworths, 1969.

15. Sotelo, C., & Palay, S. L. Altered axons and axon terminals in the lateral vestibular nucleus of the rat. *Lab. Invest.*, 1971, *25*, 653–671.

16. Wilber, K. Eye to eye: Transpersonal psychology and science. This volume.

17. Wilber, K. Physics, mysticism, and the new holographic paradigm: A new appraisal. *ReVision*, 1979b, in press.

18. Capek, M. *Philosophical impact of contemporary physics*. Princeton, N.J.: Van Nostrand Reinhold, 1961.

19. Gardner, M. Quantum theory and quack theory. *New York Review of Books*, May 17, 1979.

EDUCATION

Education and Transpersonal Relations: A Research Agenda

THOMAS B. ROBERTS

There is emerging awareness that our current educational psychology is not so much wrong as so very limited. Of course, it was never complete. But it looked like the map of the Land of Learning had most of the major features identified.

In the last half-decade this has changed. What we thought were the main features and landmarks of the land turn out to be detailed descriptions of a beachhead to a much larger continent....

The key change is that psychologists are extending their domain to include the study of consciousness.

CURRENT USES IN EDUCATION

What do ... states of consciousness have to do with education? Quite a bit, both at the immediately applicable level and in long-range possibilities. Surprising as it seems, teachers and counselors find no problem in figuring out how to use transpersonal techniques in their day-to-day work. Enough books of games and techniques for classroom use have appeared to justify the label "transpersonal education" (Roberts, 1975; Roberts and Clark, 1975; Hendricks and Wills, 1975; Hendricks and Fadiman, 1976; Hendricks and Roberts, 1977). The immediate uses stem from applying insights from transpersonal psychology to our ordinary awake state of consciousness (and consequently our ordinary schooling) rather than anything requiring an altered state of consciousness.

LEFT BRAIN/RIGHT BRAIN

The physiological locations of the abilities to visualize, fantasize, and intuit, of course, are not especially important. What is important is that we have developed a lopsided ... education (Clark, 1975; Ornstein, 1972). Fantasy seems to be a handy way to draw on the abilities of the right hemisphere.

DIFFERENT BRAIN WAVE STATES

Attending to outside stimulation, reasoning, calculating, and alertness are likely to keep the brain primarily in a beta frequency, that is, a brain wave pattern 15 or more times a second. Our current educational curricula are based on the brain operating at the beta range — at the level of ordinary consciousness.

There may be whole ranges of human abilities, however, that are primarily based on other ranges of brain wave frequencies: alpha (8–13 times a second), theta (5–7 times a second), and delta (0–4 times a second). There may also be many forms of learning that are most efficient when the brain is operating at one of these nonordinary levels. The potentials of education at these levels may be as great as those at the beta level, perhaps greater.

Dreaming, psychic healing (LeShan, 1975), and paranormal phenomena (Ullman, Krippner, and Vaughan, 1974) seem to be associated with these relaxed and inner-directed states of consciousness (Honorton, 1976; Morris, 1976). Control of the autonomic nervous system through biofeedback (Green and Green, 1973) and artistic expression may be best learned when the brain is operating at these nonnormal levels.

BIOFEEDBACK

Biofeedback bridges transpersonal psychology and behavioral-physiological psychology. By picking up bodily processes and amplifying them opens the door to learning to control bodily processes. So far the practical uses are primarily in visual attention (Mulholland, 1974), subvocal speech during reading (Hardyck and Petrinovich, 1969), counseling (Danskin and Walters, 1975; Kater and Spires, 1975; Henschen, 1976), hyperactivity (Braud et al., 1975), and in behavior therapy (Budzynski and Stoyva, 1973). These all use biofeedback in the service of current goals and practices.

The long-term implications of biofeedback go far beyond this, however, because the questions of the relationships between mind and body are raised (Green and Green, 1977). It used to be taught that we could not control the autonomic nervous system (the system that controls such things as heart rate, blood pressure, digestion, and glandular activity). Now it turns out that this system can be controlled consciously. Our area of consciousness can be enlarged to include awareness and control of areas that previously were thought to be beyond consciousness. We have the potential to be more in charge of ourselves than we had thought.

What an extension of physical education this opens! It takes us far past muscular power, competitive sports, and the hygienic aspects of health to really learning to run our bodies in the finest detail.

COUNSELING AND THERAPY

Transpersonal psychology presents a fertile field of ideas for counselors and therapists.

Different types of meditation and centering seem to bring students in touch with themselves, enabling them to relate better to others and thus assisting many counseling tasks (Driscoll, 1972; Rubottom, 1972).

Mystical experiences are another possibility. The overwhelming evidence is that mystical experiences, far from detaching one from our ordinary world, actually make daily living more socially responsible, richer, and more enjoyable. For example, Noyes (1972), Kubler-Ross (1975), and Moody (1975) find that transcendent experiences at times of near-death make people more at ease when they return to ordinary consciousness. By having given up the ego, they reduce their fear of death and feel more in touch with themselves and their day-to-day living. Clark (1973) and Pahnke and Richards (1969) found that mystical experiences triggered by psychedelics increased acceptance of self and others, willingness to confront personal problems, tolerance and compassion, and feeling more in touch with the transcendent aspects of their religions.

In the hands of specially tuned therapists and in conjunction with professional therapy, mystical experiences triggered by psychedelic drugs have improved the condition of alcoholics (Abramson, 1967), cancer patients (Richards et al., 1972), narcotic addicts (Savage et al., 1972), and autistic schizophrenic children (Mogar and Aldrich, 1969) and have contributed to creative problem solving (Harman et al., 1972). The point is not that school counselors should do psychedelic therapy with their students, for they are not specially trained to do this. The points to notice are

1. the altered state of consciousness represented by mystical experience can have beneficial effects in a person's ordinary state,

2. mystical experiences can be highly therapeutic if integrated into the person's psyche and life,

3. the natural desire for mystical experience (transcendence in Maslow's hierarchy) is basically healthy.

The third point is especially important. If our desire for transcendence is a natural one, just as sex is (e.g., Weil, 1972), then a new role for counselors and therapists is to develop this natural trait in healthy, constructive ways. Just as the last few generations of mental health professionals have worked with the human sexual drive to bring it above ground, accepted, and understood in healthy ways, the current and next generation of mental health workers may pick up the additional task of working with the desires for transcendence and exploration of consciousness. The transcendent aspects of human nature also must be brought into the light to develop healthy attitudes and appropriate behaviors.

PROFESSIONAL PREPARATION

Very little work has been done with the implications of transpersonal education for the preparation of teachers and counselors. In one of the few studies Lesh (1970) found that Zen meditation increased empathy in counselors as well as their self-actualization, and a few reported telepathic experiences.

Roberts (1976) expects transpersonal education to show up first in techniques that fit in with established practices. Then will come transpersonal content and units in current courses. Finally, there might come a reorganization and revision of curricula based on a transpersonal world view.

Exercises such as those in Masters and Houston's *Mind Games* (1973) may well provide part of such a teacher-education curriculum.

NEW RESEARCH DIRECTIONS

To summarize the main points of this paper, the realms of educational psychology may well be expandable far beyond their current limits. Instead of an educational psychology of only the left hemisphere of the brain, the right hemisphere will take its place. And there may be whole educational psychologies for each of the alpha, theta, and delta levels of consciousness. Our current beta approach will be continued, but seen in a larger perspective.

References

Abramson, H. A. (Ed.). *The use of LSD in psychotherapy and alcoholism*. Indianapolis: Bobbs-Merrill, 1967.

Braud, L. W., Lupin, M. N. and Braud, W. G. The use of electromyographic biofeedback in the control of hyperactivity. *J. of Learning Disabilities*, 1975, *8* (August/September), 420–425.

Budzynski, T. H. and Stoyva, J. Biofeedback techniques in behavior therapy. *Biofeedback and Self-Control*, 1973, 437–459.

Clark, F. V. Fantasy and imagination in T. Roberts (Ed.), *Four psychologies applied to education: Freudian, behavioral, humanistic, transpersonal*. New York: John Wiley, 1975, pp. 498–513.

Clark, W. H. *Religious Experience: Its nature and function in the human psyche*. Springfield, Ill.: Charles C. Thomas, 1973.

Danskin, D. G. and Walters, E. D. Biofeedback training as counseling. *Counseling and Values*, 1975, *19* (February), 116–122.

Driscoll, F. TM as a secondary school subject. *Phi Delta Kappan*, 1972, *54*, 235–237.

Green, E., and Green, A. The ins and outs of mind-body energy. In *Science year, the world book science annual*, Chicago: Field Enterprises Educational Corporation. Reprinted in T. Roberts (Ed.), *Four psychologies applied to education: Freudian, behavioral, humanistic, transpersonal*. New York: John Wiley, 1975, 463–472.

Green, E. and Green, A. *Beyond biofeedback*. New York: Delacorte, 1977.

Hardyck, C. D. and Petrinovich, L. F. Treatment of subvocal speech during reading. *J. of Reading*, 1969, *12* (February), 361–368.

Harman, W. R., McKim, R., Mogar, R., Fadiman, J., & Stolaroff, M. J. Psychedelic agents in creative problem solving. In C. T. Tart (Ed.), *Altered States of Consciousness*, Garden City, N. Y.: Anchor/Doubleday, 1972, 455–472.

Hartley Productions. *Biofeedback: Yoga of the West*. Cos Cob, Connecticut, 1974.

Hendricks, C. G., and Fadiman J. *Transpersonal education: A curriculum for feeling and being*. Englewood Cliffs, N.J.: Prentice-Hall, 1976.

Hendricks, C. G., and Roberts, T. B. *The second centering book: Awareness activities and transpersonal treasure maps*. Englewood Cliffs, N. J.: Prentice-Hall, 1977.

Hendricks, C. G. and Wills, R. *The centering book: Awareness activities for children, parents, and teachers*. Englewood Cliffs, N. J.: Prentice-Hall, 1975.

Henschen, T. Biofeedback-induced reverie: A counseling tool. *Personnel and Guidance J.*, *54*, 1976, 327–328.

Honorton, C. Psi-conducive states of awareness. In E. Mitchell and J. White (Eds.), *Psychic explorations: A challenge for science*, New York: G. P. Putnam, 1976, pp. 616–639.

Kater, D., and Spires, J. Biofeedback: The beat goes on. *School Counselor*, 1975, September, 16–21.

Kubler-Ross, E. Death and related experiences. Speech at the Annual Meeting of the Association for Transpersonal Psychology, Stanford, California, July 19, 1975.

Lesh, T. V. Zen meditation and the development of empathy in counselors. *J. of Humanistic Psych.*, 1970, *10*, 39–74.

LeShan, L. *How to Meditate*. New York: Bantam, 1975.

Masters, R. E. L., and Houston, J. *Mind games: The guide to inner space*. New York: Dell, 1973.

Mogar, R. E., and Aldrich, R. W. The use of psychedelic agents with autistic schizophrenic children. *Psychedelic Rev.*, 1969, *10*, 5–13.

Moody, R. A. *Life after Life*. Covington, Ga.: Mockingbird, 1975.

Morris, R. L. The psychobiology of psi. In E. Mitchell and J. White (Eds.), *Psychic exploration: A challenge for science*. New York: G. P. Putnam, 1976.

Mulholland, T. B. Training visual attention. *Academic Therapy*, 1974, *10* (Fall), 5–17.

Noyes, R. The experience of dying. *Psychiatry*, 1972, *35* (May), 174–184.

Ornstein, R. E. *The mind field: A report on the consciousness boom*. New York: E. P. Dutton, 1976.

Ornstein, R. E. *The psychology of consciousness*. San Francisco, Calif.: W. H. Freeman, 1972.

Pahnke, W. N., and Richards, W. A. Implications of LSD and experimental mysticism. *J. of Transpersonal Psych.*, 1969, *1*, 69–102.

Richards, W., Grof, S., Goodman, L., and Kurland, A. LSD-assisted psychotheraphy and the human encounter with death. *J. of Transpersonal Psych*, *4*, 121–150.

Roberts, T. B. Transpersonal education: A personal view. *J. of Humanistic and Transpersonal Education*, 1976, *1*.

Roberts, T. B. (Ed.). Transpersonal psychology in education. In T. Roberts (Ed.), *Four psychologies applied to education: Freudian, behavioral, humanistic, transpersonal*. New York: John Wiley, 1975, pp. 395–555.

Roberts, T., and Clark, F. V. *Transpersonal psychology applied to education*. Fastback Booklet No. 53. Bloomington, Ind.: Phi Delta Kappa Education Foundation, 1975.

Rubottom, A. E. Transcendental meditation and its potential uses for schools. *School Education*, 1972, 851–857.

Savage, C., McCabe, O. L., and Kurland, A. A. Psychedelic therapy of the narcotic addict. In C. Brown and C. Savage (Eds.), *The drug abuse controversy*, Baltimore, Md.: National Education Consultants, 1972.

Ullman, M., Krippner, S., and Vaughan, A. *Dream telepathy: Experiments in nocturnal ESP*. Baltimore, Md.: Penguin, 1974.

Weil, A. *The natural mind: A new way of looking at drugs and the higher consciousness*. Boston: Houghton Mifflin, 1972.

PHILOSOPHY

Two Modes of Knowing

KEN WILBER

TWO MODES OF KNOWING

When the universe as a whole seeks to know itself, through the medium of the human mind, some aspects of that universe must remain unknown. With the awakening of symbolic knowledge there *seems* to arise a split in the universe between the knower and the known, the thinker and thought, *the subject and the object*; and our innermost consciousness, as knower and investigator of the external world, ultimately escapes its own grasp and remains as the Unknown, Unshown, and Ungraspable, much as your hand can grasp numerous objects but never itself, or your eye can see the world but not itself.

Just as a knife cannot cut itself, the universe cannot totally see itself as an object without totally mutilating itself. The attempt to know the universe as an object of knowledge is thus profoundly and inextricably contradictory; and the more it seems to succeed, the more it actually fails, the more the universe becomes "false to itself." And yet oddly enough this type of dualistic knowledge, wherein the universe is severed into subject vs. object (as well as truth vs. falsity, good vs. evil, etc.) is the very cornerstone of Western philosophy, theology, and science. For Western philosophy is, by and large, Greek philosophy, and Greek philosophy is the philosophy of dualisms.

One of the principal reasons that the dualistic or "divide-and-conquer" approach has been so pernicious is that the error of dualism forms the root of intellection and is therefore next to impossible to uproot by intellection (Catch-22: If I have a fly in my eye, how can I see that I have a fly in my eye?). To detect this demands a rigorous, consistent, and persistent methodology capable of pursuing dualism to its limits, there to discover the contradiction.

Today, science potentially offers the type of rigorous approach capable of rooting out dualisms, principally because of its thoroughgoing experimentalism and its sophisticated instrumentation that allows it to pursue a dualism to its limits.

This is exactly the type of powerful and consistent methodology that is potentially capable of destroying dualisms, and although scientists didn't realize it, they had started to build upon the Cartesian dualism of subject vs. object a methodology of such persistence that it would eventually crumble the very dualism upon which it rested. Classical science was destined to be self-liquidating.

Exactly here was the problem. To measure anything requires some sort of tool or instrument, yet the electron weighs so little that any conceivable device, even one as "light" as a photon, would cause the electron to change position in the very act of trying to measure it! This was not a technical problem but, so to speak, a problem sewn into the very fabric of the universe. These physicists had reached the annihilating edge, and the assumption that had brought them there, the assumption that the observer was separate from the event, the assumption that one could dualistically tinker with the universe without affecting it, was found untenable. In some mysterious fashion, the subject and the object were intimately united, and the myriad of theories that had assumed otherwise were now in shambles.

The quantum revolution was so cataclysmic because it attacked not one or two conclusions of classical physics but its very cornerstone, the foundation upon which the whole edifice was erected, and that was the subject-object dualism. . . . It was abundantly clear to these physicists that *objective measurement and verification could no longer be the mark of absolute reality, because the measured object could never be completely separated from the measuring subject—the measured and the measurer, the verified and the verifier, at this level, are one and the same*. The subject cannot tinker with the object, because subject and object are ultimately one and the same thing.

Now at about the same time that the "rigid frame" of scientific dualism was collapsing in physics, a young mathematician named Kurt Gödel (then only 25 years old) was authoring what is surely the most incredible treatise of its kind. In essence, it is a type of logical analogue to the physical Heisenberg Uncertainty Principle. Known today as the "Incompleteness Theorem," it embodies a rigorous mathematical demonstration that every encompassing system of logic must have at least one premise that cannot be proven or verified without contradicting itself. Thus, "it is impossible to establish the logical consistency of any complex deductive system except by assuming principles of reasoning whose own internal consistency is as open to question as that of the system itself." Thus logically as well as physically, "objective" verification is not a mark of reality (except in consensual pretense). If all is to be verified, how do you verify the verifier, since he is surely part of the all?

In other words, when the universe is severed into a subject vs. an object, into one state which sees vs. one state which is seen, *something always gets left out*. In this condition, the universe "will always partially elude itself." No observing system can observe itself observing. The seer cannot see itself seeing. Every eye has a blind spot. And it is for precisely this reason that at the basis of all such dualistic attempts we find only: Uncertainty, Incompleteness.

Besides relinquishing the illusory division between subject and object, wave and particle, mind and body, mental and material, the new physics — with the brilliant help of Albert Einstein — abandoned the dualism of space and time, energy and matter, and even space and objects. ... Now this is of the utmost importance, for these scientists could realize the inadequacy of dualistic knowledge only by recognizing (however dimly) the possibility of *another mode of knowing* Reality, a mode of knowing that does not operate by separating the knower and the known, the subject and the object.

Eddington calls the second mode of knowing "intimate" because the subject and object are intimately united in its operation. As soon as the dualism of subject-object arises, however, this "intimacy is lost" and is "replaced by symbolism," and we fall instantly back into the all-too-common world of analytical and dualistic knowledge. Thus—and we will presently elaborate upon this at great length—*symbolic knowledge is dualistic knowledge*. And since the separation of the subject from the object is illusory, the symbolic knowledge that follows from it is, in a certain sense, just as illusory.

Physics and, for that matter, most Western intellectual disciplines were not dealing with "the world itself" because they were operating through the dualistic mode of knowing and hence were working with *symbolic representations* of that world. This dualistic and symbolic knowledge is at once the brilliance and the blind-spot of science and philosophy, for it allows a highly sophisticated and analytical picture of the world itself, but however illuminating and detailed these pictures may be, they remain just that—*pictures*. They therefore stand to reality just as a picture of the moon stands to the real moon. Korzybski, father of modern semantics, lucidly explained this insight by describing what he called the "map-territory" relationship. The "territory" is the world process in its actuality, while a "map" is any symbolic notation that represents or signifies some aspect of the territory. The obvious point is that the map is not the territory.

We have, then, available to us *two basic modes of knowing*, as these physicists discovered: one that has been variously termed symbolic, or map, or inferential, or dualistic knowledge; while the other has been called intimate, or direct, or non-dual knowledge. As we have seen, science in general started exclusively with symbolic and dualistic map knowledge, focusing its attention on the "shadows," but as a result of recent advances in the physical sciences, this mode of knowing—in some aspects at least—was found to be inadequate for that "knowledge of the Real" that it had so deceptively promised. This inadequacy led many physicists to draw on the second or intimate mode of knowing, or at least to envisage the necessity of this type of knowledge.

REALITY AS CONSCIOUSNESS

Now it is of the utmost significance that, of the vast number of scientists, philosophers, psychologists, and theologians that have fully and deeply understood these two modes of knowing, their unmistakable and unanimous conclusion is that the non-dual mode alone is capable of giving that "knowledge of Reality." They have reached, in other words, the same conclusion as that of the modern quantum physicists.

Throughout history, then, men have understood this one reality by temporarily abandoning symbolic-map knowledge and by directly experiencing this underlying reality, the single territory upon which all of our maps are based. In other words, they quit talking about it and experienced it instead, and it is the "content" of this non-dual experiencing that is universally claimed to be absolute Reality.

As we pointed out, the final "proof" of this consists not in logical demonstration but in experimental fact, and it is only in taking up the experiment to awaken the second mode of knowing that we will know for ourselves whether this be true or not.

We can shift this epistemological discussion to a more psychological basis by noting that *different modes of knowing correspond to different levels of consciousness*, to distinct and easily recognized bands of the spectrum of consciousness. Moreover, our personal identity is intimately related to the level of consciousness from and on which we operate. Therefore, a shift in our mode of knowing results in a shift in our basic sense of identity. Thus, while we are only utilizing the symbolic and dualistic mode of knowing, which separates the knowing subject from the known object, and then signifies the known object with an appropriate symbol or name, we likewise feel ourselves to be fundamentally distinct and alien from the universe, an identity that is signified by our role and our self-image, that is to say, the symbol-picture that we have formed of ourselves by dualistically becoming an object to ourselves. Non-dual knowledge, however, does not so operate, for—as we have pointed out—it is the nature of the non-dual mode of knowing to be one with what it knows, and this obviously entails a shift in one's sense of identity.

But before pursuing this any further, we must pause to clarify an extremely important point. Figuratively, we have stated that the "content" of the non-dual mode of knowing is absolute Reality, because it reveals the universe as it absolutely is and not as it conventionally is divided and symbolized. Speaking more strictly, however, there is not one thing called Reality and another thing called knowledge of Reality, for this is most dualistic. Rather, *the non-dual knowing is Reality*, it takes as its "content" itself. If we continue to speak of non-dual knowledge *of* Reality, as if the two were somehow separate, it is only because our language is so dualistic that it is positively awkward to state it in any other fashion. But we must always remember that knowing and the Real coalesce in the Primal Experience.

We therefore reach a startling conclusion. Since modes of knowing correspond with levels of consciousness, and since Reality *is* a particular mode of knowing, it follows that *Reality is a level of consciousness*. This, however, does not mean that the "stuff" of reality is "consciousness-stuff," or that "material objects" are really made of consciousness, or that consciousness is some nebulous cloud of undifferentiated goo. It means only — and here we must temporarily lapse back into dualistic language — *that Reality is what is revealed from the non-dual level of consciousness that we have termed Mind. That* it is revealed is a matter of experimental fact; *what* is revealed, however, cannot be accurately described without reverting to the symbolic mode of knowing. Thus do we maintain that reality is not ideal, it is not material, it is not spiritual, it is not concrete, it is not mechanistic, it is not vitalistic — *Reality is a level of consciousness, and this level alone is Real.*

By stating that the level of Mind, or simply Mind, alone is absolute Reality, this emphatically is not the philosophical doctrine of subjective idealism, although it may superficially be so interpreted. For subjective idealism is the view that the universe can be accounted for solely as the contents of consciousness, that the subject (or the ideal) alone is real while all objects are fundamentally epiphemonena. This, however, is just a sophisticated and subtle form of a side-stepping of the problem of dualism by proclaiming one-half of the dualism unreal, in this case, all objects. Furthermore, when we say Mind is Reality, this is not so much a logical conclusion as it is a certain experience — as we pointed out, Reality is "what" is understood and felt from the non-dual and non-symbolic level of Mind. Although a type of philosophy usually hangs itself onto this fundamental experience, the experience itself is not at all a philosophy — it is rather the temporary suspension of all philosophy; it is not one view among many, but the absence of all views whatsoever.

In sum: our ordinary conception of the world as a complex of things extended in space and succeeding one another in time is only a conventional map of the universe — it is not real. It is not real because this picture painted by symbolic-map knowledge depends upon the splitting of the universe into separate things seen in space-time, on the one hand, and the seer of these things on the other. In order for this to occur, the universe necessarily has to split itself into observer vs. observed, the universe must become distinct from, and therefore false to, itself. Thus our conventional, dualistic, symbolic pictures are subtle falsifications of the very reality they seek to explain.

But the split is not so much false as illusory, and the philosophies, psychologies, and sciences that depend on it are therefore not wrong but nonsensical. Man can no more separate himself from the universe and extract "knowledge" from it than a hand can grab itself or an eye can see itself. But man, relying as he does on dualistic knowledge, attempts the nonsensical and imagines he has succeeded. The result is a picture-image of the universe as composed of fragments called "things" disjointed in space and time, all alien and foreign to the isolated island of awareness man now imagines himself to be.

Thus lost in his own shadow, confined to this purely abstract and dualistic picture-map of the cosmos, man forgets entirely what the real world is in its actuality. Yet inescapably, *if* it is by the splitting of the universe into seer and seen, knower and known, subject and object, that the universe becomes distinct from and false to itself, *then* clearly it is only by understanding that, as Schroedinger put it, "subject and object are only one," that there emerges a realization of the actual world. If this be true, then this realization alone can claim the title of "absolute truth."

Now this is all the traditions are trying to tell us. See through the illusions that dualistic-symbolic knowledge has given us, and thus awaken to the real world. Because this real world as whole has no opposite, it is clearly not something that can be defined or grasped, for all symbols have meaning only in terms of their opposites, while the real world has none. Thus it is called Void, *Sunyata*, Empty, *Agnoia* — which means only that all thoughts and propositions about reality are void and invalid. At the same time, this is to say that the real world is also void of "separate" things, since things are products of thought, not reality.

If reality is inexpressible, it is nevertheless experiencable. But since this experience of the real world is obscured by our concepts *about* it, and since these concepts rest on the split between the subject that knows vs. the concepts that are known, all of these traditions emphatically announce that Reality can only be experienced non-dually, without the gap between the knower and the known, for in this manner alone is the universe not delivered up to illusion. This means that Reality and your perception of it are one and the same, which R. H. Blyth called "the experience by the universe of the universe." Now this awareness we have called the non-dual mode of knowing, the universe knowing itself as itself. And further, since we have suggested that this mode of knowing corresponds with a function, state, or level of consciousness which we term "Mind," and since to *know* Reality is to *be* Reality, then we can distill the entire essence of these traditions into the phrase "Reality as a level of consciousness," or simply "Reality as Mind-only."

Whether Reality is called Brahman, God, Tao, Dharmakaya, Void, or whatever is of no great concern, for all alike point to that state of non-dual Mind wherein the universe is not split into seer and seen. But that level of consciousness is not a difficult one to discover, nor is it buried deep within your psyche. Rather, it is very close, very near, and ever-present. For Mind is in no way different from you who now hold this book in your hands. In a very special sense, in fact, Mind is that which at this moment is reading this page.

PARAPSYCHOLOGY

The Societal Implications and Social Impact of Psi Phenomena

WILLIS HARMAN

For at least a century and a half psychic phenomena have held a fascination for some scientists and have been anathema to others. That their scientific study is gaining acceptance may be partly because improved experimentation procedures and new instrumentation have yielded better confirmed results. It is probably even more a consequence of cultural changes that allow these phenomena to "fit in" to a degree that would have been hard to foresee even fifteen years ago.

Thus it will not do to examine the impact of psychic phenomena in isolation from the changing paradigm of scientific understanding and the cultural movements evident in recent years.

IMPLICATIONS OF CONSCIOUSNESS AND PSI RESEARCH

There are presently two areas of research about which the majority of scientists still feel some discomfort — discomfort which we may assume will in time go away. One of these is the beginnings of a systematization of knowledge about different states of consciousness, including those inner experiences which have formed the bases for the world's religions and out of which have come man's deepest value commitments. The other is the important testing ground of psychic research.

The latter is a crucial area precisely because it lies midway between and links the objective world of public observation, the domain of "ordinary" science, and the "private" world of subjective experience. The phenomena of psychic research are anomalous — their occurrence is widely attested to, yet they do not "fit in." Still they speak clearly to the point that something is fundamentally incomplete about a world view which cannot accommodate them. They also serve as a sort of reality test for the universe of inner experience. They are not wholly inner—they are characterized by something being publicly observable. Neither are they wholly outer, since some activity of the mind is clearly involved. The following partial list will serve to delineate the territory under discussion:

- Telepathy, the apparently extrasensory communication of one mind to another
- Clairvoyance, the apparently extrasensory perception of aspects of the physical world, as in "remote viewing" or "out of the body" experience.
- Retrocognition, the "remembering" of events that happened to some other person, or prior to the birth of the "rememberer"
- Precognition, the "remembering" of events some time in the future
- Psychokinesis, the apparent influencing of the physical world through mental processes other than by the usual psychomotor processes (e.g., levitation, teleportation)

Evidence mounts that these sorts of preternormal knowings and abilities are latent in all persons, but typically highly represseed. . . . The implication . . . is that probably we will eventually discover that all persons have the full range of psychic phenomena as potentialities, all unconsciously understood and all thoroughly repressed.

THE EXTENT OF THE CHALLENGE

It is important to understand both why these two research areas of consciousness exploration and psychic phenomena have caused scientists such acute discomfort, and also why the reconciliation seems now close at hand. The extent of the potential impact of these areas on the scientific world view is suggested by the following list of premises which the scientific paradigm, until recently, has tended to imply:

1. The only conceivable ways in which man comes to acquire knowledge is through his physical senses and perhaps through some sort of memory storage in the genes.
2. All qualitative properties are ultimately reducible to quantitative ones; that is, color is reduced to wavelength, hate and love to the chemical composition of glandular secretions, etc.
3. There is a clear distinction between the objective world, which is perceivable by anyone, and subjective experience which is perceived by the individual alone, in the privacy of his own mind.
4. The concept of the free inner person is a prescientific explanation for behavior caused by forces impinging upon the individual from his environment, interacting with internal tensions and

pressures characteristic of the organism. "Freedom" is behavior for which scientists have not yet found the cause.

5. What we know as consciousness or awareness of our thoughts and feelings is really only a side effect of physical and biochemical processes going on in the brain.

6. What we know as memory is simply a matter of stored data in the physical organism, strictly comparable with the storage of information in a digital computer. (Thus it is impossible for a person to "remember" an event that happened to someone else.)

7. The nature of time being what it is, there is obviously no way in which we can obtain foreknowledge of the future other than by rational prediction from known causes. (Thus it is impossible for anyone to "remember" an event happening three weeks hence.)

8. Since mental activity is simply a matter of fluctuating states of the physical organism, it is completely impossible for this mental activity to exert any effect directly on the physical world outside the organism. (Thus reports of levitation or other psychokinetic events have to be nonsense or trickery.)

9. The evolution of the universe and of man has come about through purely physical causes, through random mutations and natural selection. There is no justification for any concept of universal purpose or teleological urge, either in the evolution of consciousness or in the strivings of the individual.

10. The individual does not survive the death of the organism, or it there is any sense in which the individual exists on after the death of his physical body we can neither comprehend it in this life nor in any way obtain knowledge regarding it.

The reason psychic and consciousness research is such a bitterly contested battleground is that the data in these areas challenge *all* of the above premises. Yet it was on the basis of these positivistic premises that the increasingly prestigious scientific world view was able, in the past, to dismiss as of secondary consequence the religious, aesthetic, and intuitive experiences of man, and hence to erode the value postulates based in those subjective experiences.

THE ULTIMATE QUESTION OF CONSCIOUSNESS

Let us put it another way. The reason that all these interrelated research areas — biofeedback, altered states of consciousness, hypnosis, psychosomatic illness, unconscious processes, psychic phenomena — have tended to be discomforting is that they so evidently implicate the ultimate question: "How do I know what I know—and how do I know it is 'true'?"

St. Exupery laid down (in *Wind, Sand, and Stars*) the fundamental definition of truth: "Truth is *not* that which is demonstrable. Truth is that
which is ineluctable"—that which cannot be escaped.

How do I know what is ineluctable? This question is the heart of the
discipline of epistemology, and to one with the stamina to pursue it there,
much examination of the subject can be found. Essentially there are two
quite different forms of knowing, ... and we all use both daily. One is
"knowing about" things in the manner of scientific "facts"; the other is
knowing by intuitive identification with, as in knowing another person.

Thus in opening up the exploration of consciousness, scientists are
forced to confront questions which they have, throughout most of the
history of scientific activity, managed to put aside for the philosophers to
puzzle over. What are the essential limitations of "knowledge about"?
What are the ultimate capabilities of the mind as observing instrument in
discerning intuitive knowledge of the universe, and—possibly the same
thing—of mind itself? What are the ways in which the latter knowledge is
best shared and consensually validated? In some sense all knowledge is
ultimately subjective, since the root of all experience is consciousness;
consequently, these new explorations that probe the problem of consciousness are fundamental indeed. This is where science, religion and
philosophy meet. We can hardly blame the scientists if at this point their
resolution quavers and their anxieties become more evident than usual.

In papers currently presented at scientific meetings and in articles
published in the most prestigious scientific journals are indications that,
with regard to both consciousness research and psychic research, the transition from discomfort to comfort may be at hand. This is only partly
because of the psychological effect ... of having some [data on] physical
and physiological correlates to inner experience. ... More importantly, it
has to do with the growing realization within science that it deals not with
reality in some ultimate sense, but with models and metaphors. This has
brought a change in attitude and a more promising climate for exploration
of inner experience than heretofore.

The precursor to that realization came with the resolution of the
battle in physics over the wave or particle nature of light. This was essentially resolved through recognition that both are only metaphors (as is the
mathematical equation which incorporates elements of both) — each
being useful for expressing certain aspects of the transcendental nature of
light. ... The resolution of this issue set a pattern for others.

The old-fashioned warfare between science and religion is rapidly
dissolving in a similar way, through the recognition that conventional
scientific knowledge is essentially a set of metaphors useful for expressing
certain aspects of human "outer" experience. Other facets, especially of
deeper inner experience, demand other kinds of metaphors. We have yet
to discover what particular metaphors will be most useful for our time;

many of those that had the power to move men's hearts in the past seem less useful now.

THE NEW IMAGE OF MAN

Even though these frontier scientific developments have not progressed very far, it is possible to infer which direction they will push the image of man-in-the-universe. Wherever the nature of man has been probed deeply, in Eastern or Western traditions, the paramount fact emerging is the duality of his experience. He is found to be both physical and spiritual, both aspects being "real" and neither fully describable in terms of the other. "Scientific" and "religious" metaphors are complementary; neither contradicts the other.

Aldous Huxley wrote of the "Perennial Philosophy," found at the inner core of all the world's religions, East and West, ancient and modern: "(It) recognizes a divine Reality substantial to the world of things and lives and minds; . . . finds in the soul something similar to, or even identical with, divine Reality; . . . places man's final end in the knowledge of the immanent and transcendent Ground of all being."

Before brashly attempting to sum up the primary characteristics of the Perennial Philosophy we should note first that its adherents have always insisted that it cannot be "summed up"—that it is *not* a philosophy, or a metaphysic, *not* an ideology or a religious belief, although others have typically considered it so. Perhaps the flavor of it, but only the flavor, can be hinted at in the following five statements.

Being

The basic experimental proposition is that man can under certain conditions attain to a higher awareness, a "cosmic consciousness," in which state he has immediate knowledge of a reality underlying the phenomenal world, in speaking of which it seems appropriate to use such words as infinite and eternal (Divine Ground of Being, Brahman, Godhead). From this vantage point one's own growth and creativity, and his participation in the evolutionary process, are seen to be under the ultimate direction of a higher center (Atman, the Oversoul, the "true Self"). The Upanishad puts it, "An invisible and subtle essence is the spirit of the whole universe. That is reality. That is truth. Thou art that."

Awareness

The power of suggestion is such that a person is literally and inescapably hypnotized by the suggestions he has absorbed from his culture since infancy. Thus man goes through life in a sort of hypnotic sleep, feeling that he is making decisions, having accidents happen to him, meeting chance acquaintances, etc. With more awareness the direction of the higher Self, "supraconscious choosing," becomes apparent. The person finds that decisions he felt he had come to logically or through intuition were really reflections of choices made on the higher level of the Self; that his "inspiration" or "creativity" is essentially a breaking through of these higher processes; that experiences and relationships which he needed for his growth were attracted to him by the Self and were by no means so accidental as he had assumed. Because ordinary perception, compared to this higher awareness, is partial perception, language built up from ordinary perception proves inadequate to describe the greater reality; attempts often are paradoxical in form.

Motivation

With increasing awareness the pull of material and ego needs is greatly lessened and the person finds his deepest motivation is to participate fully in the evolutionary process, achieving wholeness (haleness, health) through alignment of supraconscious, conscious, and subconscious choices. Evolution is seen not to be a random matter, but directed by a higher consciousness and characterized by purpose — this purpose including development of individual centers of consciousness with freedom of choice, gradually moving toward ever-increasing knowledge of themselves, of Self, and of the Whole.

Potentiality

It follows from the foregoing that the human potentiality is limitless; that all knowledge and power is ultimately accessible to the mind, looking within itself; and that all limitations (infirmities, illnesses, etc.) are ultimately self-chosen. The great secret of esoteric knowledge is, "I am cause." Such supernormal phenomena as telepathic phenomena, clairvoyant perception, experiencing events that happened to others, "instant" diagnosis and healing, precognition of future events, teleportation and other psychokinetic events, are in general perfectly possible. At some deep level the individual understands them, and at some deep level he chooses the ordinary "physical laws" that preclude them for the most part.

Attitude

With awareness comes a new attitude towards life. One aspect is the desire to consciously participate, to labor and serve, in the evolutionary process, the cosmic drama, the fulfillment of mankind. But the reverse side of this is acceptance, the conscious choosing of what is — since at a deep level of the self one already chooses this. Related to this is a nonat-tachment, being "divinely impersonal," unattached to specific outcomes, having "impersonal love."

THE CASE FOR SOCIAL TRANSFORMATION

No one would claim, of course, that the Perennial Philosophy has been demonstrated—or ever could be. We may only say that findings in these two fields of psychic phenomena and consciousness research point in its direction, and are compatible with it. However, if the knowledge paradigm of the society is changing to something like the Perennial Philosophy (which expands upon but is compatible with the scientific paradigm as we have known it), this implies far more—the possibility that the whole pattern of perceiving, conceptualizing, and valuing which has charac-terized modern industrial civilization may be giving way to a new order. This would involve not only changed folkways and "new-age" values, but also changed institutions and power structures and an altered economic political order.

Just what form this new social pattern might take cannot be foretold in advance. Still, we can conjecture what some of the characteristics would have to be if (a) the society were to be compatible with the new transcendentalism, (b) the dilemmas of the advanced industrial state were to become resolvable, and (c) the new social institutions are to be arrived at through a nondisruptive transition (i.e., are continous with the past).

Guiding ethic

A new guiding ethic would replace the fragmented materialist ethic (e.g., growth and consumption) which presently dominate the economic system and thence the society. This involves two complementary princi-ples. One is an ecological ethic that fosters a sense of the total community of man and responsibility for the fate of the planet and relates self-interest to the interest of fellow man and future generations. The other is a self-realization ethic which holds that the proper end of all individual expe-rience is the further evolutionary development of the emergent self and of the human species, and that the appropriate function of social institutions is to create environments which will foster that process.

Institutions

The transformation of the institutions of society would be such as to eliminate structured social and environmental irresponsiblity. That is, the overall incentive system (economic, community approval, enculturated mores, etc.) would foster ecologically wholesome behavior, in the broadest sense. The society would be synergistic—i.e., what the individual *wants* to do would be good for the whole.

Education

Education (as part of work-play-learning) would be a function of every institution in society.

Science

Under the new transcendentalism, science would be clearly understood to be a moral inquiry. Having a balanced effort of systematic exploration of both the objective and subjective realms of human experience, it could not be, as past science has tended to be, value-empty. It would deal with what is empirically found to promote wholeness—in much the same sense that present-day nutritional science deals with what foods are wholesome for man. It would place particular emphasis on the systematic exploration of various levels of subjective experience, the ultimate source of our value postulates. In this respect it would resemble the humanities and religion, and the boundaries between these three disciplines would become less sharp—as is already presaged in the recent writings of some psychotherapists.

Health Care

The new society would have a broadened definition of health, as wholeness of being. As with education, many institutions would share responsibility — medicine, psychotherapy, education, religion, welfare, environmental health. There would be a recognition that the whole society is the environment that affects health — thus, for example, equity in access to economic resources is an aspect of environmental health.

THE TRANSITION PERIOD

Finally, there is nothing in history to suggest that a social transformation of the magnitude suggested could occur without the most severe economic and social disruptions and system breakdowns. Only widespread understanding of why the transformation is taking place, and of the kind of society that might emerge following our time of troubles, can keep anxiety levels down and transition pains from becoming intolerable.

The forces of societal transformation have gathered impressive momentum. Developments in psychic research and the psychology of consciousness are part of this larger pattern. The next ten or fifteen years will show whether these forces are strong enough to bring about a major societal wrenching, or whether they will somehow quiet down and die away, or whether the confrontation between the new demands and the old rigidities is so violent that the result is destruction without a promising rebuilding. These years will not be one of the comfortable periods of history. It will no doubt be an exciting one.

SOCIAL SCIENCE

The Tao of Personal and Social Transformation

DUANE ELGIN

THE ECOLOGICAL FLOW OF THE UNIVERSE

Many persons who have explored the further reaches of human awareness agree on an essential perception: Behind the apparent disarray of random events there is a deeper harmony, a moving point of equilibrium and balance, a patterned unfolding of reality as a symbolic whole. In China, this patterned flow of the universe is called the Tao....

Congruent with the view of reality, the essence of wisdom is to act in harmony with the Tao, or natural rhythm of the universe. Smith (1958) characterizes the basic quality of life in tune with the universe as "creative quietude"—a process that combines within a single individual two seemingly incompatible conditions: supreme activity and supreme relaxation. Creative quietude (*wu wei*) is "the supreme action, the precious suppleness, simplicity, and freedom that flows from us, or rather through us, when our private egos and conscious efforts yield to a power not their own" (p. 181). Other forms of life act this way spontaneously and unconsciously. But humankind occupies a unique role as a knowing participant in evolutionary process. Humankind bears an awesome responsibility for acting in ways that do not disrupt the flowing equilibrium of the universe....

Actions that abuse our conscious, co-creative role in the evolutionary flow will rebound and, directly or indirectly, obtain their ecological retribution from persons and societies that have disrupted the equilibrium. If this is true, then it is important to examine the flow of industrialization in the West and the extent to which this flow has been resonant or discordant with the Tao.

THE DISRUPTIVE FLOW OF THE INDUSTRIAL PERIOD

The industrial revolution began with its own Taoistic-like premises — limited as they were. Adam Smith, in 1776, postulated the "Tao of socioeconomic processess":

> Every individual endeavors to employ his capital so that its produce may be of greatest value. He generally neither intends to promote the public interest, nor knows how much he is promoting it. He intends only his own security, only his own gain. And he is in this led by an *invisible hand* to promote an end which was not part of his intention. By pursuing his own interest he frequently promotes that of society more effectually than when he really intends to promote it (p. 423).

Where has the socioeconomic Taoism of the industrial period led? Judged on its own terms, the industrial transformation has been an enormous success in achieving what its internal dynamic premised as its major objective: the realization of an unparalleled level of material abundance for a majority of people. Nonetheless, it no longer seems proper to judge the industrial era on its own terms. The value premises of the industrial era, and the social form they support, fit neither the prevailing physical reality nor our growing appreciation of what it means to be human. Our powerful technologies coupled with an expressed belief in our right — indeed, obligation — to subjugate nature to our own ends have allowed us to achieve, at best, only a temporary stalemate in our struggle against nature. In struggling against nature we are gradually discovering that we have been struggling against ourselves. Only now are we finding that the mind of the human — though powerful enough to create technologies for the manipulation and destruction of nature on a vast scale — is not powerful enough to comprehend or assume responsibility for that which has been manipulated and destroyed. We mistake our power for wisdom. Indeed, our mastery of nature is a deception, for it presumes that we are apart from nature. Because we have acted with only partial awareness we have upset the equilibrium and have torn the fabric of the universe, which now returns to exact its ecological reparation. Environmental degradation, alienation, urban decay, and social unrest are mirrors of the shortness of our vision of man and the universe. Our outer world reflects our inner conditions. The arrogance of an anthropocentric perspective that places the Tao of man above that of the universe has brought us to the edge of disaster as we confront the possibilities of nuclear holocaust, world famine, population outstripping our resources, and global environmental poisoning.

RESTORING THE BALANCE (I) — THE TAO OF SOCIAL TRANSFORMATION

The idealistic vision of Taoistic action has become a pressing and realistic need. We cannot afford a lesser vision as we cope with enormously difficult and complex problems that reach global proportions. ... Presented below, in an austere simplicity that cannot begin to reflect the rich, organic complexity of reality, are personal perceptions of the natural flows of social form that seem to be emerging. Three dominant flows are considered: the failing impetus of the industrial paradigm, the pushes by natural and political ecology that are deflecting us from the social trajectory defined by the industrial paradigm, and the gathering strength of pull from an emerging image of humankind—predicated on the voluntary simplification of material aspects of life, coupled with exploration of nonmaterial/inner aspects of life. These flows are considered, in turn, below.

The Diminishing Impetus of the Industrial Paradigm

"Paradigm" refers here to the total pattern of values, beliefs, perceptions, and ways of acting that are characteristic of a culture. Thus, to say that the industrial paradigm is losing momentum is to say that the interdependent constellations of values, beliefs, and behaviors of the industrial era are collectively faltering. In short, the powerful engine of technological advance and economic growth, predicated on the seemingly unstoppable drive of our "economic will to power," now appears to be running out of steam. A number of factors may account for this.

Our cultural learning (through schools, work, and family) is supposed to mold and shape the rough outlines of personality and behavior and thereby provide a shared cultural context for existing in our society. Yet, the enculturation process seems to be breaking down; the cultural "glue" that makes our social system a cohesive whole seems increasingly ineffectual. The rapid pace of social change, the enormity and complexity of our social institutions, the demise of the extended family, the high rates of geographic mobility that further loosen once secure ties and bonds—all have converged to create an anarchic and confusing enculturation process. By organizing for economic efficiency, we have inadvertently disorganized our traditional enculturation mechanisms; it is no wonder then that we are set adrift and lost from any firm cultural moorings.

We confront a massive tangle of complexity in our social, political, and economic systems. We have aggregated comprehensible systems (small towns, and small transportation and communications networks) into supersystems of incomprehensible complexity. Our capacity to create powerful supersystems does not automatically confer a commensurate capacity to comprehend that which we have created. Consequently, we are increasingly dependent upon those supersystems but are incapable of understanding them, thus becoming the servants of a technological society that we created to serve us.

People are beginning to question that which we do best; namely, the creation of unparalleled levels of material affluence for masses of people.

We have extended a rational concern for material well-being into an obsessive concern for unconscionable levels of material consumption. . . . We are possessed by our possessions, consumed by that which we consume.

In sum, we are compelled to rethink what life means and where we wish to go. We are obliged to sort out the trivial from the significant, the ephemeral from the durable, and to find an alternative image of human and social possibility that captures our collective imagination and provides a renewed sense of direction as we proceed into the future.

Deflecting Pushes from Natural and Political Ecology

Even if the momentum of the industrial paradigm were not abating, there are strong forces that are deflecting our society from the historical trajectory of increasing material growth. The success of our industrial era has been predicated, to a substantial degree, on the existence of an inexpensive and abundant supply of energy and raw materials. Now, however, we confront a "new scarcity," which is inexorably invalidating the crucial premise of energy and material abundance.

If we were to look no further than this, the future would seem bleak indeed. An industrial apparatus faltering under its own weight and pressed to alter its trajectory by natural and manmade "limits to growth" presents a desperate picture. Without a sense of alternative possibility to pull us into a desirable future, the social prospect is analogous to that of pushing on a string—with the string of our social fabric merely bunching up in front of us the harder we push. Our constructive evolution requires an additional element—an individual and social vision equivalent to that of pulling on the string—a coherent and practical image of the future that respects and integrates the diminishing and deflecting pushes considered above.

The Pull of Voluntary Simplicity

As the pace and confidence of industrialism slows and as its direction is turned by the new scarcity, hard necessity dictates that we forge a new relationship with the material aspects of existence.

Explored below is one emerging social flow that may give greater coherence and balance to social actions—namely, the movement towards voluntary simplicity.

Historically, in the West in general and in America in particular, consumption has been viewed as a primary end of human activity. This view is reflected in the customary measure of man's happiness—his "standard of living"—which is calculated almost exclusively in material terms. We have attempted to maximize consumption, implicitly assuming that the level of consumption is directly related to the level of human well-being and happiness. This seems an ill-founded and excessively limiting assumption for approaching the totality of human satisfactions. There is much evidence that, beyond the level of material "sufficiency," money does not buy happiness.

In visceral response to this knowledge, a growing number of people appear to be adopting an alternative life-style which, though materially more modest, is overall more satisfying and enriching. Voluntarily simplifying the external/material aspects of one's life may significantly contribute to the enrichment of internal/nonmaterial aspects. The late Richard Gregg, in a prescient article written in 1936, eloquently states the rationale for voluntary simplicity.

> Voluntary simplicity involves both inner and outer condition. It means singleness of purpose, sincerity and honesty within, as well as avoidance of exterior clutter, of many possessions irrelevant to the chief purpose of life. It means an ordering and guiding of our energy and our desires, a partial restraint in some direction in order to secure greater abundance of life in other directions. It involves a deliberate organization of life for a purpose. . . .

Although voluntary simplicity may be a practical response to the new scarcity that we confront, there is little reason to think that such "frugality" would be voluntarily adopted without a compelling purpose to motivate its acceptance. What, then, is the pull to frugality/simplicity? First, whatever the purpose or magnetic pull, it needs to be strong enough to elicit a willing frugality from people. Second, it needs to be consistent with traditional values that respect individual freedoms. Third, it must be both idealistic (thereby offering a compelling image of future possibility to give direction) and pragmatic (showing respect for the real material problems that we confront). A purpose that fulfills the above needs is that of exploring, in community with others, the internal/nonmaterial frontier of man himself, coupled with voluntary simplification of the external/material aspects of life. Material necessity seems to coincide with evolutionary possibility, so that we might restrain the material aspect of life to explore more fully the nonmaterial dimensions of human existence. Rather than a passing fad or an escapist retreat from the real world, this seems a rational response to a pressing situation.

RESTORING THE BALANCE (II) — THE TAO OF PERSONAL TRANSFORMATION

Simone de Beauvoir has written, "Life is occupied both in perpetuating itself and in surpassing itself; if all it does is maintain itself, then living is only not dying." At present, it is not clear whether we can either maintain ourselves or surpass ourselves. There seem to be two fundamental reasons for this evolutionary crisis: first, a lack of "internal" evolution commensurate with our external/material evolution and, second, a failure to recognize that "internal" growth is central to human evolutionary processes. These problems are discussed in turn below.

Our present civilizational crisis emerges, in part, out of a gross disparity between the relatively underdeveloped internal faculties of man and the extremely powerful external technologies at our disposal. . . . We must right the imbalance of our present era by fostering a degree of interior human growth and maturation that is at least commensurate with the enormous exterior technological growth that has occurred in the last several hundred years. If we are to assume a co-creative role in evolutionary processes then we must do, with consciousness, care, and intention, what nature does in nonconscious and instinctive ways. Aurobindo states: "Man occupies the crest of the evolutionary wave. With him occurs the passage from an unconscious to a conscious evolution." In Julian Huxley's phrase, man must assume the position of "a trustee of evolution on this earth." In assuming that role we are obliged to act with a level of awareness or consciousness that is equal to the power and responsibility inherent in that role. . . . The evolution of our consciousness (and supportive social forms) is not a peripheral concern; rather, it is of central importance to the successful realization of our human agenda.

Evolutionary growth is more than purely physical evolution. To be sure, the primary manifestation of evolutionary growth is physical, the material world being the medium of most overt expression of change. However, the world of physical appearance is not the sum total of the world of reality. There is another and oftentimes unacknowledged aspect of evolutionary growth: the growth of consciousness in all living things. Krippner and Meacham (1968) state:

> Throughout time, the whole universe has been moving toward greater intensity and range of consciousness. "Evolution is an ascent towards consciousness," wrote Teilhard de Chardin, and man is at the frontal edge of this process (p. 154).

This persistent theme emerges from many cultural perspectives; Aurobindo (1973) states:

> An evolution of consciousness is the central motive of terrestrial existence. . . . A change of consciousness is the major fact of the next evolutionary transformation (p. 27).

Nonetheless, this is a purpose so far removed from the daily lifeworlds of most people in the West that it is almost totally unacknowledged. . . . Our cultural conditioning has rendered us perceptually deaf to our own higher human possibilities even though Western culture provides a more fertile ground for exploring these potentials than perhaps any in history.

An important dimension of the vast spectrum of consciousness into which we may evolve is revealed through so-called mystical experiences.

Though called by various names (cosmic consciousness, the absolute Tao, satori, samadhi, peak experiences), they refer to experiences that have been similarly described by persons in virtually all cultures throughout history.

These expanded states of awareness appear to constitute the *highest* common denominator of human experience. This is a profoundly hopeful discovery in that, before the people of the world can cope with the problems of our global village, there must be some degree of shared agreement as to the nature of "reality" within which we collectively exist. Mystical experiences may provide an important element of that common agreement at a level that transcends cultural differences. Yet, are these experiences so far removed from the daily life-worlds of most people that they are without significance, being essentially unapproachable and unattainable? Apparently not. Results from a recent national poll (Greely and McCready, 1975) indicate that mystical experiences "are widespread, almost commonplace, in American society today...." Spontaneous experiences of expanded perception do exist; nonetheless, they are largely unacknowledged and unintegrated into our contemporary cultural experience.

Throughout history, many persons have spontaneously attained expanded states and processes of awareness. Fewer have had the opportunity and the inclination to "train" themselves to explore the further reaches of human awareness. Further, the conscious, purposeful evolution of consciousness has not been a substantial possibility for most people, and for good reason: A vast proportion of all human history has seen the majority of the world's population engaged in one essential enterprise — that of survival. Only a few people have had enough determination in the face of material adversity to surpass themselves when occupied with the fight to maintain themselves physically. The struggle for subsistence has placed substantial constraints on any pervasive and intentional evolution of man's consciousness. Our era of relative abundance contrasts sharply with the material poverty of the past. Today, with simplicity, equity, and wisdom we can have both substantial freedom *from* want and freedom to evolve our consciousness as individuals in community with others. The industrial revolution, then, may be viewed as a major evolutionary breakthrough that provides the material base to support that pervasive, intentional evolution to expand states/processes of individual and sociocultural awareness.

Voluntary Simplicity

... Economic necessity (which dictates either enforced or voluntarily assumed simplicity), Taoistic 'necessity' (which impels us to evolve our awareness to assume evolutionary trusteeship), and human possibility (to evolve to higher levels of awareness/consciousness) all combine to create what seems to be a gentle but increasingly insistent evolutionary imperative toward individual and societal transcendence.

If we are to realize this 'new frontier' of social and human possibility, it seems likely that something akin to the following 'ethics' must emerge. First is a Self-Realization Ethic, which asserts that each person's proper goal is the evolutionary development of his fullest human potential. Accordingly, this ethic insists that social institutions provide an environment supportive of self-realization. Second, we must develop an Ecological Ethic, which accepts our earth as limited, recognizes the underlying unity of the human race, and perceives man as an integral part of the natural environment. These two ethics — the Self-Realization Ethic and the Ecological Ethic — are two sides of a single coin. Orchestrated with one another, they leave room for both cooperation and for wholesome competition, for sociality and individuality. Indeed, each serves as a corrective for possible excesses or misapplications of the other (Elgin, 1975).

Accepting the challenge of this new frontier neither denies nor turns away from our earlier, largely external/material frontier. Both necessity and opportunity require a change in proportion and balance—a shift in the center of social gravity—toward the nonmaterial dimension of an evolving human consciousness. This is not to deny our technological and economic achievements; rather, we must build on them if we are to progress into the next frontier. Yet, for some, the inward turning implied by this new frontier could be seen as an escapist retreat from the hard problems of the 'real world.' A growing interest in enhanced human awareness could be dismissed as a return to the superstitions and irrationalities of an earlier, more gullible age. Some may insist that we stand at the violent conclusion of all history, while others reassure that we now stand amid a changing stream of social evolution that reflects the first glimmerings of a profound change in human awareness. This frontier, like all new frontiers, generates both enthusiasm and despair as different people look upon its possibilities.

In conclusion, hard material necessity and human evolutionary possibility now seem to converge to create a situation where, in the long run, we will be obliged to do no less than realize our greatest possibilities. We are engaged in a race between self-discovery and self-destruction. The forces that may converge to destroy us are the same forces that may foster societal and self-discovery. The path of discovery requires us to first learn the way of the universe — the gentle imperative of the way of the Tao.

References

Aurobindo, S. *The future evolution of man*. India: All India Press, 1963.
Elgin, D. S. The third American frontier: The evolution of consciousness and the

transformation of society. Center for the Study of Social Policy, Menlo Park, Calif.: Stanford Research Institute, 1975.

Greeley, A. M. & W. C. McCready. Are we a nation of mystics? *New York Times Magazine*, January 26, 1975.

Gregg, R. Voluntary simplicity (1936). Reprinted in *Manas*, Los Angeles, Calif., September 4 and 11, 1974.

Krippner, S. & W. Meacham. Consciousness and the creative process. *The Gifted Child Quarterly*, Autumn, 1968.

Schumacher, E. F. *Small is beautiful*. New York: Harper & Row, 1973.

Smith, A. *The wealth of nations*. New York: Modern Library, 1937.

Smith, H. *The religions of man*. New York: Harper & Row, 1958.

EPILOGUE

The exploration of the highest reaches of human nature and of its ultimate possibilities . . . has involved for me the continuous destruction of cherished axioms, the perpetual coping with seeming paradoxes, contradictions, and vaguenesses, and the occasional collapse around my ears of long-established, firmly believed in, and seemingly unassailable laws of psychology.

ABRAHAM MASLOW[1]

We have only just begun. A newly recognized, centuries-old frontier is opening to us. But as yet, we know little of it and our technological expertise speaks little to this realm of consciousness, which is already proving to be far vaster than we had imagined.

The realms of the human psyche and their corresponding states of consciousness, identity, and experience extend far beyond what we had thought of as our limits. From a perspective that encompassed only a single, waking state of consciousness, we have moved toward a recognition of multiple states; from a single-layer model of the unconscious to multiple layers; from equating identity with ego to seeing ego as only one of many possible identifications; from an either-or exclusive view of psychological models that regarded one as right and others as wrong to a broader more encompassing position, which recognizes that all models and their corresponding perspectives are limited and relative; from viewing our Western psychological systems as the only ones worthy of serious consideration to the recognition that some non-Western psychologies are, in their own different ways, as sophisticated as our own; and from an automatic dismissal of the consciousness disciplines, mystical traditions, and great religions, to the recognition that some of them may represent sophisticated technologies for training individuals in the development of higher states of consciousness.

The study of consciousness has been a central concern of several Eastern cultures for millennia. By comparison, we are very recent newcomers. Our major concern has been materialistic, and we have in general sought the answers to our questions and the solutions to our problems of life in the material environment. Now we may be witnessing a quickening and deepening of interest in nonmaterialistic realms of experience and consciousness. If this interest is in part reactive to an excessive concern with materialism, then perhaps it is part of a dialectical process and we might wonder what the synthesis will be.

One possibility seems to be a potential integration and synthesis resulting from parallel developments in a number of disciplines and areas of study that were formerly seen as quite unrelated. Quantum physics, consciousness, biofeedback, meditation research, and many others are becoming linked in an interconnecting network of concepts and findings. This points to the possibility of a broad, integrated synthesis and new guiding paradigms concerning who and what we are, the fundamental nature of the universe, and our relationship to it. The possible dimensions and tenets of such paradigms have been the subject matter of this book.

New models and perspectives offer new opportunities. All that we think and do, both individually and collectively, reflects our beliefs about the nature of ourselves and the reality we inhabit. The evidence for the existence of expanded ranges of experience, identity, and consciousness affords new visions of what we can be and may well call forth our individual and collective efforts to actualize them. The recognition that we are active cocreators of our sense of self and our perception of reality shifts us from perceiving ourselves as passive victims of psychodynamic and existential givens to active cocreators, veritable gods within our own universe.

This new perspective encourages us, even forces us, to return to a consideration of the basic questions from which psychology and philosophy originally sprang. Hilgard and Bower[2] emphasize the centrality of these questions as follows:

> The really fascinating and absorbing questions of psychology were not "discovered" by modern psychologists, but rather have been matters of deep concern to philosophers for many centuries. And these are not trivial "academic" questions of only historical interest; on the contrary, they center upon the most vital motives and forces underlying Western thought and civilization: What am I to believe? What can I trust? How do we know? What kind of life is worth living? What is man's role and what is his destiny in this universe? What is Justice, the Good, the Truth? What government, if any, is worth having? What is the nature of man? Is man free? What is Mind and what is its relation to nature?
>
> These are not sterile questions because the answers we give to them impinge in countless ways upon our daily lives, providing the motives for our personal and social conduct, the rational systems of legal and governmental control over our lives, and our modes of thinking about our personal identity and about the meaning of our lives. The serious thinkers of each generation have aimed at the systematic consideration and clarification of such questions

and have proposed answers to them ... These and many other questions have provided the intellectual underpinnings of modern psychology.

In its initial strivings for experimental and conceptual rigor, modern psychology excluded such questions from consideration. But now we are finding that such an exclusion not only reduces the scope and significance of psychological inquiry but is actually impossible. For what we have discovered is that we cannot examine phenomena in isolation without introducing artificial distortions and dualities. Furthermore, we are not detached objective observers but active participants in the universe. We cannot measure without changing; the questions we ask and answers we receive are functions of our beliefs and models and ultimately of our consciousness; the subjective/objective dichotomy can no longer be maintained; we can no longer exclude ourselves from the investigation of reality, both because we are and because we create the reality we investigate.

What must we do to be adequate to these possibilities? Our first task is epistemological. As Ken Wilber pointed out in "Eye to Eye," transpersonal psychology is unique in encompassing, even requiring, knowledge from all three "eyes," or modes of acquisition of knowledge, i.e., sensation-empirical, conceptual, and contemplative-meditative. Each of these three modes of knowing yields only partially overlapping data, which cannot be reduced one to another without what is called category error. Traditionally, Western science and philosophy have used only the first two and have been guilty of category error in attempting to either ignore contemplative wisdom or reduce it to the other two realms. The recognition of this error opens the way to a balanced integration between modes and their appropriate application to the basic questions discussed above.

Each mode must be applied as skillfully, precisely, and appropriately as possible. The findings of one mode must be explored and tested and integrated with others. The insights into the fundamental nature of self and reality provided by contemplation and the theoretical interpretations and conclusions of the intellect must be grounded and tested by empirical research wherever possible. Empirical and conceptual rigor are essential if the field is to gain legitimacy and be clearly differentiated from superficial popularisms.

At the same time, we must remember the limitations inherent in empirical and conceptual knowledge. Experience, and particularly the experience of transpersonal realms, cannot ultimately be reduced to concepts but must be approached through the cultivation and practice of the contemplative mode.

The cultivation of the contemplative mode makes very different demands on its practitioner than do the others. In order to employ this mode adequately, we must make ourselves adequate for its use. Empirical observation comes relatively easily; skillful use of the intellect requires intellectual training, and deep contemplative ability requires a training of our whole being. The contemplative faculty is one of refined sensitivity to subtle, formerly subliminal experience, and, as such, is disrupted by any perturbations of emotion, intellect, personality, or lifestyle. In addition, the knowledge obtained through it may not necessarily be objective in that it may not be separable from the knower. In the transpersonal realms of experience, one must live and become that which one seeks to know. This is the difference between wisdom, what one is, and knowledge, what one has.

> Nothing can be known without there being an appropriate "instrument"... the understanding of the knower must be adequate to the thing to be known... When the level of the knower is not adequate to the level ... of the object of knowledge, the result is not factual error but something much more serious: an inadequate and impoverished view of reality.[3]

Thus we are led to the inescapable conclusion that, for deep understanding of the transpersonal realms, the first requirement is that we must work on ourselves. Attention, perceptual sensitivity, emotions, attachments, thinking, and even lifestyle, must be trained and disciplined by any individual who wishes to undertake a deep exploration of these realms. Only by commitment to a continuous, deepening discipline can we hope to explore the most fundamental aspects of transpersonal psychology, consciousness, and ourselves, and to use them to contribute to others rather than for egocentric purposes. We are the limiting factor in our exploration of this vast and timeless realm that is ultimately ourselves, and we have only just begun.

> I have been as a little child playing on the seashore, every now and then finding a brighter pebble, while all around me the great ocean of truth lay undiscovered.
>
> —SIR ISAAC NEWTON

Notes

1. Maslow, A. H., *Toward a Psychology of Being*, 2nd ed. New York: Van Nostrand, 1968, pp. 71–72.
2. Hilgard, E., & G. Bower. *Theories of learning*. Englewood Cliffs, N.J.: Prentice-Hall, 1975.
3. Schumacher, E. F. *A guide for the perplexed*. New York· Harper & Row, 1977, pp. 39, 42.

GLOSSARY

ABSORPTION. Nondualistic state of intense concentration in which there remains no separation between observer and observed.

ACCESS CONCENTRATION. Buddhist term for the first attainment in concentrative meditation; verging on full absorption.

ACTUALIZATION. To make actual; to realize all that one can become.

ALPHA FREQUENCY. Brain wave frequency of 8–13 cycles per second as measured by electroencephalography.

ANATTA. Buddhist term for no continuing or abiding self; realization of nonexistence of a solid permanent self.

ANNICA. Buddhist term for impermanence; the continuous flux of reality.

ARAHANT. Awakened being; the highest level of enlightenment recognized in Buddhist psychology; saint; perfected being.

ARCHAIC UNCONSCIOUS. The most primitive and least developed structures of the ground unconscious; not repressed; rudimentary deep structures with little or no surface content.

ARCHETYPES. Mental forms or images associated with instincts; exemplary patterns of manifestation.

ASC. Altered state of consciousness.

ATMAN. Hindu term for ultimate unitive consciousness inherent in human beings.

AWARENESS. State or faculty of knowing.

BETA FREQUENCY. Brain wave frequency of more than 13 cycles per second as measured by electroencephalography.

BODDHISATTVA. A fully enlightened being who has vowed to work for the enlightenment of all sentient beings, renouncing personal liberation until this is accomplished; a being working for enlightenment.

BODYEGO. The sense of self bound to, or identified with, the physical body.

BODYSELF. Sense of self identified exclusively with the physical body.

B-VALUES. Intrinsic values of being associated with ultimate reality; e.g. truth, beauty, love.

CLAIRVOYANCE. The power of discerning objects not present to the senses; remote viewing.

DEEP STRUCTURE. All basic limiting principles of a level of consciousness; the defining form of each level, which embodies the potentials and limitations of that level.

DELTA FREQUENCY. Brain wave frequency of 1–3 cycles per second as measured by electroencephalography.

DEVELOPMENT. Act, process, or result of developing; to unfold more completely; to evolve possibilities; to promote growth.

DUKKHA. Buddhist term for suffering; said to be inherent and inescapable in life.

EGO. Conceptual self-sense identified with individual separateness; part of the mind with which the individual identifies.

EMBEDDED UNCONSCIOUS. That aspect of the ground unconscious with which the self identifies; repressing but unrepressed; e.g., identification with superego.

EMERGENT UNCONSCIOUS. That portion of the psyche that is not repressed but has not yet emerged into conscious awareness.

EPIPHENOMENA. Attendant phenomena occuring as a secondary or peripheral result.

EPISTEMOLOGY. The theory of the method and grounds of knowledge; especially with reference to its limits and validity.

GROUND UNCONSCIOUS. The all-encompassing ground that enfolds all the deep structures of consciousness given to a collective humanity.

HIGH CAUSAL. The level of consciousness in which all forms are transcended.

HOLISTIC. Pertaining to the whole; especially the whole person.

IMPERMANENCE. The continuous flux or changing nature of reality; nothing remains the same.

INSIGHT. (Vipassana) Buddhist term for refined perceptual sensitivity that is aware of the arising and passing away of each mind moment.

INTEGRAL. Essential to completeness; lacking nothing of completeness; entire.

INTEGRATED. Formed into a whole; united, formed into a complete or perfect whole.

JHANA. Buddhist term for nondualistic state of extreme concentration.

LOW CAUSAL. A level of consciousness associated with an experience of unity with various high archetypal images, e.g., images of a deity.

LOW SUBTLE. Level of consciousness corresponding to the sixth chakra in yoga psychology. Associated in some systems with psychic ability.

MAYA. Illusory perception (samsara).

METAHEDONISM. Pleasure derived from metaneed fulfillment.

METAMOTIVATIONS. Motives pertaining to meta needs; higher order motives.

METAPATHOLOGY. Psychopathology associated with higher order needs or metaneeds.

MINDFULNESS (SATIPATTHANA). Buddhist term for state of awareness of bare attention to raw immediate experience; a meditative practice cultivating this state.

NIRVANA. Buddhist term describing a state of consicousness that is timeless, unconditioned, liberated, and nondual; end of the path of insight meditation.

OVERMIND. Embodiment of transcendent consciousness said to disclose to intuition what is prior to mind, self, world, and body.

OVERSELF. *See* OVERMIND.

PARADIGM. A comprehensive or general model or theory.

PEAK EXPERIENCE. Short-lived, intense altered state characterized by euphoria, a sense of deep knowing, belongingness, appropriateness, oneness, and perfection of self and universe.

PERENNIAL PHILOSOPHY. A fundamental description of reality and human nature found at the basis of the major metaphysical traditions.

PERENNIAL PSYCHOLOGY. A description of the perennial philosophy in psychological terms.

PERSONA. Outward appearance; social facade; masks worn by actors.

PHENOMENOLOGY. Description of phenomena without interpretation, explanation, and evaluation.

PHILOSOPHIA PERENNIS: *See* PERENNIAL PHILOSOPHY.

POSITIVISM. A system of philosophy that excludes from consideration everything but natural phenomena and their properties knowable by the senses.

PRECOGNITION. Extrasensory knowledge of the future; ability to foretell future events.

PREPOTENT. Predominant; overshadowing; demanding precedence.

PROTOEMOTIONAL. Primitive emotions appearing in early child development.

PUÑÑA. Buddhist term for insight.

PSEUDONIRVANA. A stage in which the mediator mistakes his or her experience for nirvana.

PSI. Extrasensory phenomena or abilities.

PSYCHE. The human mind; the mental life; soul.

PSYCHOKINESIS. Moving physical objects by mental activity.

PSYCHOLOGIA PERENNIS. *See* PERENNIAL PSYCHOLOGY.

PSYCHOMOTOR. Of or pertaining to muscular action directly from a mental process.

PSYCHOPATHOLOGY. Psychological disturbance; the study of mental disorder.

PSYCHOPHYSICAL. Pertaining to mind and body or mind/body interactions.

PSYCHOSOMATIC. Pertaining to the functional interrelationship between mind and body; bodily disorder induced by mental or emotional disturbance.

PSYCHOSYNTHESIS. A method for attaining psychological integration developed by Roberto Assagioli.

RELATIVE REALITY. World view as perceived by a particular viewpoint; observation as determined by interaction of observer and observed.

RETROCOGNITION. Extrasensory knowledge of the past.

SAMADHI. Meditative concentration.

SAMSARA. Illusory perception (maya).

SATIPATTHANA. *See* MINDFULNESS.

SELF-ACTUALIZATION. Bringing into existence all that one can become.

SILA. Virtue or moral purity.

SOMA. Body.

SUBMERGENT UNCONSCIOUS. The structures of consciousness that have emerged and been repressed.

SUPERCONSCIOUS. *See* OVERMIND.

SUPEREGO. The part of the psyche representing introjected values, ethics, morality, and ideals; it judges and punishes transgressions; commonly identified with conscience; the unconscious repressing, but unrepressed part of the ego with which the self unconsciously identifies.

SUPRAMIND. *See* OVERMIND.

SURFACE STRUCTURE. A particular manifestation of the deep structure of each level of consciousness.

SYNERGISTIC. Of or relating to synergism.

SYNERGISM. Cooperative action of discrete agencies such that the total effect is greater than the sum of the two effects taken independently.

SYSTEM-CONSCIOUS. Freudian psychic system differentiated from system-unconscious.

SYSTEM-UNCONSCIOUS. Freudian term for the unconscious generated by repression; the repressed or dynamically resisted impulses and experiences.

TELEPATHY. Communication from one mind to another without recourse to sense perception.

TELEOLOGICAL. Directed toward or shaped by a purpose; said especially of natural processes or nature as a whole.

TELEPORTATION. *See* TELEKINESIS.

TELEKINESIS. Transporting physical objects at a distance by mental activity.

THETA FREQUENCY. Brain wave frequency of 4–7 cycles per second as measured by electroencephalography.

TRANSCENDENTALISM. Philosophy emphasizing a priori conditions of knowledge and experience; emphasizing what transcends sense experience as being fundamental in reality; asserting the primacy of the spiritual and supraindividual as against the material and empirical.

TRANSFORM. To change the form; to change in structure or composition; to transmute; to change one form of energy into another; movement of deep structures of levels of consciousness.

TRANSLATION. Changed from one language into another; movement of surface structures on any level of consciousness.

VIPASSANA. *See* INSIGHT.

WITNESS CONSCIOUSNESS. Nonreactive observation of experience.

SUGGESTED READING

Andersen, M., & Savary, L. *Passages: A guide for pilgrims of the mind*. New York: Harper & Row, 1973.

Arguelles, J., & Arguelles, M. *Mandala*. Berkeley, Calif.: Shambala, 1972.

Assagioli, R. *Psychosynthesis: A manual of principles and techniques*. New York: Hobbs Dorman, 1965.

Assagioli, R. *The act of will*. New York: Viking, 1973.

Bateson, G. *Steps to an ecology of mind*. New York: Ballantine, 1972.

Bateson, G. *Mind and nature*. New York: E. P. Dutton, 1979.

Becker, E. *The denial of death*. New York: The Free Press, 1974.

Benoit, H. *The supreme doctrine*. New York: Viking, 1959.

Bentov, I. *Stalking the wild pendulum: On the mechanics of consciousness*. New York: E. P. Dutton, 1977.

Bonny, H., & Savary, L. *Music and your mind: Listening with a new consciousness*. New York: Harper & Row, 1973.

Boorstein, S., (Ed.). *Transpersonal psychotherapies*. Palo Alto, Calif.: Science and Behavior Books, in press.

Bucke, M. *Cosmic consciousness*. New York: E. P. Dutton, 1969.

Bugental, J. F. T. *Psychotherapy and process*. Reading, Mass.: Addison-Wesley, 1978.

Byrom, T. *The Dhammapada: The sayings of the Buddha*. New York: Vintage, 1976.

Campbell, J. *The hero with a thousand faces*. New York: Pantheon, 1949.

Campbell, J. *The masks of God* (4 vols.). New York: Viking, 1959–1968.

Capra, F. *The tao of physics*. Berkeley, Calif.: Shambala, 1975.

Davidson, J. and Davidson, R. (Eds.). *The psychobiology of consciousness*. New York, Plenum, 1979.

Deikman, A. *Personal freedom: On finding your way to the real world*. New York: Viking, 1976.

Edinger, E. *Ego and Archetype*. Baltimore: Penguin Books, 1973.

Elgin, D. *Voluntary simplicity*. New York: Morrow, in press.

Fadiman, J., & Frager, R. *Personality and personal growth*. New York: Harper & Row, 1976.

Ferguson, M. *The brain revolution: The frontiers of mind research*. New York: Taplinger, 1973.

Ferguson, M. *The aquarian conspiracy*. Los Angeles: J. P. Tarcher, in press.

Goleman, D. *The varieties of the meditative experience*. New York: E. P. Dutton, 1977.

Goleman, D., & Davison, R. (Eds.). *Consciousness: Brain, states of awareness and mysticism*. New York: Harper & Row, 1979.

Goldstein, J. *The experience of insight*. Santa Cruz, Calif.: Unity Press, 1976.

Govinda, Lama Angarika. *Foundations of Tibetan mysticism*. New York: Samuel Weiser, 1969.

Green, E., & Green, A. *Beyond biofeedback*. New York: Delacorte, 1977.

Grof, S. *Realms of the human unconscious*. New York: Viking, 1975.

Grof, S. *The human encounter with death*. New York: E. P. Dutton, 1978.

Harman, W. *An incomplete guide to the future*. Stanford, Calif.: Stanford Alumni Association, 1976.

Hendricks, G., & Fadiman, J. *Transpersonal education: A curriculum for feeling and being*. Englewood Cliffs, N.J.: Prentice-Hall.

Hixon, L. *Coming home: The experience of enlightenment in the sacred traditions*. New York: Doubleday/Anchor, 1978.

Huxley, A. *The perennial philosophy*. New York: Harper & Row, 1944.

James, W. *The varieties of religious experience*. New York: Collier, 1961.

Jung, C. G. *Man and his symbols*. Garden City, N.Y.: Doubleday, 1964.

Jung, C. G. *Memories, dreams and reflections*. New York: Vintage, 1965.

Koestler, A. *The roots of coincidence*. New York: Random House, 1972.

Kornfield, J. *Living Buddhist masters*. Santa Cruz, Calif.: Unity, 1977.

Krippner, S., & Ullman, M. *Dream telepathy*. New York: Macmillan, 1973.

Leonard, G. *The silent pulse*. New York: E. P. Dutton, 1978.

LeShan, L. *How to meditate*. Boston: Little, Brown & Co., 1974.

LeShan, L. *The medium, the mystic, and the physicist: Toward a general theory of the paranormal*. New York: Viking, 1974.

LeShan, L. *Alternate realities: The search for the full human being*. New York: Ballantine, 1977.

Levine, S. *A gradual awakening*. New York: Doubleday/Anchor, 1978.

Maslow, A. *The farther reaches of human nature*. New York: Viking, 1971.

Masters, R., & Houston, J. *Mind games: A guide to inner space*. New York: Viking, 1972.

Needleman, J. *A sense of the cosmos: The encounter of modern science and ancient truth*. New York: E. P. Dutton, 1965.

Needleman, J. *On the way to self-knowledge*. New York: Knopf, 1976.

Neumann, E. *The origins and history of consciousness*. Princeton, N.J.: Princeton University Press, 1973.

Novak, M. *The experience of nothingness*. New York: Harper & Row, 1971.

Perry, J. *The far side of madness*. Englewood Cliffs, N. J.: Prentice-Hall, 1974.

Ornstein, R. *The psychology of consciousness*. San Francisco, Calif.: Freeman, 1972.

Ornstein, R. (Ed.). *The nature of human consciousness: A book of readings*. San Francisco, Calif.: Freeman, 1973.

Pribram, K. *Languages of the brain*. Englewood Cliffs, N. J.: Prentice-Hall, 1971.

Ram Dass, *The only dance there is*. New York: Doubleday/Anchor, 1974.

Ram Dass, *Grist for the mill*. Santa Cruz, Calif.: Unity Press, 1977.

Ram Dass. *Journey of awakening, a meditator's guidebook*. New York: Doubleday, 1978.

Roberts, T. (Ed.). *Four psychologies applied to education*. Cambridge, Mass.: Schenkman, 1974.

Roszak, T. *Person/planet*. New York: Doubleday/Anchor, 1978.

Satprem. *Sri Aurobindo, or the adventures of consciousness*. New York: Harper & Row, 1968.

Schumacher, E. F. *A guide for the perplexed*. New York: Harper & Row, 1977.

Shah, Idries. *The way of the sufi*. New York: E. P. Dutton, 1970.

Shapiro, D. *Precision nirvana: An owner's manual for the care and maintenance of the mind*. Englewood Cliffs, N. J.: Prentice-Hall, 1978.

Shapiro, D. *Meditation: Self-regulation strategy and altered states of consciousness*. New York: Aldine, in press.

Shapiro, D. N., & Walsh, R. N. (Eds.). *The science of meditation: Research, theory, and experience*. New York, Aldine Press, in press.

Smith, H. *Forgotten truth: The primoridial tradition*. New York: Harper & Row, 1976.

Sujata. *Beginning to see*. Santa Cruz, Calif.: Unity Press, 1975.

Suzuki, S. *Zen mind, beginner's mind*. New York: John Westerhill, 1970.

Tart, C. (Ed.). *Altered states of consciousness*. New York: John Wiley, 1969.

Tart, C. *States of consciousness*. New York: E. P. Dutton, 1975.

Tart, C. (Ed.). *Transpersonal psychologies*. New York: Harper & Row, 1975.

Tarthang Tulku. *Gesture of balance*. Emeryville, Calif.: Dharma Publishing, 1977.

Tarthang Tulku. *Time, space, and knowledge*. Emeryville, Calif.: Dharma Publishing, 1977.

Trungpa, Chogyam. *Cutting through spiritual materialism*. Berkeley, Calif.: Shambala, 1973.

Van Dusen, W. *The natural depth of man*. New York: Harper & Row, 1972.

Vaughan, F. *Awakening intuition*. New York: Doubleday/Anchor, 1979.

Walsh, R., & Shapiro, D. (Eds.). *Beyond health and normality: Explorations of extreme psychological well-being*. New York: Van Nostrand Reinhold, in press.

Weil, A. *The natural mind*. New York: Houghton Mifflin, 1972.

Wellwood, J. (Ed.). *The meeting of the ways*. New York: Schocken, 1979.

White, J. (Ed.). *The highest state of consciousness*. New York: Doubleday, 1973.

White, J. (Ed.). *Frontiers of consciousness*. New York: Julian Press, 1974.

Wilber, K. *The spectrum of consciousness*. Wheaton, Ill.: Theosophical Publishing House, 1977.

Wilber, K. *No boundary*. Los Angeles: Center Publications, 1979.

Wilber, K. *The Atman project*. Wheaton, Ill.: Theosophical Publishing House, 1980.

Wilbur, K. *Up from Eden: A transpersonal view of human evolution*. New York: Doubleday, 1981

Wolman, B. (Ed.). *Handbook of parapsychology*. New York: Van Nostrand Reinhold, 1977.

Zukav, G. *The dancing Wu Li masters: An overview of the new physics*. New York: Morrow, 1979.

JOURNALS

Journal of Humanistic Psychology. 325 Ninth Street, San Francisco, California 94103. Four issues per year, $10.

Journal of Transpersonal Psychology. Box 4437, Stanford, California 94305. Biannual, $10.

ReVision. Box 316, Cambridge, Massachusetts 02138. Biannual, $15.

INDEX

ASC. *See* Altered State of Consciousness
ATC. *See* Altered Trait of Consciousness
Abhidhamma, 131–34
Access concentration, 142
Adequatio, 45
Aesthetic experience, LSD, 88
Altered State of Consciousness, 21, 201; consensual validation, 204–205; and cultural norms, 32; observation of, 203–204; and reality, 34; and religion, 207–208; research, 46; and science, 200–201; state specific science, 215; in therapy, 231; usefulness of, 54. *See also* Transcendental experience
Altered Trait of Consciousness, 34
Analytical psychology, 169–70
Anatta, 146
Arahant, 149
Arahat, 130–34
Archaic unconscious, 107–108
Archetypal experiences, in LSD research, 95
Archetypes, 82
Asanas, 37
Attachment, 55–56
Attention/awareness, 115
Attitude, 245
Autohypnosis, 212
Awareness, 59–60, 153, 244–45; and culture, 31–32; meditation, 139, 140; training, 150–51

Basic Perinatal Matrices, LSD research, 93
Behavioral sciences, 40–41
Behaviorism, 18, 170–71
Behavior modification, 170–71
Being, 244
Biofeedback, 21, 212, 229–30, 257
Biosocial bands, 76, 81–82
Birth trauma, LSD research, 92
Body ego, 100–101
Bootstrap philosophy, 68–69
Brain ecology, 223–24
Brain physiology, meditation, 157
Buddhism, consciousness states, 33
Buddhist psychology. *See* Abhidhamma
B-values, 123, 125, 127, 129, 130

Castaneda, Carlos, 31
Causal realm of consciousness, 216, 103–104
Chakra, 96, 102

COEX system, 89
Collective unconscious, 76, 82, 95
Communication, cross-state, 46, 60
Communication, state-specific, 72, 205. *See also* Language
Competent model, 166–67
Concentration, 142–43, 150, 151. *See also* Meditation
Condensed Experience System, 89
Conditioning, 55, 59
Consciousness, 104; ASC, 201; analytical psychology, 170; behavioral science, 41; causal regions, 103–104; cultural aspects of, 38; East and West, 41; empirical study of, 22; evolution of, 104–106, 253, LSD research, 94–95, 96–97; model, 53–55; nirvana, 148; and objects of consciousness, 186; and psychosis, 38; and reality, 26–27, 225, 237–38; research, 257; and the Self, 191; Spectrum, 75-77, 168–69; systems approach to, 115–118; transcendence of, 101–104; transpersonal context, 183–84; and well being, 119–20. *See also* State of Consciousness
Consciousness disciplines, 37–40, 49–50, 222, 225
Consensual validation, 204–205, 210, 214, 235
Contemplation, 217, 259
Continuum of inattention, 108
Core experience, 91
Cosmic consciousness, 244
Counseling, and transpersonal psychology, 230
Creative quietude, 248
Culture, 126, 196–97

Deep structure, 105
Deficiency needs, 125, 190
Dehypnosis, 159
Delusion, 131
Discrete Altered State of Consciousness, 116
Disidentification, 56, 58, 83, 186, 188
Dualism, 63, 78, 79, 82, 83, 234–236
Dynamic epistemology, 42

Eastern traditions. *See* Consciousness disciplines
Ecological Ethic, 255
Education, and consciousness states, 228–29

Ego, 58, 102, 139–140, 169, 171
Ego level of consciousness, 77, 79, 80, 185, 186, 187
Embedded unconscious, 109–10
Embryonal experiences, 95
Emergent unconscious, 110–112
Empirical validation, 296
Enlightenment, 58, 60, 151–53; goal of consciousness disciplines, 37, 40; pseudonirvana, 147
Evolution, 107, 130, 245, 253
Existentialism, 171–72
Existential level of consciousness, 76, 78, 186; therapies, 80–81, 185, 190–91
Experimenter bias, 210
Eyes of the soul, 216–18

Factors of Enlightenment, 151–53
Fetal experiences, LSD research, 95
Formal operational, 102
Formless jhana, 144
Freedom, 192
Freud, Sigmund, 30, 47, 92, 107–108
Full absorption, 143
Functionally specific states, 39
Fusion words, 128–29

Gestalt therapy, 81
Grades of significance, 45
Gross (Realm of being), 216–17
Ground unconscious, 107
Growth motivation, 125

Hierarchy of needs, 85, 120, 125
Hierarchy of pleasures, 127
High causal, 103
High subtle, 103
Hinduism, 83
Holistic medicine, 163, 180
Humanistic psychology, 19–20, 81
Humanistic psychotherapy, 171

Identity, 56, 110, 118, 186, 188
Illness, 123
Illusion. See Samsara
Imagination, 210
Impermanence, 59
Incompleteness theorem, 235
Industrialism, 249, 250–51
Ineffability, state specific consciousness, 210–11
Insight, 133, 141, 145–49
Integration, 102
Intellect, 42, 77
Introspection, 194–95

James, William, 22, 39, 50
Jhana, 143–44, 153
Jung, Carl, 48, 95–96, 108, 169–170

Karma yoga, and psychotherapy, 166
Knowledge, 202–203, 219, 236, 237

Kundalini yoga, and LSD therapy, 96

LSD research, 87–99
Language, 40, 41, 42–43; and reality, 29, 31; and state dependent communication, 46. See also Communication
Learning, state dependent, 49, 229
Logotherapy, 81
Low causal, 103
Low subtle, 102

Mahayana Buddhism, 83
Maslow, Abraham, 19, 82, 85, 120
Matter, and reality, 27
Maya, 37, 77–78
Meditation, 22, 34, 36, 58, 136, 151; and education, 230; physiology of, 156–57; processes, 141–49; psychological effects, 155–56; psychotherapy, 162, 165; research, 48, 154–59, 258; and state of consciousness, 38, 112–114; state specific science, 212. See also Concentration
Mental disorder, 133
Mental health, 48, 119–122, 131–134
Metabolism, and meditation, 156
Metacosmic void, 97
Metamotivation, 122–31, 162
Meta needs, 123, 125
Metapathologies, 123–24
Mind, 75–76, 79, 217; LSD research, 96–97; and reality, 238; therapies, 83
Mindfulness, 145–46, 151–52
Modeling, 166, 171
Model psychosis, 87
Motivation, 120, 245
Mystical experiences, 230, 254
Mysticism, 62–69, 83, 187. See also Consciousness disciplines

Nirvana, 147–49
Normal consciousness sciences, 209
Normal science, 30
Nothingness, 192

Observation, in scientific method, 203, 206
Organic world view, 63
Over-self, 103

Paradigm, 25, 26, 30
Peak experience, 60
Perception, 41, 222, 225
Perennial philosophy, 37, 216, 244–45
Perennial psychology, 74, 226
Perinatal experience, LSD research, 91–94
Persona, 77
Personal drama, 177
Personality, 56, 152–53, 177, 178, 179
Philosophy and transpersonal psychology, 234–40

Physics, 225, 235, 243, 258; and mysticism, 62–68; quantum theory, 64–68; and study of consciousness, 22, 43–44, 226; world view, 63, 187
Plateau experience, 82
Primordial images, LSD research, 95
Psi phenomena, 240–248
Psychedelics, 20, 32, 117–18; psychotherapy, 162, 230–31; research, 48, 87–99; and state specific sciences, 212
Psychoanalysis, 19, 34, 89, 169
Psychodynamic experience, LSD research, 88–89
Psychological states. See States of Consciousness
Psychosis, 38, 47
Psychosynthesis, 82
Psychotherapy, 39–40, 163; analytical psychology, 169–70; behaviorism, 170–71; COEX systems, 89; existentialism, 171–72; goals of, 165, 194; growth levels, 190–95; humanistic, 171; and meditation, 155–56, 158; personal drama, 177; psychoanalysis, 169; and state of consciousness, 39–40; therapist, 166–67; transpersonal, 16, 161–64, 167–68, 185
Punna, 141, 145
Purification, 141, 142

Quantum theory. See Physics

Reality, 27, 42, 83, 128, 139, 192, 254; Consciousness, 55, 71, 232–39, 225; consensual verification, 235; and language, 29, 43; perceptions of, 37–38, 221; and psychoanalysis, 34; quantum physics, 64–68; religious insights, 217; and science, 222
Reason, eye of, 217
Relativity theory, 66–68
Religion, 97–98, 130, 207–208
Repression, 108–109
Research: ASC, 46; Consciousness, 257; meditation, 154–59; mind, 96–97; psychedelics, 87–99

Sahaja samadhi, 104
Samadhi, 141
Samsara, 37, 38
Sat-chitananda, 59
Science, 29–30, 217–18; and consciousness disciplines, 222; in transcendental society, 247; and transpersonal psychology, 216–221
Sciences, state specific, 118, 206–207, 208–209, 214; and religion, 207–208, and states of consciousness, 200–12
Scientific method, 201, 202, 219, 223
Scientific world view, 241–42
Self-deprivation, 125
Self-actualization, 102, 122, 171, 180, 182
Self-realization ethic, 255

Self-renewal therapy, 190
Self-transcendence, 186
Shadow level of consciousness, 77
Sila, 141
Simplicity, 251–252
Society, transformation of, 246–247
Space-time, 66
Spectrum of Consciousness, 84, 100–104, 168
Spiritual disciplines. See Consciousness disciplines
States of Consciousness, 39, 72, 166, 202, 209; education, 228–229; LSD research, 88–89; psi research, 240–241; and psychotherapy, 39–40; and reality, 55; and state specific sciences, 207
Subject idealism, 238
Subjective biology, 128
Submergent unconscious, 108
Subtle (Realm of being), 216
Subtle sphere, 102
Sufism, 83
Super ego, 110
Supracosmic void, 97
Supra mind, 103
Surface structure, 105

Taoism, 83, 248–55
Theorizing (scientific method), 205–206
Therapists, 166–67, 183–84, 230
Therapy. See Psychotherapy
Third eye, 102
Third force psychology, 19
Toxic psychosis, 87
Transcendence, 106, 113, 121, 191, 231
Transcendental experience, 16, 20, 47, 48, 97–98, 165
Transcendental meditation, 155, 158
Transformation, 105, 112
Translation, 105, 109, 112
Transpersonal, 16; bands, 76, 82–83, 113; context, 183–84; content, 185; education, 229; experiences, 94–98, 185; model, 18; psychotherapy, 177–79, 181–82; realization, 182
Turiya state, 104
Unconscious, 27–28, 88
Unconscious processes, 106–12
Unity, 104

Value life, 126
Value starvation, 125
Vedanta, 83
Visuddhimagga, 141
Void, 97, 104, 145, 239

Well being, 133, 155
Wellness, 119–22
Wheel of Life (Tibetan), 33, 34
Witness, 82, 83, 178, 187

Yoga, 36–37, 163, 176